A-Z OF
BRITISH
COACHBUILDERS
1919~1960

Nick Walker

ACKNOWLEDGEMENTS

The author and the publisher are grateful to the following for supplying photographs.
Geoff Aspin: p.9, 36 lower, 56 top, 70 lower, 185, 198 left, 201 top left; Nick Baldwin: p.7 top, 8 lower, 14 lower, 17 lower, 25 bottom, 36 top, 41 centre, 43 top, 80 left, 83 centre, 92 top left, 99, 101 lower left, 103 lower, 115 lower, 117 centre, 118 top left, 126 top, 137 lower, 139, 145, 147 bottom, 148 top, 160 lower right, 171 lower, 180 top, 187, 203 left; Peter Bering: p.162 bottom; Charles K.Bowers & Sons: p10, bottom, 13 top, 20 lower, 23 top, lower, 32, 37, 41 top, 59, 50, top, 57, 58, 60, 62, 64, 72, 73 top, centre, 74, 108 top, 113 top, centre, 118 lower left, 128 bottom, 165 top, lower left, 167 lower, 179 top, 189 lower; Bridges Motor Co.: 82 top right, lower right, 202 right; Roy Brooks: p31 top, lower, 98 top, lower left; Neill Bruce: p25 top, 26 top, 65, 67 top, 68, 83 top 121, 123, 143 top, 144, 182, 183,184; Classic & Sportscar: p26 bottom; Coventry Museum of British Road Transport: p.153 lower, 176 centre right; David Culshaw: p.150 top right; Munro Donald: p142 bottom; Harry Edwards: p107 lower; Malcolm Elder: p.136 top right, 140 bottom; John Gray: p.191 centre; Doug Grinyer: p10 top, 37 top, 39, 119, 204 top right; John Grose: p.8 top, 16 top, 30 top, 35 top, 49 top, 53 lower, 116, 200 right; David Hawtin: p.124 top; David Hodges: 61 lower, 63 top, 69, 78, 85 top, 97 lower, 115 top, 135 top, 148 lower left, 149, 154 third, 155 top right, 157 bottom, 158, 166, 168, 173 centre, 174 top right, 188 top left, 192 lower, 201 right, 202 bottom left, 204 bottom right; Graham Hudson: p.152, 161 top; Ken Lea: p.66 lower; Leicestershire Record Office: p14 top, 19 lower, 34 top, 118 top right, lower right; Pat McDonald p.146; Bruce McKenzie: p.46 bottom, 88 bottom, 90 top, 163 bottom, 167 top, 177; Richard Mawer: p.102 lower, 134 centre; John Mullen: p.85 bottom, 122 bottom; Michael Mutch/ Myreton Motor Museum: p18 top, 160 top, lower left, 204 top left; Martin Parish: p.154 bottom, 178 lower; Tony Phillips-Smith: p.51 top, 76 top, 126 lower, 133 bottom; John Price-Williams: 54 lower; Pye Books 37 bottom; Quadrant Photo Library: p15, 20 top, 31 top, 52, 75 top, 79 top, 80 right, 109 top, 112, 129 top, 130 top, 138 lower, 172 top; Rolls Royce Enthusiasts Club: p21 top, lower, 34 bottom, 35 lower, 48 bottom, 54 top, 83 bottom, 91 top, 96, 101 lower right, 104, 120, 129 lower, 130 centre, 138 top right, 155 lower, 156, 173 top, 188 lower, 190 top, 191 top; Science Museum: p.7 bottom, 10 upper middle, 31 lower, 42 lower, 43 lower, 50 lower, 53 top, 56 lower, 59 top, 127, 128 top, centre, 199 top right, 201 centre left, bottom left, 202 top left, 203 top right; Dick Serjeantson: 41 bottom, 81 top right, 92 lower, 100, 159; Nick Simpson: p95 top, 105 lower, 108 lower, 140 centre, 195; Paddy Wilmer: p.61 top; Mike Worthington-Williams: p10 lower middle, 11, 12, 17 top, 19 top, 27 bottom, 28 top, 38, 42 top, 55 top, 59 lower, 67 lower, 77, 79 lower, 81 top left, lower, 82 top left, lower left, 84, 89, 91 lower, 92 top right, 93, 94, 95 bottom, 97 top, 98 lower right, 101 top, 103 top, 105 top, 107 top, 110, 111, 113 bottom, 114, 117 bottom, 124 bottom, 125, 131 top, 133 top left, right, 134 top, bottom, 135 lower, 136 top left, 137 top, 138 top left, 140 top, 141, 142 top, 143 bottom,147 top, centre, 148 lower right, 150 top left, 151, 153 top, 154 second, 157 top, centre, 161 bottom, 162 top, 164, 169, 170 top, 172 lower, 173 bottom, 174 top left, centre right, 175, 176 top, bottom, 178 top, 180 lower, 181 lower, 186, 188 centre right, 189 top, 191 bottom, 192 top, 194, 196, 198 right, 199 top left, bottom left, bottom right, 200 left, 203 bottom right, 204 bottom left

A-Z OF BRITISH COACHBUILDERS
1919~1960

AND THE DEVELOPMENT OF STYLES & TECHNIQUES

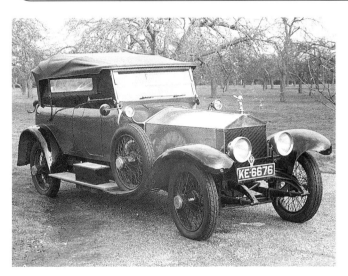
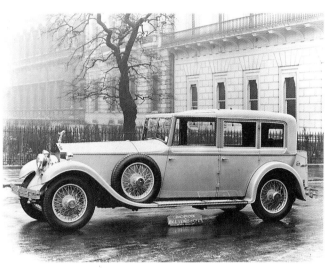

NICK WALKER

Published 1997 by Bay View Books Ltd
The Red House, 25-26 Bridgeland Street
Bideford, Devon EX39 2PZ, UK

Designed by Chris Fayers

ISBN 1 870979 93 1
Printed in Hong Kong
by Paramount Printing Co.

CONTENTS

FOREWORD

It was interesting that after I had started writing this book a number of respected figures in the world of British automotive history commented independently on the lack of a book about the coachbuilding industry. Certainly that had been my motivation when I began the project; not only was there no history of the industry but there had been little written on the subject at all, at least in the last 20 years. Yet the British coachbuilding industry was at one time a world leader, at least in matters of styling, and it seemed important to tell its story before much of the source material disappeared.

I have to confess that my initial interest had been in the development of styling, and in the technical advances which in turn allowed styling to develop, rather than in the individual firms which made up the industry. Before long, however, it became clear to me that these two threads of history were intertwined. The developments which occurred in car coachwork in Britain – particularly in the inter-war period – were both the cause and the result of changes in the industry itself. It was therefore necessary to know the history of the principal participants before one could fully understand why techniques and styling evolved in the way they did, just as it was important to know the consequences this evolution had in turn for individual firms.

Thus the book began to take on the form of a definitive history of the industry. Nevertheless 'definitive' is a relative term. The sheer number of so-called coachbuilding firms operating in every small town in Britain at the beginning of this century, even if they could have been listed and described, would have made the book far too large and expensive to be accessible to the average motoring enthusiast. I therefore set an arbitrary starting date of 1919; this is not only when recognisable trends in coachwork design became discernible, but it is also the time when many firms which previously described themselves as coachbuilders began either to specialise seriously in that branch or else began to restrict themselves to repair work – or possibly sub-contracting, or component manufacture, if they happened to be near a centre of car production.

Other self-imposed rules were that the book should be restricted to cars – no commercials, buses or coaches – and that to be included a firm must be known to have constructed at least one body, and mounted it on a chassis, for resale. A further, and I believe reasonable, restriction concerns the period after World War 2. Bearing in mind that the subject is coachbuilt bodies, and not unitary construction, space-frames or the like, I have concentrated only on those firms which continued to use 'coachbuilding' methods; for this reason the relevant chapter is called 'The Survivors'.

The one certainty about this methodology is that there will have been some mistakes. In particular, there are sure to be firms omitted from the A-Z section which had every right to be there under my rules; equally, even amongst those firms which I have covered there will be errors and omissions. I offer my apologies in advance, and ask only that I or my publisher be informed so that, if it proves possible, we can one day bring out a revised edition with any mistakes rectified.

I could not have achieved what little I have, however, without the very considerable help I have received from a great many people. Outstanding amongst these have been Michael Worthington-Williams, who gave not only active encouragement and support from the early days of the project but also very substantial help from his vast picture library, and also Dick Serjeantson, who put his long-standing and carefully-compiled database on coachbuilding at my disposal as well as giving advice on behalf of the Wolseley Hornet Special Club. Other individuals whose assistance has been particularly appreciated at different stages have been Nick Baldwin, Martin Boothman, Alan Burman, David Burgess-Wise, Giles Chapman, Rivers Fletcher, Peter Hull, Norman Johnson, Mike Lawrence, Bill Munro, John Price-Williams, Alan Stote, John Willis and many others too numerous to mention. The facilities of the various museums and libraries, and the individuals running them, have also been of enormous help, including Beaulieu National Motor Museum (Michael Ware), Coventry Museum of British Road Transport (Barry Littlewood and Barry Collins), British Motor Industry Heritage Trust, Gaydon (Anders Ditlev Clausager), IBCAM (Stuart Peck), RREC/Sir Henry Royce Memorial Foundation (Peter Baines and Philip Hall) and the VSCC Library (Messrs Hull and Willis once again). I am also grateful for specific help in preparing the appendix 'How to Buy a Coachbuilt Car' from Nick Simpson of Earley Engineering, Tony Dennett of Hightone Restorations, Malcolm Elder of Malcolm C Elder & Son, David Royle of David A C Royle and Paul Wood of P & A Wood.

Lastly, but perhaps most importantly since they represent the enthusiasts without whom there would be no car preservation movement, I must record my appreciation of the help I have been given by the one-make clubs and the dedicated experts within them, including: David Culshaw (Alvis Owner Club), Bill Smith (Armstrong-Siddeley Owners Club), John Charlton (Bristol Owners Club), Richard Mawer (British Salmson Owners Club), Sam Roberts (Ford Y & C Register), Ken Goode (Gwynne Register), Arnold Davey (Lagonda Club), Chris Clark (Lanchester Register), Philip Bayne-Powell (MG Car Club), Harry Edwards (Morris Register), Barry McKenzie and John Dyson (Railton Owners Club), David Allberry and Alan Teeder (Riley Register), Mike Evans (Rover Sports Register), Dennis Mynard (Tickford Register), Kevin Atkinson (Singer Owners Club), Bruce Dowell and John Gray (Sunbeam-Talbot-Darracq Register) and John Mullen (Vauxhall Owners Club).

Nick Walker
Ilmington, March 1997

INTRODUCTION
INDUSTRY BACKGROUND

After the First World War ended, and the heroes returned to the land they had defended, industry in general was in optimistic mood. Not only were labour and raw materials going to be in plentiful supply again, but there was so much pent-up demand in every sector that there seemed to be no problem in selling all the available production. The coachbuilding industry saw no reason why it should be an exception, and in those initial days of optimism it certainly was not. Despite the enormous inflation during the period – prices of most items, including cars, approximately doubled between 1914 and 1919 – demand for cars at all points in the price range seemed never-ending. Partly, of course, at the lowest prices, it was the normal phenomenon which is to be observed when any new market is developing: the more mass-production methods can reduce the cost and hence the selling-price, the greater the demand, and so on. In addition, many more people had of necessity become familiar with motor vehicles during the war. Far from being suspicious of them, these returnees were positively searching for an opportunity to acquire a car.

The Armstrong-Siddeley tourer on Connaught's stand at the 1919 Olympia Show (the first post-war show) gleams in expectation – but the hand-painted colour and varnish will have taken three weeks or more to lay on and dry. Connaught was a firm with a long history but by the early thirties was sub-contracting all its work.

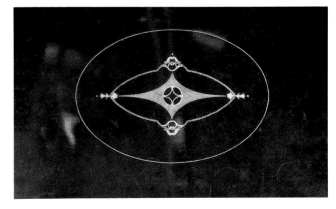

Just how expensive a bespoke body from a top coachbuilder was can be imagined from the inlay work on the door panel of a 1921 Rolls-Royce by Hooper.

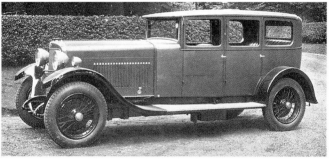

Imported chassis were often used by bespoke coach-builders, whose well-off clients were less concerned by the import duty involved. This 1924 Renault saloon (above) is by Grose of Northampton.

Sunbeam was still bodying a high proportion of its chassis itself around 1928, when this 30hp Weymann saloon was produced. Sunbeam was one of the first British manufacturers, as opposed to coachbuilders, to take out a Weymann licence.

At this bottom end of the market, the effect was a rash of companies building very small cars, initially a revival of the pre-war 'cyclecars', but soon small cars in their own right such as the Austin Seven. Above them were a host of manufacturers – some new, some well established before the war – aiming at the 'middle-class' market; many of these came and went within a few years, but some (Austin, Humber, Morris, Riley, Standard) survived until quite recent times – and one (Rover) is still with us. Many of these manufacturers, of both small and 'middle-class' cars, had large enough sales to justify their own body manufacturing facilities; others used the numerous contract coachbuilding firms which had come into existence by then.

At the top end of the market firms like Daimler, Napier and Rolls-Royce, together with the most expensive imported marques, worked primarily through 'bespoke' coachbuilders. Customers would first select a chassis – the car manufacturer and model, in other words – and were then pointed towards a limited number of coachbuilders who (it was suggested) could produce a body of the quality necessary for such a prestigious chas-

sis. At this stage the customer took at least as much trouble, if not more, in choosing the design of coachwork as in selecting a chassis in the first place. The coachbuilder was responsible for the design and manufacture of the body, and for mounting it on the chassis (usually manufacture and mounting went on simultaneously). This approach to bodywork had been the norm in horse-and-carriage days, and the same coachbuilders merely continued their existing practices when cars came along.

There was not necessarily a clear distinction between the two sorts of firm, bespoke and contract; certainly there were firms who did either one or the other exclusively, but in between came the great majority who liked the cachet of bespoke work but who also recognised the value of a contract in paying the wages. It was a habit which began early: even the most prestigious bespoke houses produced what were effectively approved standard designs for Rolls-Royce, while conversely no contract coachbuilder could resist the offer of a bespoke commission to show off his skills, especially if he could display the result at that year's Motor Show.

It is worth noting that there were exceptions to even

Martin Walter was one of the early coachbuilders to exploit the business available in building special bodies for large manufacturers. This posed 1930 shot outside the Folkestone works shows 'Cheriton' sports saloons on Vauxhall T-type chassis in various stages of construction.

a top-drawer chassis manufacturer using bespoke coach-builders. Sunbeam, for example, mostly supplied its own bodies, although buyers could opt for an outside coach-builder if they wished. Most notable at one time was Daimler, which before World War 1 believed so strongly in controlling its own coachwork quality that for a long period it would hardly let a separate chassis out of the works. As a result, its coachbuilding workforce at one time exceeded 800 employees; when one bears in mind the comparatively small annual sales of such a firm, one can begin to appreciate just how labour-intensive its methods were. Yet by the time the twenties came even Daimler was putting many of its chassis, particularly the larger ones, out to independent coachbuilders, with the result that its coachbuilding employees had dropped to around 100 by 1922.

Thus in 1919 there were a great many potential customers at the bottom end of the market, while for the middle and upper classes there was no suggestion that their numbers or spending power were any less than before the war. It added up to an ever increasing demand for cars, and initially this proved to be the case. Vehicle production, from a base of 34,000 in 1913, moved up to 73,000 in 1922. In consequence there was a dearth of skilled tradesmen in the coachbuilding industry; coupled with its labour-intensiveness, and with the huge areas required for work-in-progress (mainly because of slow paint-drying times), there began a search for more economic methods which were eventually to revolutionise the industry.

As for the designs which were being turned out at that time, the word which springs to mind is 'conservative'. Neither the mass-production car (which, bear in mind, was far more likely to be open than closed) nor the expensive, formal car looked significantly different from those being produced in 1914. The emphasis was on height – tall bodies mounted on high chassis – and, probably as a consequence, on vertical lines. It took time for horizontal lines to assert themselves, the first being the waistline. Even this development was only achieved by the expedi-

ent of raising the bonnet, which did little to reduce the impression of height.

It is interesting to reflect on the origins of this conservative attitude. There is no doubt that it ran parallel with a similar attitude to the visual arts in general, but this is merely to restate the question. The trends in art and industrial design which were already sweeping continental Europe in the twenties had very little immediate impact on the external appearance of British cars; only when the thirties arrived would the floodgates open and the resistance of the conservative forces be swept away.

While the industry tried to sort out its problems with satisfying demand and finding enough labour, the economy made its own contribution in the form of a severe and unexpected slump, which started in the autumn of 1920. Although it was relatively short in duration, its main effect on the motor industry – apart from reducing demand – was to terminate the existence of numerous small manufacturers who had set up in the first optimistic months after the war. Not that the major companies were unaffected: Austin, for example, very nearly went under in early 1922, and only the launch of the Seven saved it.

Meanwhile, at the upper end of the market the bespoke coachbuilders seem to have sailed on serenely, little affected by the 1920-22 slump. The most likely explanation for this is that there was a gradual broadening in their clientele, from predominantly aristocracy and landed gentry to what we would now call the 'aspiring' middle classes – however they may be defined. Even more interesting is the suggestion that the top bespoke firms were at first unaware of this trend, preferring to believe that they were still dealing mainly with the aristocracy. At the time, however, they were in the fortunate position of doing better than the car industry in general, and better than the majority of bodybuilding companies. The smaller firms, relying on sub-contract batch orders from car manufacturers, were the prime casualties, not only from the immediate effect of the slump but also because of the trend for manufacturers to set up their own body building facilities.

By 1930, the approximate date of this photo, tall vertical lines had clearly given way to low horizontal ones. This Mercedes-Benz fixed-head coupé was bodied by Harrington, which specialised in bodying imported chassis.

The streamlining craze was just beginning in 1932 when Hooper built this tourer body on a Rolls-Royce 20/25 chassis. There is room for more than one view on its attractiveness, but the pointed tail, extended wings and back-sloping doors at least show a consistent intent.

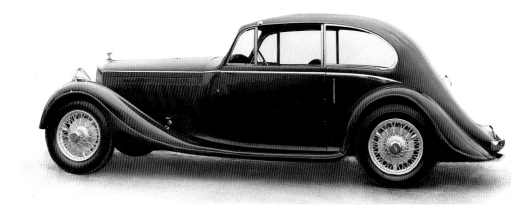

By 1936, when Barker built this Bentley 4¼-litre two-door sports saloon, streamlining had been absorbed effortlessly into the designer's vocabulary. The superb elegance of this design is underlined by a degree of restraint which had now become the hallmark of the top British coachbuilders.

Others were prepared to take streamlining much further. The design house Airstream Ltd produced a one-off study on a Ford V-8 in 1936.

The 'middle-order' coach-builders did much business in the thirties taking care of the needs of the larger manufacturers for more specialised, lower-volume bodies. Salmons (later known as Tickford) was renowned for drophead designs; this one is on a 1936 Vauxhall Light Six.

As the twenties progressed, the case for chassis makers to add in-house bodybuilding capacity became ever stronger. To begin with, the Weymann system was attractive as a route to self-manufacture, since it meant that they could avoid having to recruit many of the skilled tradesmen previously required. As a result, from a small start in 1922, by 1928 the Weymann company could claim no less than 50,000 cars made under its licences. Moreover, the attractions of the Weymann system – lightness, cheapness, reduced skill content – tempted smaller manufacturers to produce their own 'fabric' bodies. Many of these, while looking outwardly like Weymann's, did not use its essential (and patented) feature – ie separated joints – and thus squeaked and rattled like any other body. It could well be this crude plagiarism which led to the demise of the Weymann body.

Another important factor in persuading manufacturers to build their own bodies was the arrival of quick-drying cellulose paints in around 1925. This removed what had been previously a huge bottleneck, and allowed companies to contemplate a bodyshop which did not require an inordinate amount of space. Yet a further reason was the availability of large-tonnage sheet-steel presses; these were increasingly used for parts (mudguards, bonnets, rear panels) which had previously required the skills of a panel-beater or wheeling-machine operator. Finally, of course – and this only applied to the very largest manufacturers at first – it became possible to produce an all-steel, welded body when the Pressed Steel Company opened its doors in 1927. Initially it worked only for William Morris's firms, but by 1930 it was available as a sub-contract supplier to all and sundry.

So there was great uncertainty for those coachbuilders who had been relying on sub-contract orders from manufacturers. And quite apart from the loss of business to in-house body shops, as the end of the twenties drew near another threat loomed – that such customers as they still had might go out of business. Over

the period 1920 to 1929, the number of British car manufacturers dropped from 130 to 50. But this was a nett number for during this same period 205 new car-producing companies had been formed. Thus the decade had seen the disappearance of no less than 285 manufacturers; it is no wonder the smaller coachbuilders were disappearing too.

It is usual to blame this carnage amongst the ranks of manufacturers on the 1929-31 depression, but this is only a very partial explanation. To begin with, the great worldwide slump affected the British car industry far less than in America, and indeed less than most other European countries: the UK car market only declined some 13 per cent between 1929 and 1931, compared with between 33 per cent in France, 50 per cent in Germany, and a near-unbelievable 75 per cent in the United States. Secondly, the shake-out in British car manufacturing happened throughout the twenties, not just in the last two years of the decade, so there must have been another factor at work. This factor was, of course, the growth of the small-car market, driven by the major firms of Austin and Morris who were bringing down prices so relentlessly that most of their competition were unable to keep up. The small (under 10 hp) car segment of the car market had grown to a 24 per cent share by 1927, and would reach an amazing 60 per cent by 1933 (helped by the arrival of the Ford Eight). For the coachbuilding industry this was very bad news since it meant that outside coachbuilding was being replaced by in-house manufacture.

This was the industry background against which the coachbuilding industry continued to trade in the twenties and early thirties. On the face of things, its corner of the market seemed relatively stable. One measure of its strength was the coachwork section of the Olympia Motor Show each year: from a total of 50 British firms exhibiting in 1923, the numbers peaked at 61 in 1926 and then declined to 43 in 1934, which hardly amounted to decimation. However, concealed within these figures is an

Through the thirties the bespoke houses continued to provide 'town carriages' for the top of the trade. This 1938 Rolls-Royce Wraith has been given a touring limousine body by Rippon, the famous Huddersfield coachbuider.

abrupt change in the kind of firm involved. Many of the bespoke houses went out of business at this time, and so did some of the big-volume sub-contractors, but they were replaced by a new breed of low-cost coachbuilder who could turn out batch quantities of special models for the larger manufacturer.

Another change during the slump was in people's attitudes. There was a new-found desire for restrained looks; if, in the late twenties, there had been the start of a trend away from the typical vertical, conservative lines of the time, and towards a more horizontal, flowing appearance, then for a year or two it seems to have been stifled. It might even be argued that the restrained look remained, to an extent, throughout the thirties. Certainly in comparison with some of the outlandish French designs, or the massive German ones, the typical British coachbuilt car – particularly if it was a closed model – was simpler and less excessive. At the time, this was regarded as a quintessentially British quality, and generally admired; looking back, one wonders whether it also marked the beginning of the end of British leadership in the field of coachwork design.

Not that innovation was finished in the British bespoke trade. Immediately after the slump came the most important trend to occur in body design for the whole of the two decades: streamlining. We shall look at streamlining in much more detail, but it is worth recording at this point that the British bespoke industry embraced the concept as quickly as anyone, at least at first. Its imaginative designs during the crucial years 1933-1935, displayed on such occasions as the RAC Rally coachwork competitions, as well as Motor Shows,

were as much responsible for fuelling the industry's rush towards streamlining as any trends imported from America or the Continent. Yet once this new fashion had been adopted by the volume manufacturers, the bespoke industry began to retreat into its shell and reverted to producing the sorts of designs it felt it knew best, for the customers it knew best. Needless to say, these were elegant but dignified creations, for the very top of the trade – indeed, for the sort of clientele who would never have been happy to be seen in a daring new streamlined style of coachwork.

At the same time the middle-order coachbuilders continued to win contracts from major manufacturers for those special models – often drophead coupés – where sales volumes made it more economic to sub-contract. This became a substantial business in the thirties, and seemed to point to a possible route to the industry's survival, but at the same time it was intensively price-competitive, and many of the less efficient firms gave up. There was also work available in bodying those marques which were imported from the Continent or North America; import duties ensured that their numbers would be small, but they also made it worthwhile to bring in the bare chassis and have them bodied in Britain. Even these additional sources of business, though, did not provide enough work to fill the industry's capacity.

By the late thirties, no one with any perception could doubt that they were watching an industry doomed to decline. This was even true of those working on the shop-floor. One former employee of Cross and Ellis recalled the final years of the firm (Cross and Ellis went into receivership in 1938): 'You don't apprentice your son to bodymaking when you know full well it's going to fold up in ten years' time'. One strategy for survival which many of the remaining firms decided to follow was to ally themselves with those manufacturers, and those potential clients, who could be foreseen to require bespoke bodies

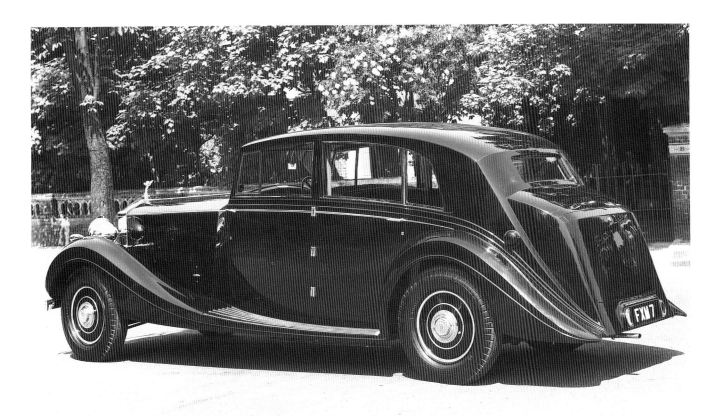

The 'razor-edge' style was a British innovation of the late thirties which persisted after World War 2. This beautifully-proportioned Rolls-Royce Phantom 3 limousine of 1939 is by Freestone & Webb.

for as far in the future as possible. If this meant producing conventional town carriages on Rolls-Royce and Daimler chassis for the older members of the upper classes, so be it. The alternatives were to be a supplier to a small manufacturer, or to build small-volume variants for a major manufacturer. The first was a risky choice, judging by the continuing trend to concentration in the industry; the second had its own problems, because traditional coachbuilding methods demanded a separate chassis, and there was no optimism that this would continue when Vauxhall, for example, were already making an integral-construction, chassis-less car.

The Cross & Ellis employee was both right and wrong: the coachbuilding industry was indeed in decline in the late thirties, but it survived for much longer than ten years, even allowing for the six years' pause brought about by World War 2. Unfortunately it was the wrong part that survived for so long – the dignified creations for the top of the trade. As things turned out there were more people than one might have expected, not only in Britain but throughout the world, who were prepared to pay for these superb examples of craftsmanship but they were a dwindling band and gradually the number of coachbuilding firms involved shrank until, by the end of the sixties, there were effectively only two participants left.

And what about the alternative strategies for survival? The forecast of further concentration in the motor

The best strategy for survival post-war, in hindsight, was to build or convert small-volume bodies for major manufacturers. Carbodies followed this course for more than 20 years; this is the Zephyr Six convertible they were making for Ford in the mid-fifties.

manufacturing industry proved all too true, and by the fifties there was no future in being a sub-contract supplier of bodies to small manufacturers. That left the building of small-volume variants for the major manufacturers, but the universal adoption of integral construction, as expected, meant that there had to be a total change in technology if a firm was going to compete in this field, and very few seemed ready to face up to the challenge. Of those that did, two were swallowed up by manufacturers, and a third became bogged down by its parent company's finances. In the end, the British coachbuilding industry simply faded away.

THE TWENTIES

Hamshaw of Leicester showed this Daimler 30hp limousine-landaulet at the 1920 Olympia Show, but it could almost have come from the pre-World War 1 period with its low bonnet, massive windscreen and lack of protection for the chauffeur. Note the horizontally sliding division and the window blinds with their silk pulls.

On a superficial view, the twenties were not an era of major advance in body design and the typical 1929 car was not drastically different in appearance from a 1919 model. The major points were that it was somewhat lower, had balloon tyres on wire wheels, and possibly had some rudimentary luggage accommodation. Yet this apparent slow rate of evolution concealed dramatic changes beneath the surface, which in some cases were only to come to fruition in the thirties.

Crucially, the twenties were the decade when manufacturers realised that looks could sell, that car buyers were far more influenced by a car's appearance than they

A Vauxhall all-weather built by the Cheltenham firm of Martin & Young in about 1920 clearly demonstrating the complicated system of folding door-pillars which the more expensive all-weather bodies employed. V-windscreens had arrived by this time, making hood-frames even harder to handle. Note lack of driver's door.

would admit to or indeed were even aware of. Nowhere was this more clearly understood than in America, where the principle of annual cosmetic model changes was established at General Motors as early as 1925. Already at that date there were some 17 million cars in use in the United States, and to sell more was increasingly a matter of persuading existing owners to change to a new model.

Even in Europe the concept of making a car's appearance 'attractive' – whatever that word meant at the time – through careful body design was increasingly understood as the decade progressed. The difference from America was that in Europe it carried more weight at the expensive end of the market, where the decision was which car to have rather than whether one could afford a car at all. Thus the bespoke coachbuilding industry carried the burden, far more than volume manufacturers, of pioneering new body styles.

It took time for the realisation that customers would respond favourably to designs that were aesthetically pleasing to make its mark on the coachbuilding industry, and even then it had to be applied with caution. There can be little doubt that the typical British buyer was conservative in his views – certainly more so than his Continental counterpart – and so innovations in design had to be introduced little by little. Gradually, spurred on in part by changes in the artistic and design environment at the time, the form of the coachbuilt product began to change, and with it in due course the corresponding designs from volume manufacturers. The rate of change only accelerated towards the end of the decade, and reached its full flowering in the thirties.

Before such considerations became important, however, there were other problems to be solved. First and foremost was the technical question – just what was the best way to build a body? For the volume manufacturer this was fundamental: with the methods used at the start of the decade he could foresee nothing but rows of buildings filled with work-in-progress, as the coachbuilders laboriously made their wooden frames, the panel-beaters clothed them, and the painters hand-painted each coat of varnish and waited for it to dry.

The volume manufacturers' answers were essentially twofold: steel pressings and cellulose paint. In between came the fabric body – started, interestingly, at the bespoke end of the industry but adopted with enthusiasm by the cheaper end of the trade until its limitations became more evident. It solved the panel-beating problem but little else, and eventually steel pressings became the norm. Wooden frames were harder to eliminate, unless you had such massive sales that you could go to an all-steel, welded body. William Morris had just such sales volumes, and encouraged the American Budd company to open up a plant (Pressed Steel Ltd) adjacent to his Cowley factory in 1927 (first in Britain but not in Europe, that honour going to Citroën). Other large-scale manufacturers followed on, but the medium-sized firms had to remain with the 'composite body' – a wooden frame on which were mounted pressed or fabricated steel panels.

For the coachbuilding firms the technical problems took a different form. There was no question of their using steel pressings; the cost of the dies could never be justified by the volumes in which they dealt. Hence they were committed to building up individual, hand-made

It is difficult to believe that an owner could have specified a dickey-seat for his (her?) footman in a new car. Nevertheless Cunard was asked to build one into a 40/50 Napier in 1921.

panels on some form of frame, and this was a business in which they were knowledgeable and proficient. Uppermost in the minds of these producers of high-quality, expensive bodies were such questions as how to make them lighter, and how to stop squeaks and rattles – and the related, longer-term question of the life expectancy of their product.

The coachbuilt body of the early twenties was beautifully made, but it was still very much a 19th-century carriage in its manner of execution. Steel or aluminium panels had replaced the previous wooden ones, but the framework and ironmongery involved had changed but little. The result was that the typical closed body was heavy – some 8-10cwt (400-500kg). Furthermore, it was very carefully mounted at numerous points to the chassis, so it took the full force of any chassis flexing – and there was plenty! (For example, there was even a suggestion in the motoring press at the time – 1923 – that the 'rigid saloon' was taboo in certain industrial areas, because the poor street surfaces soon produced incurable rattles 'even in the most expensive bodies'.)

Thus the coachbuilders at the time faced the twin – and to some extent linked – problems of weight and flexing. The former sapped the performance of the chassis,

the latter led initially to squeaks and rattles and eventually to more serious problems: splitting in the panels, cracked or broken glass, and eventually the scrapping of the whole body. They therefore set about trying to solve both problems as a matter of urgency. It was a sufficiently serious problem to occupy numerous column inches in the motoring press, as witness this extract from an article in 1922:

'Most have experienced at some time or other the nuisance of that brain-racking tapping or creaking noise somewhere in the body, whatever the conditions of the road, which, should it happen to occur in a closed body, amounts to an incessant drumming noise, which the faster the car travels, the increased vibration intensifies, until it becomes a veritable tattoo on the panels. It may be further added to by a movement in the door or windows squeaking, which, however well built, is inevitable if the bodies, as is often the case, are fixed directly to the chassis.'

There was at this stage no agreement as to what an ideal body mounting method might be. A 1922 article seriously suggested that the most effective answer would be to suspend the body from each corner by leather straps and C-springs – presumably as coaches had been in the last century – and that only cost considerations prevented this method being adopted.

The initial solution was to try and insulate the body from the flexing of the chassis by use of a subframe insulated by some elastic medium – either rubber or spring steel. A great deal of ingenuity was devoted to such systems throughout the decade, and indeed into the thirties. Daimler, still building some although far from all of its own bodies, was an early devotee of a subframe system;

There were many designs of dickey-seat; Grose of Northampton had a version with a fold-down flap which both acted as a step and made access easier. The car is an Alvis 12/40 sports of 1922.

The 'Eclipse' one-man hood of 1922 was an early attempt to ease the effort involved with all-weather bodies by using counterbalancing springs. Stowing the folded hood was not made easier by the fashion for V-windscreens.

its own, first described in 1921, used a patented steel frame, hinged at the rear and with rubber buffers at the front. The Lanchester version in 1922 used a form of double insulation in which the body was separated by rubber washers from mounting brackets, which in turn were also rubber-insulated from the chassis. Later (1925) both Connaught and James Young brought out their own variants. Connaught's, shown on a Daimler limousine at Olympia that year, used a four-point mounting, while the

By 1923 bonnet lines had risen to match the waist level, although vertical lines and an impression of height still predominated. This is a Vauxhall 14/40 saloon by Warwick Motor Body of Croydon.

Blake of LIverpool described this 1923 Wolseley two-seater with dickey as 'sporting', but it looks rather staid to modern eyes.

James Young version sounds even more complex, with Hardy Spicer flexible disc couplings used at five separate points and seats fixed directly to the chassis. The following year London Improved Motor Coachbuilders showed a Crossley saloon which again seems to have used a subframe and steel springing.

It is worth noting that the same debate was raging, and the same solutions were being sought, on the Continent. In 1925 the French coachbuilder Kelsch combined the national affection for fabric bodies with a subframe mounting by developing a lightweight plywood structure which was attached to the chassis in a novel manner: it was fixed rigidly at the centre, but flexibly at each end via ball-and-socket joints. Just what advantages this method brought is hard to see, and indeed little was heard of the Kelsch system – at least in England – thereafter.

The search for the ideal body mounting method continued. A thoughtful paper in *The Automobile Engineer* in 1926 compared the merits of the different systems. It made the important point that it was possible to have *too large* a relative movement between body and chassis – what we would call today 'compliance' – and that this was exacerbated by the sheer mass of the body, often moving out of harmony with the chassis. The same point was made even more graphically by the designer E.C.Gordon England in an address in 1927. He noted how difficult it was to make people understand that 'weight and bulk are not proof of strength, and more often than not are definitely signs of weakness'. His crucial argument was that 'apart from chassis distortion the

greatest factor tending to destroy the body is its own inertia'. The Gordon England patented system once again used a subframe, insulated from the chassis through the medium of rubber, but needless to say the distinguishing feature of the body was its lightness.

Finally, Rolls-Royce itself decided to enforce a subframe mounting system on its coachbuilders when it launched the Phantom II in 1929. Once again the system used three compressed-rubber mounts – one at the front, two at the sides – although there was an additional 'supplementary' support at the rear. Rolls-Royce naturally produced a set of superbly printed instructions for the coachbuilder, in which it pointed out the system would not only reduce chassis shocks on the body, but would also greatly reduce the time that the chassis spent in the coachworks, since the body could be built in advance on the subframe. It was probably the last widely-used subframe system, if we exclude the MG N-type of 1934.

An alternative approach to subframes was to use steel framing instead of wood; this would either reduce weight for the same strength or give increased rigidity with no further weight penalty. There had been pre-war attempts along these lines, notably from BSA with their two- and four-seater open cars. Early pioneers of all-steel frames post-war were Morgan (the coachbuilders of Leighton Buzzard, not the three-wheeler manufacturers from Malvern) and Bowden Brake (known at that period for its coachwork). A Bowden saloon from 1922, on a Morris Oxford chassis, even boasted a sliding door, which says something about the maker's confidence in the rigidity of the body. Yet none of these much-praised systems lasted. We can only guess at the reason, but it is likely to be that the claims for rigidity were found to be exaggerated.

In the end, it seems that there was no really successful system of metal-framed body until the famous Park Ward design of the mid-thirties. This is not to say that no steel was used for framing; on the contrary, it was increasingly employed at high-stress areas such as windscreen pillars, as well as substituting for the previous very heavy

Compared with the Blake Wolseley shown on the previous page, Penman of Dumfries made this 1923 Bentley 3-litre coupé look lower and better balanced.

A Weymann patent drawing showing the way in which the frame members were held together, without touching, by steel plates.

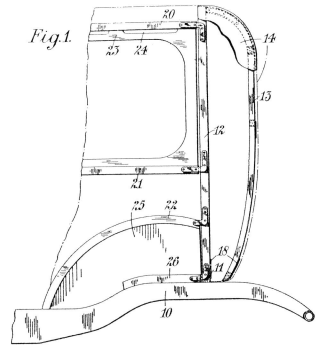

Fig. 1.

timber bottom rails (where it brought the added benefit of reducing the overall height of the body).

While development of subframes and all-metal frames had been proceeding, a wholly different approach to the twin problems of weight and flexing had arrived on the scene from France. Why, mused M. Weymann, try to make your bodywork more and more rigid? Instead, make it flexible, let it ride with the twists and turns of the chassis, and let anything of importance – especially seats – be mounted directly on the chassis, independent of the body. The bodywork's sole function, in effect, would be to protect the passengers from the elements, and hence it could be made both flexible and much lighter. Thus was the Weymann system born: a light, cellular wooden frame covered with padding and fabric ('imitation leather'). In later versions there were also aluminium panels, or sometimes expanded metal, to give curved rather than square corners.

As well as dramatically lightening a conventional body – maybe by as much as 50 per cent, which would typically mean 3-4cwt (150-200kg) – the system 'eliminated' squeaks and rattles from the framework. It did this by introducing a gap of 4-6mm between the members of every joint, these being held together – or rather apart – by metal plates. To give an idea of the detailed development which eventually went into the system, each plate was itself separated from its wooden member by a strip of greaseproof paper, and fixing was not by woodscrews but by countersunk bolts and nuts. In the few cases where it was not possible to avoid wood contacting wood, such as in fabricating certain complicated shapes, then leather or canvas was inserted between the two parts. Similarly, felt was used between the bottom bars and the chassis when the body was mounted. The whole assembly was covered in leathercloth, the space between the outer covering and the interior lining being sometimes filled with cotton wool or horsehair. Doors were not a tight fit, but instead shut on to soft seals; the doors themselves were extremely flexible, and were fitted internally with strain-

ing wires to allow their shape to be adjusted if necessary.

The claim was that the body would remain absolutely silent even after long service – something that was especially desirable in France with its *pavé* surfaces. As an added bonus, the light fabric roof also solved the problem of drumming which plagued the owners of steel-roofed saloons for most of the decade (and which was probably cured through the widespread adoption of the sunshine roof). A further advantage claimed was that these bodies were much easier to keep clean, and compared with the varnished paintwork then in use it was certainly true. Although early versions tended to be rather square in shape, users of the system soon found ways of adding curvature at the right places, to the point where a Weymann body and a coachbuilt one looked very similar in outline; the one difference – and a major one in the end – was the matt surface finish of the Weymann.

Landaulets were becoming less formal by 1923; this 30hp Daimler by Knibbs of Manchester has no division (and technically is therefore a saloon landaulet).

By around 1924 when Hamshaw bodied this Hispano-Suiza, limousines were already adopting the D-back form which would persist right up to World War 2, with a fold-out grid for luggage. Note the domed roof, which was a common measure to try to prevent drumming. The bonnet-line has now moved up to the level of the waist-rail.

As far as Britain was concerned, the first news of this impending revolution arrived in the early part of 1923 in the form of a description of the system, followed by the announcement of the start of full production in Paris (although it would appear that development work had begun as early as 1920). Incidentally, it is a telling comment on the insularity of the coachbuilding trade at that time that the motorist could find out much more about Weymann from his weekly magazine than the professional could from his monthly journal. Learning from experience in France, where it made all its own bodies and was hard put to keep up with its growth rate, Weymann decided that in Britain licensing was to be the initial way forward (this was also a means of keeping initial capital investment to a minimum). The first two licences appear to have been granted to car manufacturers, Talbot-Darracq and Rover, while the first to coachbuilders were probably to Chalmer and Hoyer (forerunners of Hoyal) for a four-door saloon body on a 3-litre Bentley chassis, and to Elkington for a Peugeot 12 saloon. By the next year's Olympia Show Cadogan, Gurney Nutting and Windover had been added to the list, and in 1925 Harrington and H J Mulliner; there were probably others not recorded.

The Weymann system took both France and Britain by storm. In Britain the company achieved rapidly increasing success until the late years of the twenties, although the peak was somewhat earlier in France. The British company's policy of licensing continued but it decided to build bodies itself as well, and in 1925 moved into a factory in Putney; it soon outgrew it, and in 1928 Weyman moved again to Addlestone. While numbers are hard to come by, it is known that some 12,000 Weymann bodies were produced in France in their best years of 1926-7, and that the British figures, while somewhat lower, were of the same order. It is therefore possible that Weymann bodies formed roughly a third of all British coachbuilt production in these peak years. At the 1928 Olympia Show 37 per cent of the exhibits had fabric bodies, mostly Weymanns, and in the same year it was claimed that there were 50,000 Weymann bodies in use in the two countries combined. By that time, though, the

Gurney Nutting was amongst the first to take out a Weymann licence, exhibiting this Sunbeam 20hp Weymann saloon at the 1924 Olympia show.

Also quick to take up the Weymann system were Freestone & Webb. This 3-litre Bentley saloon of 1925 has the typical squared-off lines of the earlier Weymann bodies.

system's attractions had been whittled away by numerous competitors, as we shall see later.

It is interesting to compare the different approaches of Charles Weymann and E.C.Gordon England – both with a background in aviation design – to the question of body design. England did it for us, in 1927:

'M. Weymann believed that the solution was to build a light structure that was flexible and cover it with a flexible material, which, while adjusting itself to the movements of the structure, would, at the same time, prove quiet. On the other hand, I provided a very light, rigid structure, entirely insulated from the chassis distortion and the weights of passengers, and because of this was able still further to reduce the structure weight beyond what would seem safe practice.'

Thus weight reduction and insulation from flexing were the critical questions which the bespoke coachbuilders worried about for much of the twenties. In the meantime, subtly but inexorably, the overall shape of cars was evolving. One of the first Edwardian features to be jettisoned

was the low bonnet, the purpose behind this being to achieve a continuous waistline on one level, from radiator to back panel. Such a feature was deemed particularly desirable on touring cars, and no doubt led to some early attempts at a disappearing hood: William Arnold, the Manchester coachbuilder, showed three examples of their version at the 1920 Motor Show.

Hoods in the early twenties usually had a V-shaped top rail to match the V-windscreens then fashionable, so folding away such an ungainly device – let alone concealing it – was quite a feat, but most buyers were prepared to put up with this task. By far the majority of cars purchased at that time were open, and this was the case for most of the decade: even in 1927 there were some 89,000 open cars newly registered, as against 76,000 closed ones. Not that this necessarily represented car buyers' aspirations, for in the early part of the decade an open bodied car, being much cheaper, was all that most buyers could afford. Initially they were fairly unpleasant places to be in the wet, having little if any weather protection at the

The London Improved Co. used a sub-frame in 1925 when they rebodied this 1920 Rolls-Royce Silver Ghost – and they paid a licence fee to the Gordon England company for the privilege, so it must have employed the latter's three-point mounting system. Note the roof ventilator, a common mid-twenties feature.

The 1925 Rolls-Royce 20hp by Harrison shown here is described as a cabriolet, since it has an early example of the Tickford folding head (made by Salmons of Newport Pagnell); here the cant-rails remain in place.

sides. Later on, with the advent of rigid, removeable side-curtains (pioneered by the Standard company) they became known as 'all-weather' bodies, and were much more acceptable in their own right even disregarding price. However, once volume manufacturers could produce a saloon at a competitive price, the true nature of demand asserted itself and open car registrations dived – down to a mere 13,000 in 1931.

At the bespoke end of the trade, by contrast, the majority of production was of closed bodies. Where a coachbuilder did produce an 'all-weather', it was a very different concept from the mass-market version. Typically there would be glass windows which folded down against the inside of the doors; alternatively, they would wind down into the door itself, and the appropriate pillar would then fold down into a horizontal position. The hood itself would frequently be lined, and of course the general standard of upholstery and fitments was much higher. There was considerable progress during the decade in producing 'all-weather' designs that were gen-

uinely weatherproof, easy to convert, and not too costly to build, starting with the Gwynne head, which replaced the previous heavy wood hood sticks with slimmer, lighter steel ones. The 'Tickford' system, introduced by Salmons and Sons of Newport Pagnell in 1925, which used a series of gears turned by a handle from the outside, became one of the best known, and both Beadle of Dartford and Alexander of Glasgow had similar 'demountable tops' on offer two years later.

There were still diehards who preferred to be in the open air as much as possible, and for them the tourer continued to be made. It would appear that their passengers did not always share their enthusiasm, judging from the plaintive cries in the motoring press for better weather protection in the back of such cars. Strangely, passengers were worse off in the back of a coachbuilt tourer than in a cheaper car, if only because in the more expensive (and therefore bigger) models they were further away from the windscreen. Eventually such devices as the Beatonson or Auster screen, which could be folded out from behind the front seats, came to their rescue. Some of these would also convert into a division, thus preserving the social niceties between chauffeur and employer when the car was in its closed form. Incidentally, the social order was rarely so strongly emphasised as in a Cunard-bodied Napier coupé-landaulet of 1921 (shown on page 15), which incorporated a fold-out dickey seat for the footman.

The V-windscreen fashion began to die out by the middle of the decade. The newer designs were not only flat, but sloping as well, often to match up with a sloping door-pillar line. They also changed gradually from being split horizontally, with the top half opening, to the one-piece version which opened in its entirety from a hinge at the top. There was even a move, started by Brewster, the Rolls-Royce coachbuilder in America, to a 'retreating' (ie reverse slope) windscreen which allegedly helped to disperse rain-drops; but this did nothing for aesthetic appearance and little more was heard of it.

Around 1923 and 1924 came the first signs of a development that would change the shape of cars probably more than any other single feature – the luggage boot. At first these tended to be no more than separate trunks, attached to the rear of the car, although in 1924 Arthur Mulliner did manage to build space for four cases into the back of a D-back Farman limousine, and the following year Hill and Boll produced one of the very first sloping back treatments containing a luggage boot, on a Chrysler. These were the exceptions, however, and the norm – where luggage accommodation was provided at all – was the separate trunk, fixed to the body but looking as if it was detachable. This style became much more developed in France, so much so that it eventually gave its name to the 'Continental coupé'; by 1927, indeed, there was acceptance even amongst British designers that the French were ahead in the matter of providing accommodation for luggage.

The position was very soon redressed. The British industry recognised the pressures to provide covered space for luggage, even in relatively small cars, and the result was the 'sportsman's coupé', a two-door, four-light style which arrived so quickly and from so many different coachbuilders that the 1928 Olympia was dubbed 'the Show of the Sportsman's Coupé'. By moving the rear passengers forward within the wheelbase – often by making room for their feet under the front seats – designers were able to add luggage space behind the rear seat, within the overall outline of the body; in many instances there was no external door to this space, access being gained by folding down the back seat.

The built-in boot in fact arrived from two directions, as it were, since it also developed from the dickey-seat of the typical two-door, two-light coupé. These had a flush-fitting lid covering the seat when it was not in use, and it did not take a feat of imagination to realise that the compartment so formed, which often contained the tool-kit, could also carry luggage. Another popular addition on this style of body was the golf-club locker, which ran the full width of the car behind the front seats and was reached by a small trapdoor in the near side.

The interesting point about the more expensive saloons and (especially) limousines is that they resisted the trend to luggage trunks or boots longer than any other body style (apart maybe from sports cars); instead they made do with a folding or concealed luggage grid. There was a good reason: these were normally town cars, and on the rare occasions when they were employed on longer journeys the luggage would be sent on ahead – by rail, by steamer or in the second car with the staff. These cars were the last to retain the 'D-back' shape of the early twenties; other styles moved gradually to a straight, and then a sloping, shape of back in order to harmonise with the luggage trunk. At the same time the pronounced domed roof of the earlier years disappeared, in spite of its being less prone to drumming. No doubt this was not only for aesthetic reasons but also to accommodate the popular sliding roof.

An unusual symptom of light-heartedness – or, putting it another way, of bodywork being designed to attract buyers – entered the scene in the early years of the decade, and persisted for a number of years. This was the craze for 'boat' or 'skiff' bodies on sports cars in which by some contrary thinking, the rear part of the body was made to look like the prow of a boat. As with so many fashions, it became popular in France before England, but in this case there was a difference: it seems to have been seen first on the English side of the Channel. No doubt there were earlier examples than 1919, but certainly in that year Barker displayed a Rolls-Royce with a boat-shaped body, and it had what became almost the trademark of such designs – mahogany planking held down with copper rivets. Such a no-expense-spared display of conspicuous consumption was unusual for the immediate post-war period, and it was another couple of years before other builders felt confident enough to follow suit, but at the Paris Salon in 1921 the boat body had suddenly become *de rigueur* for small sports cars, and the same situation applied during the following year.

Meanwhile the British, having apparently started the craze, seem to have been slow in exploiting it. Nothing further appeared at Olympia until 1924, when Egerton produced a three-seater example on an AC. By the next year boat designs were plentiful; Grosvenor had its well-known Vauxhall 30/98, Jarvis showed its two-seater Aston Martin, and even stately Lanchester produced a design, using teak for the planking. Jarvis, particularly, seem to have made a speciality of the boat style, showing Bugattis in both 1926 and 1927 with tulip-wood planking and a Darracq in 1927. Then, suddenly, the craze died out on both sides of the Channel, far more quickly than it had begun. Another possibly related fashion of the same period, for wood-grain finish, in which Barker seemed to specialise, was equally short-lived.

Boat-shaped bodies are a very early example of a styling fashion which developed purely in its own right

Freestone & Webb had a long association with Mercedes chassis during the twenties. This is a Weymann-style limousine from 1926; even at this stage not all sharp angles had yet been eliminated from Weymann bodies.

At the 1926 Motor Show Freestone & Webb exhibited a 37.2hp Hispano-Suiza Weymann saloon upholstered in suede calf, with cabinet work decorated in 'ornamental French Lacquer'.

rather than being the result of any new technical influence. One can speculate about the psychological motivation behind it; probably one factor was a reaction against the horrors and the sadnesses of the Great War, which manifested itself in many other ways during the twenties, and particularly amongst the well-off young. Yet there may have been a serious point behind this craze and similar exercises such as the Alvis ducks-back, in that they were satisfying an early subconscious desire for streamlining.

The year 1925 saw the arrival of a major technical innovation which was to have enormous influence on the appearance of coachwork thereafter. This was the cellulose painting process, which not only transformed volume manufacture by its speed of application, but also opened new opportunities for the specialist coachbuilders. Like so many other technical advances, it had been developed in America, and first used (by Cadillac

and Oakland) as early as mid-1923. Its use was preceded by the perfection of paint-spraying techniques, which were being used with the older style lacquers before the arrival of cellulose; indeed, Ford was using spraying at its Trafford Park factory as early as 1912, and it was in wide use by 1921, though more for simple components such as wings than for the body itself. Dipping and flow-coating were also highly developed by 1922, and the larger factories were using artificial drying by 1924.

All these techniques, but especially the introduction of cellulose paint with its quick-drying properties, were aimed at cutting down the inordinate amount of time a body took to be painted. The traditional coach-painting process up to then had been a laborious matter of laying on successive layers of primers, fillers, guide coat, stopping coat, 'common colour' and 'best colour' – each one by hand, and each one having a long drying time – followed by the fearful business of hand-varnishing; this was

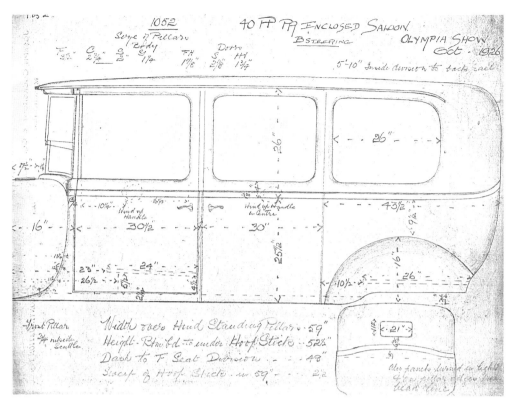

It is hard to believe that the drawing reproduced here, no more than a sheet of foolscap notepaper, could have been turned into the beautiful example of coachwork shown below. To appreciate the panel-beater's skill one need only compare the drawing of the scuttle with the complex shape which eventually emerged.

The Rolls-Royce Phantom 1 saloon which took shape in the Manchester coachworks of Joseph Cockshoot from the sketch shown above. It was exhibited at Olympia in 1926, finished in primrose and black. Note the suggestion of 'brougham' shape to the front pillar.

This is how coachbuilt bodies looked at the start of the twenties – low bonnets, V-windscreens, peaked roofs; the hand-painted finish has no doubt been replaced by cellulose in the intervening years. The 1920 Napier 40/50 coupé-cabriolet shown here was bodied by Cunard, at that time Napier's own 'in-house' coachbuilder.

The 'Town Brougham' of around 1925 advertised on the 30hp chassis by Armstrong-Siddeley was built by Burlington, another in-house coachbuilder. It shows most of the brougham characteristics, including carriage-lamps and peaked roof at the rear, but not in this case the forward-curved rear door.

Gurney Nutting's reputation was at its peak in 1928 when the firm bodied this ultra-expensive Hispano-Suiza 8-litre 'Boulogne' sports saloon. Polished aluminium bonnets were often specified at this period.

Albany Carriage made an early, and brave, attempt at streamlining in 1927 with the 'Airway' saloon. It was inspired by aviation practice at the time, with three wickerwork seats and a specification which included an airspeed indicator. Albany's solution to providing headroom in a swept tail was unconventional, and less than beautiful.

Lea-Francis provided Avon (strictly speaking New Avon) with much of its work during the twenties. This 1927 Model K boat-tailed two-seater, with underslung spare wheel, probably looks more elegant with the hood down.

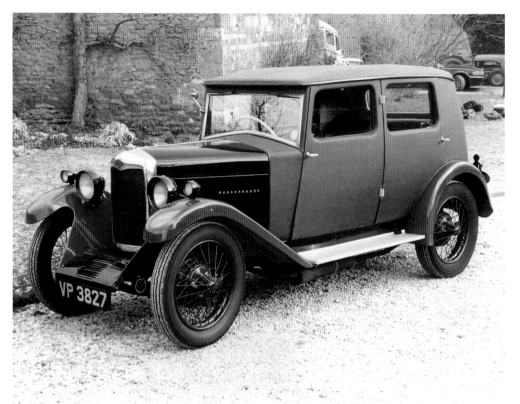

The Riley Nine, bodied by yet another in-house coachbuilder in Midland Motor Bodies, was a landmark design in the way it used footwells to achieve a lower seating position. This is the Monaco fabric saloon of around 1927.

Gordon England was probably the best-known supplier of special bodies for the Austin Seven. This is the Cup model, introduced in 1925 although this particular example is from 1928. The fabric-covered body was unusual in having both running-boards and a louvred chassis valance.

fraught with the risk of dust entering the atmosphere before the varnish had dried, and both coachbuilders and volume manufacturers used filtering and other tricks to minimise it. A coachbuilder described in 1921 just what the pressures were on his coach-painting department: the 'ideal' process, using all the successive coats desirable, would take no less than 48 working days, and even what he termed a 'practical' sequence took 20 days. 'When a customer asks how long it will take to paint his body, the answer from the foreman coach-painter is always "Oh, twenty to thirty days", whereas in practice the shop could not afford to take so long'.

With such benefits on offer, it is surprising that the industry was rather slow to take up the cellulose process. Vanden Plas, with its aircraft-painting connections, and Lanchester claimed to be among the first users, which is likely to have been in 1925, but even though suppliers were advertising the product to the trade and offering use of their demonstration plants, only two other coach-builders (Beadle and Short) featured cellulose finishes at Olympia that year. A year later it was still being treated as a novelty, and only by 1929 was it considered as near universal. Needless to say, it was the more traditional end of the trade which was the slowest to make the change; even in 1928 Hooper was only conceding that 'in some cases cellulose paint is used', before going on to describe lovingly the various stages of hand-painting.

Slowness in changing over to cellulose could not be blamed on the reluctance of the customer. It is hard for us to imagine from this distance the impact on a potential buyer when he saw a cellulose-painted car for the first time; its surface was as deeply lustrous as the finest hand-varnished product from an expensive coachbuilder, and its colour was many times brighter. More than that, its toughness allowed it to be cleaned easily without fear of scratching, something which could never have been said of varnish finishes. This was a significant point even at the bespoke end of the trade, at a time when chauffeurs were becoming less common and the 'owner- driver' was unimpressed by the time and care necessary to look after the traditional type of paintwork. Furthermore, if an owner was unlucky enough to find a scratch, he could now in many instances polish it out, something which had not previously been possible.

The new range of bright colours available was soon exploited by coachbuilders. In place of the dark reds, dark blues and purples which had previously been the norm, colours such as primrose, ivory and light blue suddenly began to appear and even the previously obligatory black wings became the same colour as the body. The gaiety of these colours seemed to capture the spirit of the age, one which was unfortunately to change all too soon with the onset of the Depression.

It is probably true to say that cellulose paints were responsible for the death of the Weymann body and all its fabric-covered imitators. Some loyal users of the system fought on, firstly by using cellulose paints themselves (so that they could at least compete on colour, if not on finish) and then by using the newly available glossy fabric known as *Tôle Souple*, which from a distance made the body look like one with coachbuilt metal panels. From contemporary accounts, incidentally, it would seem that *Tôle Souple* was a very difficult material to work. Another innovation was to apply dummy hood-irons to the rear quarters, thus giving the upper fabric the appearance of a drophead; this was the start of the many *faux cabriolet* (false cabriolet) treatments beloved of Continental coachbuilders in the thirties.

Another, and in the long term more significant, attempt at a halfway house was the so-called 'semi-Weymann' body, which combined the usual Weymann lightweight frame and fabric covering to the upper half with metal cladding below the waistline. Certain commentators at the time called into question the validity of trying to mix a flexible frame with rigid metal panels, but it would seem that they missed the fundamental basis of the revised Weymann method, which was to make the body frame act as a series of rigid cells flexibly connected to each other. Thus the scuttle, rear quarter and doors were each in themselves rigid enough to take metal panelling, but their flexible connection to each other allowed the body as a whole to flex with the chassis as before. Relative movement between these cells was taken up by allowing the doors to move in two directions within the door openings. The bottom frames were jointed as before with metal plates, and care was taken to avoid trouble in critical places by not turning over the edges of the metal panels.

The 'semi-Weymann' development undoubtedly gave a renewed impetus to the Weymann system, and to fabric bodies in particular. H J Mulliner made a speciality of this treatment for a couple years, and other exponents were Avon, Freestone and Webb, Hoyal, Gurney Nutting, and Martin Walter. Nevertheless, the significance of the semi-Weymann development is that it pointed the way to building flexible coachbuilt bodies, in other words, bodies that were inherently flexible and yet which could still carry metal panelling. This in turn led to such innovations as Silent Travel, which although strictly speaking started in 1929 is really more appropriately regarded as a thirties phenomenon.

In the end the buyers were not deceived. Fabric bodies were just not as attractive to look at as metal ones. They were dull instead of shiny, and they had sharp corners and flat panels instead of seductive curves. One damning summary was that 'some people live in tents and are satisfied; others prefer houses'. Even their earlier advantage of being easy to clean had been nullified by the advent of cellulose paints. On top of this, their general reputation had suffered at the hands of cheap imitators, since at the lower end of the market there were fabric bodies which were not noted for their longevity. This is not to denigrate, however, those perfectly respectable fabric body systems which grew up alongside Weymann.

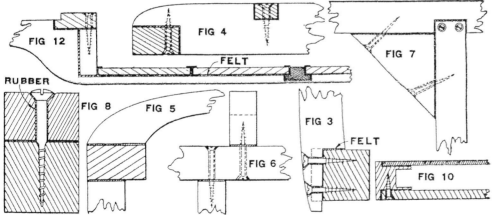

Another 1926 Show exhibit was a smart Darracq 20/98 Six 'sports special' from Grose. It was finished in grained sycamore, a fashion at the time. The extended tail carried only tools, not luggage.

The 'British Flexible' construction system of 1928, developed by Harrison, used felt between the joints and screws encased in rubber.

One such was the 'British Patent Flexible Fabric Body' developed by the well-known coachbuilding firm of Harrison and Sons. Here the flexibility was provided by sandwiching a layer of felt between the two halves of each joint, and then encasing the woodscrews which held the joint in rubber sleeves. As with Weymann, the framework itself was very light and the seats were fixed directly to the chassis. No doubt this would have been an attractive proposition to coachbuilders in the middle of the decade, but by the time it was introduced in 1928 the swing against fabric bodies had begun, and there is only one known example – Vanden Plas in 1929 – of the system being used under licence.

Another development along Weymann lines was the 'Alvista', built for Alvis by Cross and Ellis in both closed and open forms. This bore a surprising resemblance to Weymann techniques in that the main joints were held together – but not in contact – by metal plates, sometimes with felt inserted in the gap. Although the plates were said to be of a special design, they again echoed Weymann by providing the necessary flexibility to the framework. More importantly, there was a unique method of mounting the body using sheet steel brackets which clamped the side pillars rigidly to the chassis, thus ensuring that any flexing occurred only in the upper part of the body framework. The Alvista system ran from 1927 to 1930 and was developed for a short period into a semi-panelled form on the 1929 Atlantic saloon.

The demise of the Weymann body, and of fabric bodies generally, did not happen overnight. At the 1929

Pytchley launched its sliding sunshine roof in 1925. By the time of the 1926 Show there was so much interest in it that the company mounted a special demonstration on a Standard 18-36hp saloon (it did not normally open in this manner!).

By 1926 the 'continuous waistline' was firmly established, especially for tourers. The Hooper Phantom 1 shown here also boasts a hood which folds much flatter than those of a few years previously. Note the chromed hood frame and the ship-type scuttle ventilators.

Motor Show, *The Autocar* calculated that no less than 30 per cent of the exhibits in the coachbuilding section were of fabric in some form; even this figure is misleadingly low given the preponderance of limousines, landaulets and so on, which were always of conventional – ie composite wood-and-steel – construction. Yet by the early thirties a new Weymann body was a rare event. In France the disappearance was even quicker: *The Automobile Engineer* reported that at the 1931 Paris Salon not only was there no Weymann body or licence plate to be seen, there was no fabric body of any description.

One design innovation for which the Weymann system can claim some credit is the full-length door; that is, the door carried right down to the running board, obviating the need for a valance between the two. Certain coachbuilders (Hamshaw, Offord) had tried such a style in the early twenties, but it was much easier to achieve with a Weymann body, not only because of the lightweight construction of the doors but also because these bodies could easily be built out beyond the width of the chassis. Eventually, of course, it was copied by non-Weymann builders. This was one area where French coachbuilders could certainly claim to have been in the lead, to the extent that after the 1927 Paris Salon *The Autocar* portentously announced 'the death-knell of the valance' – prematurely, as we shall see, but the full-length door was to remain a dominant feature in most future designs.

Running parallel with this development was another theme which was to dominate design thinking thereafter

A Windover Rolls-Royce Phantom 1 limousine of 1927 finished in polished aluminium. The transparent opening roof panels were an unusual feature. An interior shot (opposite) gives some idea of the standard of finish which a buyer expected. Note the speedometer and chronometer, with companion-set between – not to mention the cut-glass vase.

– the desire to reduce a car's overall height. Very probably this started as a result of early work on streamlining, but designers soon realised its aesthetic benefits. The key to achieving a lower profile was of course to seat the passengers lower – particularly those at the rear – and the quickest way to do this was to provide footwells for them. It would be a brave man who claimed to identify the first car to incorporate footwells; the 1922 Lancia Lambda was an early such design, although the wells came about more as a result of its pioneering monocoque construction than through a desire for reduced height in itself. Amongst British manufacturers, the Riley 9 of 1927 was one of the very first to use footwells, and in that case it is clear that the objective was to reduce height.

The alternative means of lowering seats in the car was by lowering the chassis. Once again the Riley 9 was an early example, but that was because Riley built its own coachwork and could see the benefits. Other manufacturers soon responded to the entreaties of their coachwork suppliers, however, and underslung, downswept or 'dropped' chassis became the norm by the end of the twenties. One immediate effect could be seen in the design of sports bodies: their drivers could no longer reach over the door either to operate an outside handbrake or to give a hand signal, and around 1928 the cutaway sportscar door was born. Another oddity to emerge was the 'observation body', in which the rear row of seats faced backwards, presumably to give occupants a better view than they could have had from a shallow, high-waisted side window. Hill and Boll and James Young produced examples in the 1927-8 period, and James Young's Chrysler saloon even had a rear-opening door.

What did not happen immediately was a corresponding lowering of the bonnet line. Why this should have been the case is not totally clear; possibly there was a perceived need for the radiator header tank to be placed high up, even when many engines had moved from thermosyphon cooling systems to pumped ones (by 1928, 67 per cent of British production models had a water pump).

Whatever the reason, retaining a high bonnet line meant retaining a high waistline as well, even though the roof had been lowered. Thus there came about the shortlived fashion for dramatically deep doors, surmounted by equally dramatic shallow windows – the 'letterbox windscreen' era, as it has been called.

To modern eyes this trend is retrograde; it seems to be moving further from the low, balanced lines which became the norm in the thirties. And there was more to come: the next fashion was for cycle wings. Why they should have arrived just at this period is uncertain, but it is possible that they were associated with racing-car practice at the time. Their adoption was understandably coupled with the removal of running boards, since these no longer flowed naturally from the line of the wing. In most cases the running board was replaced by a simple metal step, usually fixed but sometimes folding out when the door opened.

The result of eliminating the running board was that the chassis members which had been concealed behind it were now revealed. Realising that – even if the body width would permit it – the current deep doors simply could not be deepened further to hide the chassis, designers instead found a new device: the chassis valance. Frequently they added louvres to it, not for any functional purpose but merely for aesthetic reasons; possibly louvres also suggested that the car sported an undertray, which in turn smacked of a racing pedigree.

During the period that they were becoming lower, cars were also, towards the end of the twenties, changing their interior layout. This was one of the most significant developments of the decade, and was triggered by a perceived need to accommodate the rear seats within the

wheelbase. There was a variety of reasons for this: primarily, as we have already seen, designers at this period were trying to incorporate the luggage-boot within the overall outline of the body. At the same time there was a reaction against the two-light coupé with a dickey-seat – understandably in view of the increasing speeds of which cars were capable – and the pressure was therefore to accommodate the 'occasional' seats under the same roof as the front seats. The result was a rash of 'close-coupled' designs, initially the 'sportsman's coupé', and then only a year or so later the 'sportsman's saloon', a four-door/four-light style which was to some extent a reaction against the cramped access to the rear of the sportsman's coupé.

Connected with this trend towards more roomy accommodation was a parallel one towards widening the rear seat by bringing the body out over the rear wings. Interior comfort was also improved by the introduction of sponge rubber, which proved invaluable for such things as armrests, and which also began to replace coil springs and horsehair in cushions and squabs. Trim materials continued to be leather in medium-priced and open cars, and cloth in the passenger compartments of more expensive ones. There had been some more adventurous experiments including suede leather (Barker in 1925) and lizard-skin (Hooper and Weymann in 1928). The French, not to be outdone, tried both lizard-skin and snake-skin and the French had also been responsible for a truly over-the-top interior in 1922 when Gaborit produced a Louis XVI interior on a Sizaire-Berwick complete with carved *fauteuil* seats. Britain's riposte was not until 1927, when Charles Clark of Wolverhampton produced a Rolls-Royce coupé de ville – 'built to the order of a lady' – with an equally outrageous Louis XV interior (see page 34).

At the same time as the designer was trying to reconcile the two conflicting needs – for seating within the wheelbase yet for sufficient room for two rows of seats – he was beset by another fashion trend for longer bonnets. One has to accept that this was entirely a fashion-driven move as there are no obvious technical reasons for it to have happened. No doubt it was motivated in part by the streamlining craze, just becoming a force in the late twenties, but more importantly a longer bonnet suggested racing-car design and therefore power. Designers resorted to new levels of inventiveness to make their bonnets appear longer. The easiest way was to extend the bonnet over the scuttle, and the next was to move the scuttle itself, with the windscreen, further back, while leaving the seats where they were (which did nothing for ease of access). The front seats themselves, incidentally, were by now (1927) generally adjustable fore-and-aft, the well-known 'Leveroll' mechanism having been introduced two years earlier; adjustable back seats were by no means uncommon either. Pneumatic cushions were being increasingly used in smaller or lower bodies where the room for stuffed spring-cases, or even foam rubber, was limited.

We have already mentioned the word 'streamlining' in this review of the twenties, in connection with boat-tails, with reduced overall height, and with lengthened bonnets. It is now an appropriate moment to stand back and look at the streamline movement as a whole – possibly the single most important influence on the aesthetic design of cars between the wars – and how it grew during the twenties, even though it was not to come to full fruition until the following decade.

The word 'streamline' goes back a long way – cer-

Hamshaw was one of many Weymann licensees and exhibited this Humber 14-40 Weymann saloon at the 1927 Olympia Show. The fabric could now be made to follow curves very similar to those of a steel panel. Note also the dummy hood-irons, full-length doors and peaked roof.

In 1927 it was possible to order coachwork to any design you wanted. Here is a Louis XV interior, on a Rolls-Royce Phantom 1 'brougham de ville', produced by Charles Clark of Wolverhampton 'to the order of a lady'.

tainly to the early part of the nineteenth century. In modern scientific parlance, it implies what is called laminar flow, as opposed to turbulent flow. When air flows over a smoothly shaped body, such as an aeroplane wing or a car, it moves along lines which are closely parallel to the surface; we can visualise such lines as 'streamlines'. If the surface is insufficiently smooth, the lines of air movement break away from the surface and form whirls and eddies: this is turbulent flow. Turbulent flow is the enemy of the aerodynamicist, because the vacuum which it creates at the back of the surface causes drag. In modern terms it increases the Cd or drag factor.

All this was well understood by the experts at the beginning of the twentieth century, and led to the development of the aerofoil-section wing which made powered flight possible. These same experts were on less sure ground when they went on to state that, for minimum air-resistance, the ideal shape was a 'teardrop' – a spherical front to meet the air, followed by a long pointed tail. Such a statement seemed to embody no more than everyday experience – after all, was this not the form into which fish and dolphins had evolved? – and it was readily accepted for at least the first three decades of the century. It determined, amongst other things, the shape of U-boats and Zeppelin airships in World War 1, and influenced a great deal of the work on streamlining of cars thereafter.

However, the assumption was fundamentally wrong. To begin with, droplets of liquid – be they water, tears or anything else – falling freely in air do not take up the elongated shape attributed to them; high-speed photography shows clearly that, after breaking up into smaller drops,

they assume a spherical form. Secondly, the aerofoil or teardrop shape is inappropriate for an object such as a car moving close to the ground: there is no benefit in reduced drag by extending the tail to a point. (When Professor Kamm, working in Stuttgart in 1935, showed conclu-

Pytchley and Tickford were the most successful designs of opening roof, but they were by no means the only ones. This version was the work of Grose of Northampton on a Talbot Darracq M67 16hp saloon of c.1927.

Few designs encapsulate their period so precisely as this 1928 Rolls-Royce Phantom 1 sports saloon by Crosbie & Dunn of Birmingham. It is of semi-Weymann construction, and the fabric material is 'tôle souple' which looked from a distance like cellulosed metal. The design also boasts dummy hood-irons, a separate luggage trunk and float-type running-boards (which appear to incorporate a toolbox).

sively that this was so, the scientific community at first refused to believe him, and treated his results as a joke.)

This background is necessary if we are to understand how streamlining began as a movement, and why it had so many false starts before it grew into something the public would accept. Not that we should think of streamlining as something which only affected cars. On the contrary, it was a word on everyone's lips, put there by the artists and industrial designers of the time who tried to apply it to all aspects of modern life, but it was applied to cars at least as soon as it was to any other form of transport. Indeed, this is one field where the car can be said to have been the pioneer, since the first streamlined train (the famous 'Flying Hamburger') and streamlined plane (the Douglas DC-1) only appeared in 1933, well after even production models of streamlined cars had come on the scene.

Although there were a number of early intuitive

The 1929-30 period typified by a Type 44 Bugatti with two-door coupé body produced by the Weymann company. It has cycle wings, steps instead of running-boards, a louvred chassis valance, glass louvres over the doors, dummy hood-irons and a separate luggage trunk. The sloping windscreen is quite an advanced feature.

attempts at producing a streamlined body, it was only after World War 1 that scientific experiment took over. In 1921 Paul Jaray began testing scale models of car bodies, using the wind tunnel at the Zeppelin airship works where he was chief engineer. In the following two years the Zeppelin company made at least three prototypes, using Ley chassis, presumably to test public reaction. Since the cars did not go into production, one can only assume that they were found to be too radical to be acceptable, in spite of the fact that their engines were in the conventional position at the front, which made them far less outlandish in appearance than some of the rear-engined experiments which were to follow. Jaray's cars nevertheless had the distinction of a true teardrop tail – ie one which tapered in both plan and elevation.

At the same time, another aircraft engineer was testing prototypes in another wind-tunnel. Dr Edmund Rumpler used the Eiffel laboratory at Auteuil in France to test his prototypes. From a technical point of view these were highly advanced: the engines were placed at the rear, to keep the car's width to a minimum at this point, and their six cylinders were arranged in a novel 'broad-arrow' configuration to minimise overall length. Rumpler also developed his own swing-axle suspension at the rear. The arrangement gave an approximation to a teardrop shape in plan, but not in elevation (although the open sports version was much closer to this ideal than the saloon, and prettier as well). Further reductions in drag were achieved by concealing the springs (four semi-elliptics) within the bodywork, and by using solid-disc wheels and minimal mudguards.

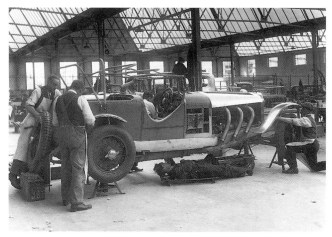

A supercharged Mercedes-Benz 38-250 with racing-type body takes shape in the Folkestone coachworks of Martin Walter in 1929. Unusually, its panels were 'covered with smooth, glossy fabric which was then sprayed in cream cellulose'. Note also the early style of cutaway driver's door.

Rumpler's work did at least produce some results, since the startling rear-engined Benz Grand Prix cars, entered at Monza in 1923, were based on his work. In fact Benz only used the swing-axle portion of his design, and the engines were in-line sixes, with the transmission behind and in unit with the crankcase. They also brought the radiator outside the main body shell, sacrificing aerodynamics for cooling capacity. This seems to have been the end of the road for Rumpler's design, and no more was heard of it.

Whatever the fate of their prototypes, these two men, Jaray and Rumpler, seem to have determined later designers' thinking about streamlining. Both assumed unswervingly that the teardrop shape was essential while Rumpler went further and assumed that this shape could only be achieved with a rear-engined configuration. From the early twenties on this rear-engine fixation ruled any dis-

By 1929, the Brighton firm of Thomas Harrington was beginning to body some cheaper chassis in addition to its normal fare of expensive imports. This Austin 12-4 fabric saloon is an example; note the glass door-louvres, chromed scuttle ventilators and radiator stoneguard (an unusual feature). The roof peak has by now almost disappeared.

Rumpler rear-engined streamliner of 1922. Dr Rumpler's ideas influenced thinking about streamlining for the next ten years.

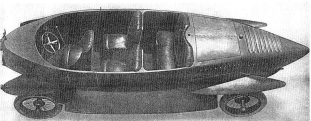

The Burney Streamliner prototype was completed in 1929. Below is one of the production cars of 1930, bodied by Carlton and using a Beverley-Barnes straight-eight 3-litre engine. They were not a commercial success, though how much this was due to the £1500 price and how much to the car's appearance will never be known.

cussion about streamlining. Next to fall in line was Sir Dennistoun Burney, at the time (1928) Chief Designer of the Vickers R101 airship at Howden in Yorkshire. Presumably in his spare time, he designed and built a prototype streamlined car, based on a reversed Alvis front wheel drive chassis; later cars were powered by Beverley-Barnes, Lycoming and Armstrong-Siddeley engines. The design approximated to the desired teardrop shape, but showed the other typical characteristics of these rear-engined exercises: poor rearward visibility and unattractive – some would say ugly – lines. In fairness to Burney, his devotion to the teardrop was based not only on aerodynamic principles, but also on his theories of optimum mass-distribution for passenger comfort.

Burney persisted with his cars for several years, setting up production in a factory at Maidenhead; at one time (1931) there was even talk of his design being taken up by a major US manufacturer. However it never caught the public's imagination – particularly at a price of £1,500 – and only a dozen or so examples were built. A revised version based on the Burney patents was launched by Crossley in 1933 at a more reasonable price of £750, but it was just as unattractive to look at and achieved just as little commercial success.

One might have thought that America would have been the home of streamlining, whether for cars or for anything else, but it was not so. The interest was certainly there, but in the twenties it did not get beyond designers like Norman Bel Geddes producing speculative designs, all of them rear-engined, and many with tail fins. One design had been commissioned by the Graham-Paige Company, but a combination of reservations about its acceptability and the onset of the Depression stopped it being built. However, some wind tunnel work went on,

A Rolls-Royce Phantom 2 sports saloon built by Gurney Nutting in 1929 with the then-fashionable lower roof line, brought about by using footwells to lower the seating. The Phantom 2 was one of the last models to use a subframe to mount the body.

both in universities and at the Bureau of Standards.

With such emphasis on the necessity for rear-engined chassis for streamlining, and with such poor commercial results whenever it was tried, it is not surprising that the coachbuilding industry, whether in Britain or on the Continent or in the US, steered clear of streamlined designs throughout the twenties. Clearly none of their clients, however anxious to make an impression at the next *concours d'elegance*, was sufficiently brave to order a streamlined body, even on a conventional front-engined chassis (although there was the occasional honourable exception like the 1927 Albany 'Airway' saloon on a Lancia Lambda chassis). Nevertheless, the industry and its clients did take note of the streamlining movement, and would often describe a design in such terms even though it bore no relation to a teardrop shape. There was also an increasing tendency to give the teardrop treatment to individual parts of the body, starting with the tail – hence the many 'boat-tail' designs, as we have already seen. Other areas subjected to streamlining at this time were such things as 'float-type' running boards, 'flared' wings (the vestigial, eyebrow-type wings popular on mid-twenties sports cars) and, later, 'swept' wings which continued in an unbroken line to form the running-board. Windscreens were sloped back, peaked roofs were made peakless ('eddy-free'), and sunshine roofs were made flush-fitting, all in the name of streamlining.

This, then, was the status of streamlining at the end of the twenties. It was known and used as a word, and possibly as an aesthetic movement to the more knowl-

edgeable, but showed no sign of taking over as a dominant force in car body design. Yet within two or three years that was exactly what was to happen, not only in Britain, but throughout the car-manufacturing world. In the meantime, the last forces of traditionalism could have their sway: limousines could stick doggedly to their D-backs (with a luggage-grid, often concealed, in case a visitor was vulgar enough to arrive carrying his own luggage), and designers could continue to indulge themselves by producing 'brougham' bodies. This last was a notably persistent influence: it was deemed old-fashioned even in 1922, when an exhibit at the Paris Show included a 'Brougham front pillar, with its characteristic outward curving toe', yet in 1925 a Windover Rolls-Royce limousine is gushingly described as built 'on angular lines of the brougham pattern. It clearly shows that,whatever style may be fashionable, the angular type of body on modern lines has too many inherent good qualities to admit of it ever being abandoned or superseded.' Although reeking of conservatism, these words were prophetic, since the brougham tradition was to lead to the razor-edge style of the late thirties – as modern in its day as one could wish.

There were two other important developments during the latter part of the decade which we should not overlook. First was the introduction of chromium plat-

By the 1929-1930 period, when this Austro-Daimler coupé was bodied by Harrington, low roof-lines were all the rage, resulting in ultra-shallow windscreens. Note the very long bonnet, dummy hood-irons, sloping windscreen and also the boa-constrictor horn.

ing, which superseded nickel plating in the period 1927-8. Its obvious benefit to the owner-driver, namely the ability to restore its lustre just by wiping it with a chamois leather, meant that coachbuilders had little difficulty in deciding to make the change. Even so, Britain was behind both America and the Continent in taking up the new process.

The second development was in the field of ventilation. In the early part of the decade this was hardly a problem; those few cars which were not open to the elements were not built for speed, and could manage with a simple roof ventilator for the passenger compartment, with the driver's needs taken care of by either an opening windscreen or indeed by sides open to the weather. As speeds increased, however, and as owner-drivers became the norm, something more sophisticated was required. Thus came scuttle ventilators, side-pillar ventilators, and eventually opening quarter-lights – initially only at the rear. An important late-twenties innovation, quickly adopted by coachbuilders and mass-producers alike, was the glass louvre over each door-window, which allowed the window to be lowered a little without causing draughts. There were also some early experiments in interior heating; one Hooper body, on a Rolls-Royce cabriolet, had the 'rear compartment warmed by an

exhaust heater, to which the effect of a live fire is given by switching on lamps fed by the car accumulator'. However, the single most sought-after ventilating device at the time was the sunshine roof. Without getting into a discussion as to when this was invented, it is certain that the design launched by coachbuilders Pytchley Autocar in 1925, and subsequently licensed to countless others, was the catalyst for its widespread adoption. Subsequently designs from SOS and Weathershields also became popular, and before the end of the decade there were examples of electrically-operated roofs – and even a 'suction' operated one from Howes, the Norwich coachbuilder.

So as the decade reached its end, the general outlines of a coachbuilt body had advanced markedly from what had prevailed in 1920, though it was still a long way from the pinnacle of achievement which we now recognise in the thirties. Yet, we should not underestimate what had been achieved. All cars – whether from volume manufacturers or built by a bespoke coachbuilder – were vastly more attractive to a potential owner. As well as being cheaper both to buy and to run, and easier to drive, they were much more comfortable to ride in. The body designer's contribution to this last factor was not only in providing more room; he had made the car quieter and better protected from the elements, and was starting to find ways to ventilate it better and even to heat it. Most importantly, though, he had made the car more attractive in its appearance. In doing so he had showed manufacturers that this was the most important way by far to influence sales.

THE THIRTIES

Although the Depression was to have its effects, and major ones, the new decade started very much where the old one had left off. Two-door bodies on both saloons and coupés, and four-door close-coupled saloons, were still numerous at the 1930 Olympia Show, although some claimed to detect a falling-off in popularity. 'Semi-Weymann' construction was to be seen on many stands, and an increasing trend towards long, swept wings was a foretaste of things to come.

The major difference was that Britain, and indeed the whole western world, was beginning to feel the full impact of the Depression. It was a common observation when each Show came around that 'some well-known names are absent this year', and although the total number of coachbuilder exhibitors did not drop too alarmingly during these difficult years, this was because the old-established firms, catering for the higher class of trade, were being replaced by more modern, go-ahead businesses which were aiming at the cheaper, high-volume – often sub-contract – end of the market. There were other signs of the times: colours were subdued, with greys, dark blues and blacks predominating, and observers complained of an absence of novelty – not surprising when no one wanted to spend money on speculative development work.

As far as aesthetic design was concerned, quite the most important influence in the thirties was the movement which became known as 'streamlining'. That apart, there were technical and economic developments which had an equally significant impact – and to a great extent they were linked. The question which worried bespoke coachbuilders as they tried to climb out of the Depression, expressed in modern marketing jargon, was: 'How can I prevent my client base continually shrinking?' They were being attacked on two fronts, for while the major manufacturers were producing ever more attractive products at lower and lower prices, the bespoke version was becoming more expensive, and – what is worse – in some respects inferior in quality.

The great advantage of the mass-produced, all-steel body was its inherent strength and rigidity. It was both lighter and quieter than one of composite construction, which was the only type a coachbuilder was capable of producing. His challenge was therefore to find a form of construction which was, ideally, both lighter (for the same strength) and cheaper than his traditional methods, without giving up his two main advantages – design flexibility and attractive appearance. It was, in effect, the search for a successor to Weymann.

The next innovations came, like Weymann, from France. First, in 1929, was the De Vizcaya system, which

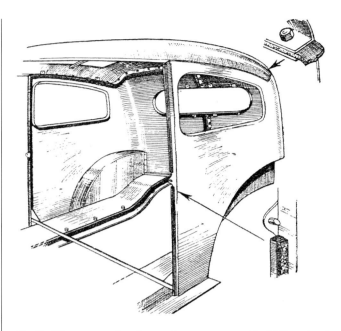

The De Vizcaya construction system, announced in 1930, gained some favour in France in the thirties but none in Britain. It used the strength of the flanged panels, bolted together with rubber in between, to do away with a separate frame.

used flanged aluminium panels bolted together with rubber sandwiched in between as the sole bodywork medium, without any supporting framework. Thus a two-door saloon built in this manner consisted of only six elements – two doors, two rear quarters, the roof and a front frame forming the door pillars and windscreen frame. As with Weymann and others, the seats were fixed directly to the chassis. The result was a body of satisfactory rigidity coupled with notably low weight: it was claimed that a five-seater body for a 16hp Darracq weighed only some 633lbs (287kg).

When the system was first announced it was linked with the French coachbuilder Marbeuf. This link seems to have died early on, however, and from 1930 it was taken up with particular enthusiasm by the Million Guiet company. With one intriguing possible exception, it does not seem to have crossed the Channel to Britain. Its more ready acceptance by the French public is understandable, since the rather flat, square panels which the system demanded were not out of tune with trends in French coachwork design at the time. One can speculate, however, that a corresponding shift in French taste in the ensuing few years was responsible for the De Vizcaya system's demise, at least as far as car bodywork was concerned, although Million Guiet persisted with it for many years afterwards in bus bodies.

Then in 1931 the Daste system was announced, and

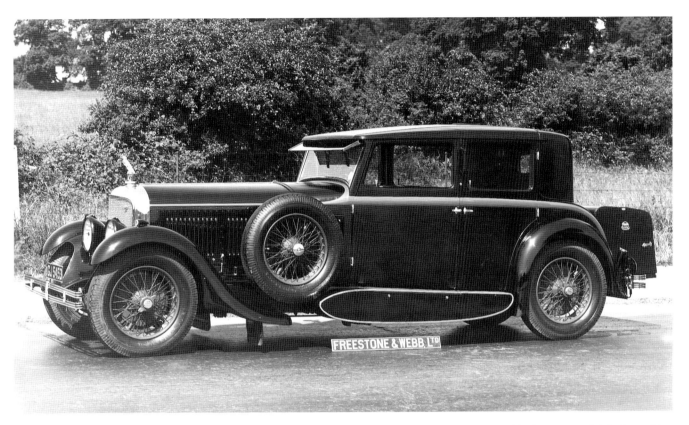

Gordon of Birmingham had a long-standing connection with Austin, which served the firm well during the battle for survival in the early thirties. The 1930 'Kaye Don foursome fabric sun coupé' offered a potential buyer numerous special features, including yet another form of folding roof.

Swallow was the most successful producer of special bodies on standard chassis between the wars. Here, in about 1930, the Coventry factory is turning out bodies for Wolseley Hornets.

Possibly one of Freestone & Webb's less successful designs, this 1930 Speed Model 6½-litre Bentley pillarless saloon is struggling between the styles of two decades – helmet wings and float-type running-boards from the twenties, but a suggestion of the falling waistline which was to become popular in the thirties.

was licensed in Britain to the Silent Travel Company. It had in fact been in use since 1929 by the Van Vooren coachbuilding company of Paris, but not initially under that name. Van Vooren described such bodies as being constructed on 'modified Weymann' principles, in that the separate plates were 'hinged on Silentbloc bushes throughout'. (The Silentbloc bush was one of the first examples of the newly developed ability to bond rubber to steel; it consisted of two concentric bushes, with rubber bonded in between.) When the Daste system was finally launched, it was based on the Silentbloc bush, both at framework joints and where the frame was mounted to the chassis. As with the 'semi-Weymann' approach, the body frame was effectively three separate cells which could move relative to each other. The difference was that any flexing was taken up entirely at the Silentbloc bushes; thus each cell could be made totally rigid, and could be metal-panelled all over instead of having to be partially fabric-covered, with all the advantages (primarily cellulose finish) which that brought.

This was probably the most successful of the post-Weymann systems appearing to satisfy all the requirements – lightness, quietness and the finest coach-built appearance. *The Autocar* subjected it to a scientific noise test which brought it high commendation; *The Automobile Engineer* commented that it was 'expected to

Another coachbuilder who adapted quickly to the demand for special bodies on volume chassis was Martin Walter, believed to have been responsible for this attractive Hillman Wizard foursome drophead coupé of 1931. Note the dual windscreen-wipers – an early application on other than a luxury car.

The bespoke coachbuilders, meanwhile, continued with expensive chassis. Hooper built this tourer, with a lengthened bonnet and an attractive design of flared front wing, on a Rolls-Royce Phantom 2 chassis in 1930-31. Note that a sloping front door line has already emerged.

be adopted by builders of quantity-produced bodywork', though failing to mention whether that term meant six bodies a week or six hundred. In the launch year it is certain that Lancefield, Gurney Nutting and Harrington were using the system while by the time of the 1932 Olympia Show a number of other prestigious coachbuilders – such as Arnold and Windover, not to mention the French houses of Figoni and of course Van Vooren – were offering bodies built under Silent Travel licences. A year later the Silent Travel Company was claiming no less than 76 licensees. Thereafter its attraction seems to have declined, but that could have been because fewer constructors bothered to take out licences, as there must have been many other ways of incorporating Silentbloc bushes into a body frame.

Weymann itself had at the same time brought out yet another version of its own method. 'New Weymann' was based even more closely on what was then aircraft prac-tice and gave further weight saving by using spruce spars instead of ash, with the spars hollow. Major components such as the bottom rails also had steel tubes inserted to allow them to be attached to the chassis. The most surprising aspect, though, was that this assembly was then covered with plywood – with canvas glued to the inner face and 'fine quality linen' to the outer. This outer face was then filled to give a smooth surface and cellulosed. Although it was announced in all seriousness in 1931, no examples of the New Weymann system are known to have been built in Britain, and even in France it seems to have died a rapid death.

Meanwhile, other coachbuilders were experimenting along quite different lines. In 1929 the French coachbuilder Hibbard et Darrin produced a system, later named 'Sylentlyte' when it was announced in Britain, which used aluminium almost entirely. The frame was built up of castings made of Alpax, an aluminium alloy,

The 1930 Daimler Double-Six four-door close-coupled saloon shown here is said to have been bodied by Martin Walter as late as 1932, although the style is more 1930-31 – especially the shallow windows.

Hooper was also responsible for this 1932 interior, again on a Phantom 2 but this time a limousine. It shows remarkably modern influences, especially in the design of the chromium-framed occasional seats which might almost have come out of the Bauhaus school of design.

and these were moulded in modular fashion in 'expandable moulds', thus giving a large range of sizes which could fit most chassis. The frame was then covered with aluminium panelling in the normal way. Although the Hibbard et Darrin company exhibited examples at the 1931 Paris Show nothing was heard of the system thereafter; very probably it proved too expensive.

British coachbuilders were also continuing to experiment with all-metal bodywork. Thrupp and Maberly claimed to have such a method in 1929, using alloy castings for such things as door frames, door pillars and wheel arches, but although no other details are available the suspicion is that wood had not been entirely eliminated. In 1931 Barker announced a framework system which was entirely of Birmabright aluminium alloy, using a combination of extruded sections and gusset plates rivetted together; the aluminium cladding was then also rivetted on, with felt interposed for silence. It was suggested that there would be a potential weight saving of 2cwt (100kg) on a large closed body. The one chassis known to have been bodied in this way, as a prototype, was none other than Earl Howe's racing Mercedes, but in spite of such a searching test programme the new method apparently came to nothing; once again, cost was probably the decisive factor.

In spite of these failed attempts to produce a cost-effective all-metal framework, the need for some such method was widely recognised. The problem was that coachbuilt bodies were increasingly being seen to perform badly in comparison with their mass-produced counterparts insofar as durability, and therefore silence, were concerned. Not that the bodies on cheaper cars were totally rigid by any means, but their all-welded construction combined with chassis which had become far less flexible meant that they were becoming much less prone to develop faults. *The Automobile Engineer* in 1935 put the point succinctly: 'It is hardly reasonable to suppose that purchasers of high-priced vehicles will remain indifferent to faulty or noisy bodywork when perfect satisfaction is given by cars costing from a third to a half the price.' They therefore concluded that 'the builder even of hand-made bodies may be obliged to provide a virtually all-metal construction'.

An immediate product of this thinking was the Park Ward 'all-steel' body of 1936. Designed in the first instance for Bentley chassis, and tested on them for a year prior to its announcement, the system used a frame built up from fabricated steel ribs, which were pre-formed and then welded together, usually in jigs, depending on the number of bodies to be made. The framework's sheet steel sills were then attached to the chassis through Silentbloc bushes, and the panelling – again steel – attached by clinching over and then spot-welding. Park Ward claimed a weight saving, compared with a traditional wood-framed, aluminium-panelled body, of ½cwt (25kg).

The crucial part of the whole Park Ward system was the ability to form curves in the box-section ribs. These ribs were made by closing the flanges of a top-hat rolled steel section round a flat strip, in such a way that the strip was captive but could still slide within the flanges; the top-hat section was slotted along its length to facilitate bending. Thus the complete assembly could be formed into a curve, after which the two parts were brazed

The Wolseley Hornet Special chassis continued to be popular with coachbuilders throughout the first half of the thirties. This 1932 fixed-head coupé is by R.E.A.L. Back-seat room was limited in the extreme.

together along their length. Park Ward was coy about these details at the time, probably because it did not want to reveal that the process had been invented not by itself but by the three Meltz brothers, who thereafter acted as consultants to the firm.

It is not clear why this highly significant development did not have more impact on the British coachbuilding industry. Certainly at the time it was recognised as offering the crucial advantage which the industry had been looking for, namely the ability to produce something like a traditional coachbuilt body but with the rigidity of steel. It was also no coincidence that it had been developed on a Bentley chassis by a coachbuilder in whom the Rolls-Royce company had a financial interest (and whom they would purchase outright a few years later). There are those who consider that the all-steel system could and should have been developed much further, and that it could have changed the history of the firm, if not the whole industry, after World War 2, but in the event it did not come near to replacing the traditional composite body either at Park Ward or anywhere else.

At the same time as the coachbuilding industry was trying to compete with the mass-producers, however, new opportunities opened up for the two to cooperate. This was in the field of so-called 'special bodies', on what would otherwise have been rather ordinary chassis. This desire to own a car which looked different from the general mass, while not a new phenomenon, became quite a vogue in the early thirties. No doubt it reflected an increase in prosperity amongst the middle classes. The trend was accelerated by certain manufacturers deciding to make their chassis freely available to the coachbuilding trade, rather than regarding them as competitors. Some even reversed their previous policy and agreed to supply chassis without bonnet and wings.

A favourite for such treatment had for a long time been the Austin Seven; well-known special bodies on this chassis were those from Swallow (soon to become SS Cars), Compton (Arrow) and Wright. Standard, Morris, Hillman and Singer were other small-car makers whose chassis were often used, but the one model which seemed to attract most attention, from the moment of its introduction in 1930, was the Wolseley Hornet, which by 1934 had ten different coachbuilders listed as producing special bodies for it.

The key to success in this section of the market was to keep costs down, as potential buyers were only prepared to pay a limited premium for the privilege of being different. In all cases, this was achieved by standardising on one body style and then producing it in batches. The differences were in the means by which the product was marketed. Some bodybuilders decided to sell through sole agents, as with the Arrow Austins sold through H A Saunders. Some agents reversed the process and commissioned a bodybuilder to produce a design under the agent's name: this was the case with the Eustace Watkins Hornet, which was made by either Whittingham and Mitchel, Salmons or Abbey. The more confident bodybuilders, however, such as Avon and Swallow, advertised and sold direct to the public.

One might have thought that an opportunity like this – volume production of special bodies – would have been snapped up by the traditional bespoke coachbuilders, concerned as they were by their diminishing market. In practice only a few of them did: Cunard with Morris, and Maltby with the Wolseley Hornet, come to mind, but few

Carbodies of Coventry bodied many MGs during the twenties and thirties, including this 1931 MG 18/80 fabric sportsman's saloon. It is a typical example, with four doors, close-coupled seating and an integrated luggage boot.

One can begin to appreciate from this interior shot of a 1931 Austin Seven Swallow saloon the superior standard which a buyer of a special body might expect. Note the ship-type scuttle ventilator.

A bespoke coachbuilder's normal work was producing not sensational designs but totally conventional ones, such as this 1931 Park Ward saloon on a Rolls-Royce 20/25 chassis. The only ususual feature, presumably requested by the client, is front-hinged front doors. The designer has had difficulty resolving the change in width from bonnet to door-pillar – especially tricky on the shorter Rolls-Royces.

Abbey Coachworks bodied several Railton models in the mid-thirties; this pillarless two-door saloon is from 1935. Note the sidelamps faired into the wings, and also the swage-line used as a boundary between two tones of colour, an increasingly popular device in the later thirties.

Lancefield built this advanced disappearing-head coupé design in 1937 on both an Alvis Speed 25 chassis, as shown here, and later on a Bentley. Note the Art Deco fluting carried right through from front to rear.

Avon Bodies was responsible for this pretty prototype drophead coupé for the Morgan company in 1937 (above), but cost considerations unfortunately prevented it being put into production. By this time even sports cars were receiving the full width body treatment.

At the 1935 Olympia Show James Young attracted much attention with the 'parallel-action' door, an attempt to reduce the pavement space needed when a normal – particularly two-door coupé – door was opened. This example (below) is on a 1937 4¼-litre Bentley.

Grose produced the 'Harleston' fixed-head coupé on the Alvis Speed 20 chassis in 1932. It involved replacing the manufacturer's bonnet with a new lengthened one. The leading edge of the door curves forward in 'brougham' fashion – something of a Grose trademark.

Carbodies was a contract coachbuilder to Alvis for many years; this is its 1932 'beetle-back' on the 12/60 TL chassis. Sports cars persisted with cycle wings and chassis louvres longer than saloons and coupés did.

others. Mostly the business was taken by relatively new firms, who presumably had less in the way of overheads and traditions and were more easily able to organise for batch production.

There was, however, a related area of business which was exploited by many of the traditional firms. This was the supply of cabriolet bodies to the larger manufacturers, to be listed as standard catalogue models of those manufacturers. The term 'cabriolet' was in vogue in Britain in the mid-thirties, meaning what we would now call a drophead coupé (a term which in fact began to take over in the later thirties). This was a two-door, or sometimes four-door, close-coupled open car, with winding windows in the doors (and sometimes disappearing quarter-lights). There was much discussion at the time about the market for cabriolets appearing to be on the increase. Some attributed it to the availability, from about 1932 on, of stiffer, cross-braced chassis which put less strain on the body and thus encouraged both manufacturers to offer cabriolets and the public to buy them. Certainly most manufacturers seemed to think it worth their while to list a cabriolet version; possibly the good summers of 1933 and 1938 played their part.

A number of coachbuilders had in any case long-standing alliances with certain manufacturers to supply catalogued models, for example Gordon with Austin, and

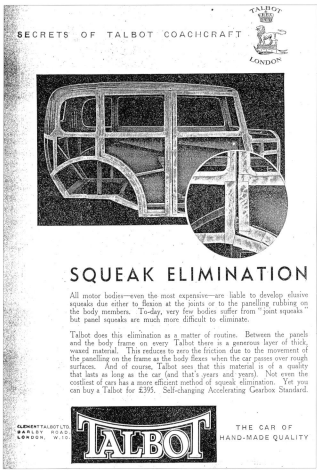

There could be no doubt that body squeaks were a serious problem when Talbot chose to call attention to it in this 1933 advertisement.

Grosvenor with Vauxhall. Others decided to make cabriolets their speciality. In 1933 Martin Walter took out a licence from Glaser of Germany, set up a dedicated factory and started to manufacture German-style cabriolets. 'German-style' meant, firstly, a hood which when closed had a more pronounced side-to-side curvature than

By 1933 coachbuilders had the Ford 8 chassis on which to offer special bodies. This version was by R.E.A.L., although it was probably only a one-off.

Another classical Hooper design: a 1933-34 sports saloon on a 3½-litre Bentley chassis. The swept wings and running board integrate perfectly, as do the sloping lines of windscreen, front door, bonnet and bonnet-louvres. Note the direction indicators recessed in the door-pillar. The falling waistline, however, has yet to arrive.

British practice at the time – because of a curved top rail to the windscreen – and secondly, because of the hood's very solidity, a slightly more cumbersome appearance when it was lowered. Maltby also became a cabriolet specialist, and in 1935 was the first British supplier to offer a hydraulically-operated head, which very ingeniously worked (manually) off the same pump as the Jackall built-in jacking system; by the following year it had motorised the process. (Incidentally, this was by no means the first electrically-operated head, even in Europe, examples having existed from 1927 if not earlier. Carbodies went on to offer their version in 1937, using a chain drive and toothed quadrants.) Yet another firm, Vehicle Developments, used German experience – including that of the Ambi-Budd company – to produce a standard pressed-steel door and pillar for cabriolets. Its claim was that such a door could be integrated into cabriolet bodies on a wide range of chassis sizes, from Austin 12 to Chrysler, without looking out of place.

Hood materials developed rapidly at this period. At the start of the thirties they were still often leather, with black enamelled leather being particularly popular, but canvas-like fabrics soon took over, initially unlined, but later with elaborate linings to offer saloon-like comfort when closed. Cant rails were in some cases made from fabric filled with rubber. There was a fashion at the end of the decade for the hood material to be in a contrasting colour – often fawn – to the bodywork.

Another body style became popular around the early thirties, and again its arrival was not unconnected with the development of more rigid chassis. This was the pillarless saloon, which was effectively a sportsman's saloon, but it provided an answer to the criticism that the door-widths on this style were rather small. It had front-hinged front doors and rear-hinged rear doors, and no centre pillar, so that when the two doors were open there was no central obstruction for either front or rear passengers. Its two-door counterpart the pillarless coupé, where the door closed directly on to the quarter-light glass, became something of a vogue slightly later, probably because of its appearance. Usually the door-windows were frameless, so when they and the quarter-lights were

Lancefield built two very similar streamlined designs in 1934 for their designer/client Mr Haworth-Booth – a Siddeley Special, and the Alvis Speed 20 shown here. As well as a streamlined tail, it featured a full-width body with no running boards, three-abreast seating front and rear, semi-recessed headlamps and front wings brought forward below the wheel centre-line.

The Chrysler Airstream created a sensation at the 1934 New York Auto Show. Not only were both front and rear heavily 'streamlined', but by moving the radiator and engine forward the designers could in turn allow the seating to move forward to within the wheelbase. Note also the louvre-doors on the bonnet.

wound away there was a clear, unbroken space between the windscreen pillar and the rear quarter.

We have noted previously how, during the twenties, coachbuilders seemed aware of the streamlining movement yet reluctant to produce a totally streamlined body; they were content merely to 'streamline' individual components such as the wings. The interesting question is why this attitude amongst coachbuilders – and indeed amongst volume manufacturers as well – should ever

have changed. Change it most certainly did, for from around 1932 onwards there was an upsurge of interest in streamlining throughout the industry. Not only were more and more bodies appearing with individual items – wings, running boards and so on – described as streamlined, but so were occasional complete designs. The key point about these was that – for a closed body – they used a sloping tail which flowed in one continuous line from the roof.

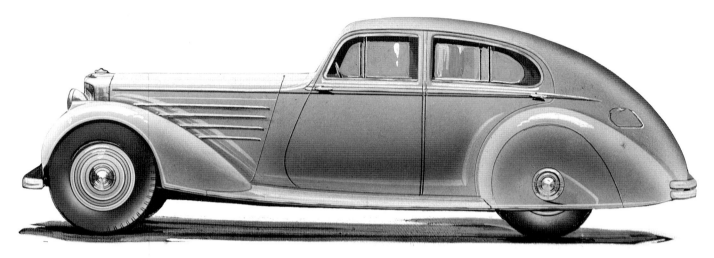

Thrupp & Maberly's streamlined 3½-litre Bentley sports saloon was one of the 1934 Olympia Show sensations. Its rounded tail, enclosed rear wings and minimal running boards helped define the style for the second half of the decade.

Just why a more receptive attitude should have arrived at this particular time is difficult to say: possibly it is connected with the increasing availability of lowered chassis, which permitted a balanced, flowing treatment for the first time. Undoubtedly it was also a reflection of what was happening in the wider world, with streamlining being discussed in connection with all forms of transport and even consumer electrical goods. There were also more prosaic explanations in some cases. Running boards would have had to make a come-back in some form, as the cycle-wing fashion had shown just how much protection from mud had been lost, and the 'parabolic wing', although commended as being a streamlined form in itself, was in reality a halfway house between the cycle wing and the fully 'swept' version.

In a sense, it was an anti-climax for all the work of Jaray, Rumpler and others to be subsumed into the rather simplistic concept of a closed car with a sloping tail, yet the logical thread was there. For the previous ten years designers had been force-fed with the twin assumptions that, firstly, streamlining meant a teardrop – that is, a tail which came to a point – and, secondly, that the only way to achieve a tail of this shape was to mount the engine in the rear. All at once, they began to realise that it was possible to achieve the *illusion* of a teardrop shape on a conventional chassis by sloping the tail in one plane only. In other words, the car would be streamlined in side view, even though it was not if seen from the top (and who looks at a car from the top?).

It would be fruitless to try to pinpoint the first such design but they existed during the twenties. The more important point is that there was a sudden rush of them in the early thirties. Whereas only one was on offer at the 1931 Olympia Show (a 40-50 Rolls-Royce saloon from Barker), there were more in 1932 – and, most significantly, one was from a volume manufacturer (the Hillman Aero Minx, which was designed not by Rootes but by the famous Freddy March). The real activity, however, started in 1933, and not only in Britain. *Carrosserie aerodynamique* was the talking-point of the Paris Salon that year, with sweeping tails featuring on such chassis as Bugatti, Delage and Hispano-Suiza. One manufacturer,

Chenard et Walcker, managed to produce an unattractive, befinned design that appeared to have a rear engine even though it did not.

The 1933 Olympia Show was important in that it marked the start of real interest in streamlined design from both bespoke coachbuilders and volume manufacturers. The standard Talbot 95 saloon, for example, with its flowing tail treatment, described itself as 'semi-streamlined'. Meanwhile, in the coachwork section, Abbott were showing an advanced design of two/four-seat Talbot 105 sports body which incorporated both streamlined wings and a tailfin, but many of the bespoke coachbuilders seem to have been caught out by the upsurge in interest in streamlining, and only brought out their first efforts in early 1934, some being entrants for the coachwork competition of the RAC Rally. Notable designs from around this time were a Park Ward 3½-litre Bentley sports saloon, and a Lancefield sports saloon on a Siddeley Special chassis which was notable for a full-width bonnet and faired-in headlamps. The fact that both these interpretations of streamlining were carried out on close-coupled, two-door 'sports saloons' was no coincidence, since the limited rear headroom which such designs assumed made it much easier to incorporate a dramatically sloping line for the roof and tail.

Thus from 1933 onwards, the streamlining movement had a major effect on the way that cars looked, and it influenced designers in other ways which could hardly be said to affect a car's aerodynamics. We have already noted that a trend developed in the late twenties for bonnets to be lengthened, partly as an expression of power. This continued in the thirties, in spite of the fact that it moved designs away from the ideal 'teardrop' shape; in aesthetic terms, though, it appealed to designers and customers because it made the car look lower. It is probably true to say that this style was initiated by French coachbuilders, who not for the first time took it to extremes: its

The wing treatment on this 1934 Hooper 3½-litre Bentley three-position drophead coupé is at an interesting transitional stage. It has overtones of the late-twenties parabolic wing, but also looks forward to the separate wings and lack of running boards of the late thirties. Note also the falling waistline.

The 1930s British motorist still preferred fluted or pleated leather for his interior trim. This treatment was in a 1934 Grose 4½-litre Lagonda sports coupé, and was carried out in green leather. The 'sunray' fluting, another Art Deco influence, was very popular at the time.

most outlandish expression was a coupé by Fernandez in 1931, on a Hispano-Suiza chassis, where the scuttle was extended *over* the steering-wheel, the latter being enclosed by a hump with a matching hump on the opposite side.

At the same time, where streamlining dictated that windscreens should become more sloping, designers realised that appearance benefited if everything else sloped to match; thus suddenly bonnet louvres, bonnet shut-lines, windscreen pillars and door leading-edges started to line up in an attractive uniformity. The last of these, the sloping or cutaway leading edge to the front doors, was justified at the time as giving more legroom under the scuttle when entering the car, but this explanation smacks of post-rationalisation. Two other trends which affected the appearance started to grow at about the same time. Horizontal louvres instead of vertical, possibly influenced by the Art Deco movement, became increasingly common by 1934, further accentuating the length of the bonnet. Then came a move imported from

the Continent to replace louvres altogether and substitute individual doors; most probably this was a change controlled by the chassis manufacturers, who usually supplied the bonnet and who were becoming increasingly concerned about engine compartment temperatures.

Occasionally, too, a designer would not be able to resist the temptation to slope the rear – ie hinge – line of the doors on a saloon, to match up with the slope of the bonnet and the door shut line. This was a triumph of art over practicality, as it caused the door to rise as it opened; French open cars managed this in the twenties, but their doors were much lighter. Sports cars at the start of the thirties were taking on a style of their own, with cutaway doors and 'double-flare' scuttles, sometimes with separate aero-screens. Neither of these features could be said to have any aerodynamic effect, but they were in the spirit of the times. Doors on two-door coupés, on the other hand, gave the opposite problem, in that they were becoming long and heavy, making them difficult to open in a confined space; James Young brought out their solu-

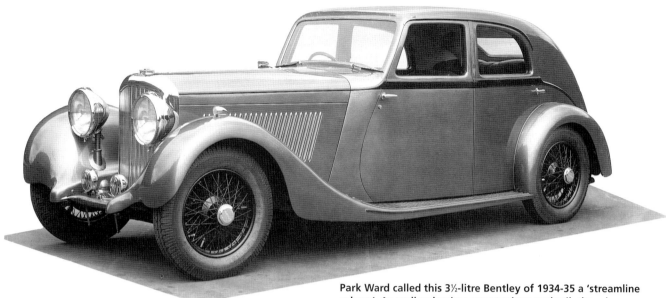

Park Ward called this 3½-litre Bentley of 1934-35 a 'streamline saloon'. As well as having swept wings and tail, the wings are heavily valanced and are brought forward in front to just above the wheel centre-line. Note that even front bumpers, let alone rear ones, were still not deemed essential.

tion in 1935 with the swinging 'parallel action' door on a Bentley drophead (shown on page 48), an idea which Bertelli emulated on an Alvis drophead two years later.

In October 1933, at both the Paris and the London Shows, the overwhelmingly dominant theme was streamlining. The French bespoke coachbuilders showed designs which were at least as advanced as those of their British counterparts. The striking thing about the Olympia Show, however, was the wholesale adoption of streamlining by the British volume manufacturers as well; every other stand seemed to contain an 'Airline' or 'Airstream' version. As for the British coachbuilders, they were now beginning to show the exceptional skill which brought their reputation to a peak in the thirties. Their designers were learning how to combine the curves and proportions of roof and tail to give that particularly British sense of grace and restraint. Part of this style was the 'falling waistline', much in evidence at the Show which involved curving the lower line of the rearmost side-window downwards so that it blended with the roof and tail. It was claimed at the time that this device was invented by the French coachbuilders Letourneur et Marchand, but its origins were evident in Britain at least two years previously, from Lancefield to cite just one example. A more likely explanation is that the falling waistline was a designer's device to conceal the fact that bodies were increasing in height at the rear, because of more supple springing, and that it therefore occurred to more than one individual at the same time. Whatever the reason, it remained a feature of most thirties designs until the end of the decade, when – possibly because of American influence – the fashion once more became to have a straight waistline.

Other features of the new style, intended to give genuine reductions in air resistance, were front wings brought forward to level with the wheel centre-line, and rear wheels enclosed by spats. The latter device was seized on by British designers of upmarket bodies, and they were soon followed by the French; there was something about enclosing the rear wheels which spoke not only of stream-

THE MAN WHO SAID HIS BODY NEVER RATTLED

Charles Follett was a well-known London car-dealer, specialising in up-market makes such as Alvis. His New Year card, from what would seem to be around 1935, shows that he had no illusions about the coachbuilt bodies he was selling.

lining but of opulence as well. It later evolved into a form of half enclosure, and then by the end of the decade had largely been dropped again, possibly because the spats had a tendency to loosen and rattle.

There were a number of landmark designs at the 1933 Show, all on Bentley chassis: four-door sports saloons from Arnold, Rippon, and Thrupp and Maberly, and a concealed-head drophead coupé from H J Mulliner. The last two, particularly, were outstanding achievements, and could still have passed for new designs five years later.

There was one other major trend to emerge from the streamlining movement, and its start can be pinpointed more accurately than most. When Carl Breer and his team at Chrysler were developing the Airstream they realised that its sloping tail was in danger of reducing rear headroom to unacceptable levels. They therefore took the bold step of moving the engine and passenger cabin forward relative to the rear wheels, by no less than 20 inches. As well as solving the headroom problem, this layout gave

The car with which Freestone & Webb single-handedly started the 'razor-edge' fashion – the Bentley 3½-litre 'brougham' shown at Olympia in 1935.

improved ride characteristics, but it also profoundly changed the frontal aspect of the car. European manufacturers soon found the same headroom problem in their streamlined designs, and moved towards the same solution. The rapid adoption of the forward radiator and engine position was not just for reasons of passenger space; it also gave better weight distribution, increased luggage space and improved visibility (by bringing the front seats nearer to the windscreen).

This trend was of course one which only the chassis manufacturers could initiate, although no doubt the coachbuilders were pressing them as well. Its acceptance by British volume manufacturers was marked by Standard launching their Flying Standard range in 1935. This family of designs worked particularly well in the larger models, where the combination of swept tail and forward engine position gave both an attractive appearance and good passenger accommodation. For the remainder of the thirties, the forward mounting of engine and radiator became the norm. Radiators, now more prominent than ever, were increasingly sloped back in a further attempt to reduce drag.

After streamlining, the other major influence in the thirties was the razor-edge style, variously known when it was introduced as 'angular', 'chamfered' or 'mitred' treatment. Although there will be many claimants as to how and when this style started, it seems clear that it emanated from the British side of the channel, and that a seminal design was the Freestone and Webb Bentley 'brougham' exhibited at Olympia in October 1935 which had a sharp ridge along the outside edges of the roof. By the following year Thrupp and Maberly had taken the

Rover was an important contract customer for Carbodies. This is their 1935 12hp sports saloon (with non-standard knock-on wheels).

hint, showing both Rolls-Royce and Bentley saloons with the full razor-edge treatment, while Hooper and Mayfair both used angular roof corners. From 1937 onwards this style became widely used, and of course it survived well into the post-war era.

Meanwhile, coachwork designers were keeping up the pressure on the chassis manufacturers to produce ever lower profiles. One of the effects was to eliminate footwells, in the sense that floors remained as low as before but chassis rails were lowered to the same level; this gave a supposedly 'flat' floor, which was so if one disregarded the transmission tunnel. The combination of lower floors with an unchanged seat height tended in itself to give increased leg-room to rear-seat passengers. At the same time, a change in the way in which front seats were constructed, by adopting tubular steel frames with spring suspension of the cushion, also gave more footroom. Designers gradually learned not to try and conceal these frames but instead to treat them in a modern, almost Bauhaus, style, often chromium-plating them. The two developments together gave a new lease of life to,

Martin Walter was quick to exploit the need for cabriolet bodies on major manufacturers' chassis, and set up a production line in an old airship shed. This late-1935 shot shows Vauxhall Light 6 chassis being fitted with 'Wingham' four-door cabriolet bodies.

The introduction of the Rolls-Royce Phantom 3 chassis inspired the top bespoke houses to even more magnificent creations. This Hooper sedanca of 1936 has a roof echoing the falling waistline, and the newly fashionable rear-wheel spats. The pillarless treatment of the rear door and quarter-light is interesting.

amongst other things, the four-door close-coupled saloon.

A crucially important result of lowering the chassis was that it also permitted bodies to be built out further over the chassis side-frames, thus ushering in the era of the full-width body and the elimination of running boards. If one had to select one way above all others in which a late thirties car differed in appearance from one of 10 years before, it would be in this feature. The style was quite different from the cycle-wing era of only a few years previously when running boards were eliminated purely for fashion reasons, only to be reinstated as soon as their mud-protection properties were appreciated. This time the wider bodies were used to advantage, by carrying the doors outwards at the bottom and so preventing mud splashing up on to doors and rear wings. Probably the first such treatment was on the H J Mulliner Bentley drophead coupé that was shown at the 1934 Olympia show, and by 1937 the majority of volume manufacturers had followed suit. Needless to say, the new style's impact on passenger comfort, because of the increased

interior width it provided, was no less dramatic.

Another, rather short-lived, fashion to emerge in the latter half of the thirties was one for increasing vision in an upwards direction. Started by Offord in 1935 with the 'High Vision' saloon on the Austin 20hp long-wheelbase chassis, it was picked up two years later by H J Mulliner on a Daimler saloon. Offord's version involved doors with curved glass panels extending into the roof, while H J Mulliner managed with glass let into the front and top of the screen. The motivation may well have been to allow passengers to cling to the idea of an open car without experiencing the discomfort which came with it in a world of increasing speeds. Ranalah came up with an interesting variation in the same year with the Lanchester 'Clear View' saloon, in which forward vision was improved by totally eliminating the windscreen pillars. The windscreen was thus held at the top and bottom only, and the door glasses butted up against it, leaving 'a gap of about $3/16$ of an inch which has an excellent extractor action giving good ventilation'. Judging by this design's

At the 1937 Earls Court Show Ranalah introduced the Lanchester Clear View saloon, which did away with windscreen pillars in the interest of improved vision but which necessitated leaving a gap between screen and door glasses.

lack of success, the ventilation was a little too good.

One other external influence on appearance should be mentioned in any discussion of the thirties – namely, the movement known as 'Art Deco'. The name came from the title of an exhibition in Paris in 1925 – the International Exhibition of Modern Decorative and Industrial Arts – which had a formative effect on all areas of design thereafter. Its impact on car bodywork came later than in some fields but was noticeable nevertheless. Early examples were Avon adding chrome strips to relieve the wide valances on their parabolic wings in 1932, and the same fashion being noted on a Maybach at the Berlin Show in 1934. In 1938 Lancefield produced some concealed-head coupés, on Alvis, Bentley and Mercedes-Benz chassis, using an *avant-garde*, fluted treatment on the wings and waistline. Carlton produced a Bentley saloon around the same time which showed similar influences. Many coachbuilders used Art Deco motifs, for example, to enliven the appearance of rear-wheel spats. Even the shaping of waist-mouldings – often picked out with a chrome flash – could be said to be influenced by Art Deco ideas.

As far as surface finishes were concerned, there was no development in the thirties as revolutionary as cellulose paints were in the twenties, but the development of metallics was of major importance. One might almost consider that they began in the twenties, since in 1923 and 1924 there was something of a vogue for 'granite' finishes – usually in a steel or bronze colour – which were said to give a 'varied glistening colour effect'. Why granites did not survive is not clear, but the lofty opinion that they were 'not judged suitable for closed cars' may tell us something about prevailing attitudes. The metallics story really begins in 1932, however, when paints based on 'pearl essence' first appeared in Europe. This magical substance was made from guanin, obtained from beneath the scales of herrings and appears to have been used on its own as a base coat, then mixed with lacquer for the final coat. It lasted for only a couple of years, however, before being superseded in 1934 – primarily on grounds of cost – by what we would now recognise as the true metallic paints, although initially these went under such names as 'metallic lustre', 'jewelescent' or 'polychromatic'. Although the initial view was that such finishes would be confined to the most expensive coachwork, by 1936 they were relatively common.

Paint colours became brighter again after the dull trend of the Depression years, and particularly so in 1936-7 when Coronation Red was a popular colour; this shade, and its companion Coronation Blue, had been specified by the British Colour Council in honour of the great occasion. There was also a tendency towards single colours (or sometimes two tones of one colour) instead of the previously common two contrasting ones. Where two colours were used it was often in dramatic fashion, with a sweeping swage-line dividing the two so that even front and rear wings were in different colours. After the celebrations in 1937 there was a reaction, with a preference for pastels and 'sober shades' being commented on. It is not too fanciful to suggest that this trend, as in the Depression years, could have been reflecting the mood of the times. There was also an increasing use of chromium-plate or stainless steel, both on mouldings and on ever more elaborate radiator grilles. Chrome had replaced nickel around 1928, with stainless steel starting to be used a couple of years later.

In 1930 there was evidence of an increasing demand for cloth upholstery and it seemed reasonable at the time to predict that this upward trend would continue. After all, it was only in open cars that leather was to be preferred for practical reasons, while cloth had long been the mark of the passenger compartment of luxury closed cars. More importantly, closed cars were now the larger segment of the market. Yet the expected trend did not materialise, at least in Britain, although pleated cloth trim did become the norm on the Continent by the mid-thirties. The British buyer still preferred his car to have leather trim – pleated or fluted at first, but later in the decade perhaps plain with occasional horizontal piping. This latest example of the contrary taste of the British buyer did not suit the industry and in 1939 *The Automobile Engineer* summed up the situation as follows:

> 'Several attempts have been made to introduce cloth upholstery, and while this form of covering material is widely used on imported American and Continental cars, it does not find ready acceptance on cars produced in this country. From a manufacturing viewpoint, cloth would appear to be a very desirable trimming material, for it reduces cutting waste, but despite repeated attempts to popularise it, there does not appear to be any immediate possibility of cloth-trimmed cars.'

These remarks applied, of course, to lower- and medium-priced cars; at the top end of the market such trimming materials as West of England cloth were frequently found – and so indeed was satin on at least one occasion. As for the construction of the seats themselves, these became typically Dunlopillo over a spring case, Dunlopillo moulded sponge rubber having become available for volume orders in 1931 and on general supply a year later. Some bodies, usually the more sporting ones, continued with air-cushion seats. Later on, from about 1935, adjustable air-bags started to be fitted to seat squabs. There was also a movement towards simplicity in interior fittings: on mass-market cars plastic mouldings began to be used for fillets instead of wood veneer, and even at the top end of the market there was less involved cabinet work and trimming.

Numerous extras which might previously have been fitted as after-market accessories became commonplace during the decade. Bumpers were initially fitted at the front only – doubtless because of their role as harmonic stabilisers, to damp out axle-tramp – but within a few years rear ones were being supplied as well, often the split type, enclosing a built-in illuminated rear number plate. Direction indicators were being fitted from the late twenties, but it is only in 1932 that we first encounter 'signalling arms recessed in the pillars'. Similarly, although windscreen wipers for the driver date from the early twenties, it is only from about 1934 onwards that 'dual' wipers became common. A later refinement was the 'concealed' wiper, which initially meant merely that the blades dropped below the level of the screen, but later implied that the motor was concealed behind the dash. Pressed steel wheels became the norm from 1935 onwards, replacing the previous wires, but in turn were starting to be replaced by the plain disc wheel – often with a large-diameter hubcap – by 1939. This style of hubcap is not to be confused with decorative wheel-discs, used to cover up the spokes of wire wheels, which were common on the more expensive chassis throughout the first half of the thirties.

H. J. Mulliner joined the fashion for increased all-round vision with the 'High Vision' Daimler of 1937-38. The additional transparent panels could be covered by internal blinds when necessary.

Finally, before we leave our review of the thirties, we should note the progress that had been made in the field of ventilation and in the related area of noise reduction. Whereas the late-twenties driver had been more than content with an opening windscreen, opening rear quarter-lights and glass louvres over the side-windows, the level aspired to by the end of the thirties was much more sophisticated. One of the first innovations was opening quarter-lights at the front to match those at the rear; a very early example was a 1930 40-50hp Rolls-Royce faux-cabriolet by H J Mulliner, which had 'hinged ventilating devices in the edges of the front windows'. This date makes all the more interesting the publication of a patent in 1933 by the Fisher Body Corporation, part of the great General Motors, which purported to patent swivelling quarter-lights both front and rear – the front ones in the doors, the rear one in the fixed panel – as part of a 'no-draught ventilation system'. The legal advice to the British coachbuilding industry must have been very clear, since the Olympia Show later that same year had numerous examples of opening front quarter-lights, not to mention those at the rear which of course had existed for a number of years. Their popularity spread rapidly over the next few years.

By 1938 the subject of ventilation was being treated scientifically on mass-produced cars as much as coach-built ones. It began to be realised that a positive pressure within a (saloon) car was desirable, both to control the flow of air and to prevent unwanted fumes from entering, and that to achieve this the fresh-air entry had to be sited at a point of high pressure such as on top of the scuttle. As for heating the car's interior, the early experiments with exhaust heating were clearly unsatisfactory, and heaters using water from the engine's cooling system began to appear around 1933. At first these were proprietary makes, such as the Clayton, developed from those used in motor-coaches. One of the first cars to have a heater fitted as standard was the Vauxhall 25hp of 1937;

Even in 1938 the D-back limousine sailed serenely on, untouched by the streamline movement. This Hooper Rolls-Royce Wraith hints at its modernity only by the forward placing of the radiator and the opening front quarter-lights.

It was inevitable that designers would try to match the slope of the front door leading-edge with a corresponding slope at the rear. The difficulty of raising a heavy door such as the one in this 1938 Park Ward Rolls-Royce Wraith sedanca can be imagined.

the heater, of AC manufacture and no doubt American design, was built in to the dash rather than being a mere add-on. All these devices had up to this point heated the air that was already in the car, but 1939 saw the SS Jaguar become the first British-produced car to have what was then called 'air-conditioning' as standard, in the form of a combined heater and demister which heated the incoming fresh air.

The question of demisting had become a subject of much discussion as the decade progressed. The opening windscreen was still an almost universal fitting, but its use was being increasingly confined to driving in fog, and the need for some other device to keep the inside of the screen clear was clearly recognised. One or two coachbuilders even fitted a wiper blade on the inside of the screen, on the driver's side. The solution was to come with combined heaters and demisters, but not in general before the forties. In this respect Continental practice was ahead of British: Peugeot was fitting 'defrosters' to all its models as early as 1937.

Noise reduction was attracting more attention, not only because of higher speeds but also because of the increasing availability of car radio. It was for long an area where the coachbuilt body had claimed superiority, but

the all-steel body was catching up. It was comparatively simple in this type of construction to introduce a so-called 'false dash' between engine and passenger compartment which reduced engine noise and also, incidentally, helped to prevent engine heat being conducted back to the passenger compartment or to sensitive components such as petrol-pumps. Flush fitting of windscreens was another measure to reduce what was known as 'storm noise', and became common practice from around 1937. Windscreens were listed amongst the six most common causes of such noise, the others being door gaps, (sunshine) roof, windows, louvres and external fittings.

The contribution which apertures in the bodywork made to noise transmission, and hence the necessity of sealing them, was also just beginning to be appreciated by the end of the thirties. In addition more use was being made of sound-deadening materials to eliminate the drumming which had become a characteristic of all-steel bodies at that time. The material normally used was a bitumen compound, with a high sand content in order to give sufficient weight for it to be effective. As for coachbuilt bodies, although they suffered less from drumming they had instead to contend with 'panel squeak', whereby a metal panel moved slightly relative to the correspond-

By the late thirties the concealed-head drophead coupé could look neat when open or closed. This is a 1938 Bentley 4¼-litre by H J Mulliner. Note the rear-wheel spats, which show Art Deco influences in both shape and ornamentation.

ing part of the framework; a typical example would be where the roof-panel curved over the cant rail. Various solutions were tried, such as inserting waxed material between the panel and the frame, but it was difficult to find one which cured the problem permanently.

It could be said, therefore, that the thirties ended for the bespoke coachbuilders where they began – searching for a type of construction which was as inherently quiet, yet as attractive to look at, as the all-steel body from the mass-producers. Weymann and its derivatives had failed on the test of appearance while the orthodox composite body – even in a sophisticated form such as Silent Travel – failed on durability and, by implication, on noise. Park Ward's all-steel frame had probably showed the most promise of all, but was not sufficiently well developed or marketed.

Meanwhile, the mass-producers had certainly not stood still. At the start of the decade an all-steel body was something of an exception. The Pressed Steel company had only just been freed to supply such bodies to other manufacturers than the Nuffield Group, and most producers were still putting together composite bodies on wood frameworks, albeit in many cases from steel pressings rather than hand-formed components. Ten years later, however, the 'Big Five' manufacturers were using all-steel construction as a matter of course. Its attractions were not merely that it was cheaper, given sufficient volume, but that it was far more rigid than a composite body and hence much less prone to develop squeaks and rattles.

This was not all. Encouraged by the way in which the American market had developed, European mass-producers were working hard throughout the thirties to produce the ultimate in all-steel methodology – the elimination of the chassis, known as 'integral construction'. This approach made no distinction between body framework, body panelling and chassis, but designed all three as one component as economically as possible; it is essen-

tially the way in which cars are designed today. There are numerous claimants to the title of first producer of an integral design, going back to the early years of this century. In any such list, the Lancia Lambda of 1922 would have to have an honourable mention, since it managed to apply the integral form of construction to open bodies as well as closed ones. However, if we concentrate on those designs which were mass-produced, then we would have to consider (in Europe) Citroën in 1934 or Opel in 1935 as the main contenders, with the final decision being clouded by disputes as to what was true 'mass-production'. The first British producer of an integral construction model is clear – Vauxhall, with its Ten-Four announced in 1937. In France, Panhard started using integral construction early in 1937; the Gregoire system, announced later the same year and used by Hotchkiss, involved Alpax (light alloy) castings rather than welded steel sections for the main strength-giving members, but it can still be regarded as an alternative form of integral construction.

Not everyone, either in America or Europe, was convinced of the overwhelming merits of integral, sometimes called 'unitary', construction. An alternative, offering most of the benefits in terms of rigidity but without the very heavy capital costs, was a method dubbed 'semi-unitary'. Here there was a separate chassis, but its final strength was added only when the body was mounted. In some cases the body sill closed off the outer face of the channel-section chassis rail to form a box-section side member, in others the body had its own sill. The common feature was that the body contributed a significant amount to the rigidity of the final combined structure, and it did this by using tubular steel side framing built up

This late-thirties scene, with an MG WA drophead coupé bodied by Salmons (Tickford), is tinged with foreboding when we spot the headlamp mask – an early consequence of the Defence Regulations introduced at the outbreak of war in September 1939.

Even though it still has running-boards, the forward radiator position and flush-fitting windscreen confirm that this is a late-thirties design. Barker built this pillarless fixed-head coupé on a V-12 Lagonda chassis in 1939. Note yet more Art Deco scrolls on the rear-wheel spats.

on correct engineering principles (referred to as the 'bridge truss' method).

Integral construction represented the greatest challenge yet to the coachbuilding industry as a whole; if this was the direction that car body design was to take, then neither the bespoke builders nor the sub-contract firms could contemplate being part of it. Even the semi-unitary approach was largely untried. What was to be their answer? In most senses of the question there was no answer. For one thing, the approach of World War 2 made a nonsense of any long-term planning. In such circumstances, the response of many firms was to ensure their continued existence by obtaining war contracts in some form – and who can blame them? There were neither funds nor sales to justify any further experimentation on coachbuilding methods. The best that most coachbuilders could hope for was to use the expertise they already had on similar work, and that is what happened in many cases; Vanden Plas made components for the wood construction Mosquito aircraft, Charlesworth made sheet-metal bomb-bay doors, and so on.

The pity was that this work was enshrining existing, obsolescent skills rather than developing new ones. If

only, for example, coachbuilders had been widely experienced in building frames from aluminium extrusions, or from lightweight steel tubing, then they could have developed their knowledge and experience throughout the war years and thus been in a strong position to obtain contracts for, say, prototypes or concept cars from the major manufacturers after the war. But it was not to be.

Even before the onset of war, some bespoke coachbuilders took a quite different attitude towards their future business – they got out of it altogether. In many cases this was merely bowing to the inevitable; demand was falling, no technical break-through was in sight, and as a result the industry was having to shrink. In the five years from 1933 to 1938 the number of British coachbuilders exhibiting at Olympia dropped from 41 to 27, and even this figure concealed the number of older, traditional firms withdrawing from coachbuilding to be replaced in part by newer firms concentrating on the sub-contract market. Others took what we would now describe as a strategic decision: Martin Walter, having built up a substantial cabriolet business from 1933, then sold it in 1937 and later switched to building the Utilecon and the Dormobile.

POST-WAR: THE SURVIVORS

After World War 2 the bespoke coachbuilders picked up where they left off. This 1946 Rolls-Royce sedanca by Freestone & Webb could just as easily have been produced in 1938-39.

If prospects for the coachbuilding industry had looked gloomy in 1939, they were deeply depressing in 1945. Britain had emerged from its second catastrophic war in 30 years, with its economy shattered, its empire crumbling and its upper and middle classes under attack from socialist and egalitarian thinking. Who could possibly contemplate spending large sums on coachbuilt bodies – even if they could get hold of a chassis in the first place?

Indeed, the first two or three post-war years very much reflected this kind of thinking. Steel shortages meant that car production was held back, and the steel allocation system ensured that such production as there was had to be directed towards exports. Once a coachbuilder had managed to get hold of a chassis, he then had to obtain his own steel allocation before he could make any progress. This shortage of steel is the prime reason for the proliferation of 'woody' estates which emerged in those early post-war years – that, and the fact that they were very much easier to construct than a steel-panelled body, so that many more small firms were tempted to try. There was a stage when it was easier to find aluminium than steel, so a surprising number of bodies built in the early years were made of the more expensive material.

The coachbuilding firms, of course, were planning their own salvation. Many had already left the industry: of the 26 firms (excluding Pressed Steel) which had exhibited at the last pre-war Earls Court Show in 1938, only

14 were present at the first post-war event 10 years later (plus two which had not been there in 1938 for their own reasons – Barker and Vincent). Within the 12 which had dropped out, one (Ranalah) had disappeared, one (Maltby) had been bought out, and the remainder were pursuing business in related branches of the motor industry – retailing, commercial bodywork, repairs and so on.

Even amongst the 1948 exhibitors, a number could only be counted as half-hearted in their dedication to traditional coachbuilding. Barker was no more than a trading name of Daimler-Lanchester, while Thrupp & Maberly as part of the Rootes Group was soon to find itself involved in painting and trimming only. Vanden Plas was now part of Austin and confined to that firm's products. Gurney Nutting had drawn the short straw in the Jack Barclay group, and would not be seen again at Earls Court; that privilege was to be reserved for James Young. Within the independents, University (Coachcraft), Lancefield, Rippon, Vincents and Windover would leave car coachbuilding within the next few years. Two others – Carbodies and Mulliners of Birmingham – decided to go the mass-production route in cooperation with major manufacturers, and soon moved away from traditional

Harold Radford was the only major new post-World War 2 firm to use traditional coach-building methods, including ash framing. The company initially made estate conversions of Rolls-Royce and Bentley saloons; this 'Countryman' is Radford's first model, launched in 1948.

coachbuilding methods. (Of these last two, however, only Carbodies would remain independent, Mulliners being drawn into the Standard-Triumph fold in the late fifties). Tickford (Salmons) soon began working closely with the David Brown group prior to being taken over by it.

Thus by the start of the fifties there were only six significant firms still undertaking the role of bespoke coachbuilder: Abbott, Freestone & Webb, Hooper, H J Mulliner, Park Ward and James Young. This was a huge drop in the industry's capacity, but hardly a surprising one. Of the two markets available to a coachbuilder in 1938 – luxury bodies on large cars, or special (usually drophead) bodies on smaller ones – the second had virtually disappeared. In the early post-war years car buyers were little interested in out-of-the-ordinary bodywork as it was sufficient achievement to obtain a new car at all, so there was no pressure on volume manufacturers to provide drophead coupé or tourer versions of their saloon cars. Indeed such was the power of the manufacturers in the market place that in order to make life simpler for themselves they even omitted the thirties' favourite extra, the sunshine roof; a whole generation of motorists grew up unused to this benefit, and it had to be reinvented in the seventies. However, by the time car supplies began to catch up with demand and manufacturers could see an advantage in offering drophead designs, all volume cars were of integral construction, so that the drophead models were made by converting saloons – a quite different technology from making composite bodies, and one which only Carbodies chose to espouse.

As to the alternative market – luxury bodies on larger cars – there were precious few chassis available on which the coachbuilders could practice their skills. *The Autocar* magazine analysed the problem at the time of the 1948 Motor Show. They listed chassis with a wheelbase of 10 feet or more, and came up with only 10: Rolls-Royce Silver Wraith, Bentley Mark VI, two Daimlers, two Austins (A125 and A135) and one each of AC, Armstrong-Siddeley, Riley (2½-litre) and Wolseley (25hp). Possibly this was a somewhat harsh analysis, as the arbitrary wheelbase rule left out such models as the Alvis TA14, which provided the basis for many special bodies at that time.

Mann Egerton of Norwich had effectively withdrawn from car bodybuilding in 1939, but made one last effort in 1951 with a limousine on the Austin Sheerline long-wheelbase chassis – a model which was normally monopolised by Vanden Plas. It was at the 1951 Motor Show but not thereafter.

One of the few companies to specialise in conversions for the major manufacturers was Carbodies of Coventry, which at the beginning of the fifties was working for Austin, modifying A40 Somerset saloons into convertibles.

On the other hand, it was raising coachbuilders' hopes too much to expect that low-volume models such as the last four listed, which already offered manufacturer's standard bodywork, could attract many buyers for special coachwork. Even the two Austins were available with standard coachbuilt bodies from Vanden Plas, leaving lit-

There was a period in the fifties, in the 'Lady Docker' era at Daimler, when Hooper could be guaranteed to produce one of the talking-points of the Motor Show. This Daimler Straight Eight fixed-head coupé appeared in 1952, painted in two-tone metallic blue with quatrefoil motifs.

tle room for an independent design (although Mann Egerton was the one exception in 1951, with a limousine on the long-wheelbase Sheerline chassis).

Thus the shape of the post-war market was already ominously clear even in 1948. For the independent, traditional coachbuilder there could be little hope of work from the major manufacturers in providing special bodies for their catalogues as there had been in the thirties. That left the 'luxury' segment: apart from Daimler, who in any case had Hooper and Barker available in-house, there would only be Rolls-Royce and Bentley chassis which could offer the hope of worthwhile business. Yet the larger part of potential Rolls-Royce and Bentley coachbuilding business had been destroyed at a stroke when the company announced that it would for the first time be offering standard bodywork – and pressed-steel at that – on both the Silver Dawn and Mark VI chassis. Although the Silver Dawn would be available only to export markets, this still meant a loss of business to the British, and especially London, coachbuilders.

No wonder, then, that there was such a rapid and drastic shake-out in the industry's capacity. The only clients left for these six firms were those at the very top end of the market, who wanted not just a Rolls-Royce or Bentley but one that was different from anyone else's – not a standard body, thank you. Once a firm had captured such a client, the sky was the limit, but there were not too many around to be captured. A high proportion of such bodywork went for export, as the cachet of British craftmanship on such prestigious chassis was even more of an attraction in overseas markets than at home. The home market, meanwhile, struggled to lift itself from both post-war austerity and high taxation – not only personal income tax and surtax but also the prohibitive rate of purchase tax which was added to these expensive cars, virtually doubling them in price.

The six coachbuilding firms which found themselves in this bracket had only one strategy for survival: they would sell their work on a combination of design – both aesthetic quality and exclusiveness – and craftmanship. Price, on the other hand, was so far out of the equation that it was in effect ignored. If you had to ask, you could

not afford it. Of the two, craftsmanship always had the upper hand for these remaining firms had at least retained all the necessary skills and were now dealing with such a demanding level of customer that the quality of their work was if anything better than ever. Design, on the other hand, carried on where it had left off at the end of the thirties, both literally and figuratively. The same influences prevailed: those who were in a position to pay for such work were also, in general, of a conservative disposition (with major exceptions, such as Lady Docker's attention-grabbing Hooper-bodied Daimlers at Motor Shows in the first half of the fifties). The early post-war designs from the top firms were indistinguishable from those of 1938-9 as indeed were the products of the volume manufacturers, but the difference was in the rate of progress thereafter. To take just one example, Ford moved in one bound in 1951 to eliminate separate front wings and produce a true full-width body while the top London coachbuilding firms were still trying to resolve the problem ten years later. Their designers, if taxed with this criticism, would certainly have used the defence that they were only moving as fast as their clients would let them, but it would not alter the facts: British bespoke coachbuilding design, which led the world in the mid-thirties, was lagging way behind by the mid-fifties.

This is not in any way to denigrate the aesthetic standards which prevailed in the post-war years. Some quite stunning designs emerged from five, at least, of these six firms (one could argue that Abbott sometimes looked like a second-division player). Particularly noticeable was the instant 'rightness' of any HJ Mulliner or James Young design, the occasional quirkiness of a Hooper, the slightly heavy look from Park Ward and the elegance of any Freestone & Webb product. Judged as works of art, they all passed, many with honours. Nevertheless they bore less and less relation to the real world of motoring and motor manufacture. Design innovation hardly existed; in a

R.E.A.L. was almost entirely a commercial bodybuilder after World War 2, but one car contract it did carry out was the bodying of the HRG 1500 sports car – effectively a continuation of a thirties design.

Land-Rover chose Tickford in 1950 to build its Station Wagon model. This was constructed by traditional coachbuilding methods, using aluminium panelling which avoided the problems of obtaining steel sheet at that time.

There was still a limited demand for special versions of standard models after World War 2, and Abbott initially decided that it would continue in this market. This is a 1950 drophead coupé on the Bentley Mark 6 chassis.

Another early post-war Tickford contract was to build drophead coupé bodies on the Humber Super Snipe chassis, although why this work did not go to Rootes' in-house firm Thrupp & Maberly is a mystery. This is a 1950 Mark IIA model, the design very much a continuation of 1930s thinking.

The Healey company quickly built a reputation after World War 2, and its relatively small volumes provided an opportunity for the traditional coachbuilders. Abbott gained the contract for the drophead version; this is a 1951 model.

Park Ward continued post-war with its steel-frame system, although it was soon over-taken by several competitors who adopted aluminium for their frames. This is PW's 1951 fixed-head coupé version of the Mark 6 Bentley.

One of the outstanding designs of the post-war period was H J Mulliner's 1953 Bentley Continental, with its dramatic flowing lines at the rear. It also marked an early attempt by a bespoke coachbuilder to produce a full-width body from front to rear – something which the mass-manufacturers were already doing.

Freestone & Webb continued as long as possible on bespoke work, producing some very fine designs. This Rolls-Royce Silver Wraith limousine, shown at Earls Court in 1954, demonstrates the elegance of line which the firm consistently managed to achieve. Only two years later, however, it withdrew from coachbuilding altogether.

Harold Radford's later design of Countryman, shown here on a 1954 Rolls-Royce Silver Dawn. Note the boot opening extending above the rear window.

bizarre role reversal compared with pre-war practice, new features had to become common amongst volume cars before the coachbuilders' clients would accept them on their own exclusive models.

On a technical level, there was progress of a sort, but of questionable relevance. At the end of the thirties Park Ward had been significantly ahead of its competitors, with its all-steel system by then well developed while everyone else was using frames entirely or almost entirely of wood. Even then, though, there had been signs that PW was not exploiting its new system as quickly as it might have done, and the six years of World War 2 inevitably resulted in its technical lead being further eroded. Not only did others learn the techniques of sheet-steel folding and low-temperature brazing, but newer possibilities emerged – particularly the aircraft industry's use of light-alloy frames of fabricated or extruded sections. Hooper was probably the first into such methods: from 1949 onwards its body frames were mainly light-alloy, using a combination of extruded sections and alloy castings, with steel only as a reinforcement where necessary. Hooper was followed three years later by H J Mulliner, whose Bentley Continental was proclaimed as 'all-metal, light alloy', again indicating that steel had not been entirely eliminated. James Young appears to have adopted similar methods the year after, in 1953.

This left only Abbott and Tickford using traditional ash-framing, together with one newcomer to the industry who deserves a mention at this point. Harold Radford, although not a 'survivor' from the thirties, used traditional coachbuilding methods in constructing his 'Countryman' bodies. These were conversions of standard saloons, typically Bentley or Rolls-Royce, and occ-

asionally other marques, but they were carried out to the highest standards. They appear to have satisfied a demand which the bigger companies had failed to observe for a type of up-market estate car which would come into its own at country events such as point-to-points. This is possibly the only post-war example of the coachbuilding industry showing the way to the volume producers; Radford first revealed his design in 1948, well before any of the major manufacturers started to offer estate-car variants.

Abbott and Tickford can be considered the last of the middle-of-the-road coachbuilders, happy to supplement a smaller manufacturer's range with, usually, a drophead coupé (or convertible as they were increasingly being called), or indeed to build anything they were asked, from a prototype to a full production run. Abbott was particularly known in the early to mid-fifties for its drophead bodies on Mark VI Bentley, Healey and Bristol 405 chassis. Tickford's main work from the late forties for some years was constructing drophead coupés for Alvis, firstly on the TA14 and then on the 3-litre TA/TC21 models, but it also bodied Humber Super Snipes and Healeys. However, Tickford became increasingly bound up with contracts for the 3-litre Lagonda, leading to its acquisition by the David Brown group in 1955.

Abbot of Farnham changed its post-war business strategy totally, moving from bespoke coachbuilder to conversion specialist. From the early fifties, for about 10 years, the firm converted the larger Ford saloons into estate-cars; shown here is a Zephyr from the mid-fifties.

Martin Walter made a late attempt to re-enter the car bodybuilding business in 1956 with this Vauxhall Velox estate-car conversion (below), seen at that year's Earls Court Show. It was not successful, although Friary Motors later showed that such a conversion could be a commercial proposition.

Park Ward, meanwhile, had been left behind by its main competitors, clinging to its 'patent steel framework' where the others were using aluminium completely or partially. This changed in 1954 when PW announced its own aluminium and light alloy system, using extruded sections, on the Bentley Continental chassis. They claimed a 50 per cent weight saving over the equivalent steel frame, which makes their tardiness in changing over even more poignant. Such methods were now the norm for the latter part of the fifties; in what was something of a repeat of the thirties, coachbuilders were desperate to keep down the weight of their creations so that they did not take the edge off the car's performance. Nevertheless, H J Mulliner showed that there were other solutions to the problem when in 1959 it announced its Silver Cloud convertible in 'pressed-steel, stressed-skin construction', with aluminium confined to bonnet, doors and boot lid.

In summary, although there had been progress and refinement in techniques, virtually none of the key firms had managed to break away from the principle of constructing a framework on a chassis and then panelling it. Thus the bespoke coachbuilding companies were in the unhappy position of being leaders in neither design nor technical innovation; the one skill they still possessed was to produce something, whatever it might be, to the highest standards of quality. Their products were held up as outstanding examples of British skill and achievement, but fewer and fewer people wanted them, and even fewer could afford them. Yet the industry continued to produce them, because it was the only thing it knew how to do. It had allowed itself to become a magnificent irrelevance.

Needless to say, the gloom in the industry was terminal. What all the firms knew, although the public did not, was that Rolls-Royce's successor to the Silver Cloud 3 and Bentley S range was being designed without a separate chassis, which meant – apart from the few Phantoms each year – an end to traditional coachbuilding methods.

Hooper's reaction was swift: by the 1959 Motor Show it had already announced its imminent closure. H J Mulliner, which to a great extent had taken over Park Ward's former role of technical innovator, was paid the ultimate compliment – Rolls-Royce bought it in that same year; two years later it was merged with Park Ward. Freestone & Webb had ceased coachbuilding three years previously, Abbott was now only interested in its Ford estate car conversions, Mulliners (Birmingham) and Tickford had been subsumed by Standard-Triumph and Aston Martin respectively, and James Young struggled on building bodies for a few years longer. The British coachbuilding industry was as good as dead.

The story of the post-war British coachbuilding industry reads like a Greek tragedy: the ultimate ending is clearly predictable for a long time in advance but no less terrible when it happens. Yet it is reasonable to ask whether there was any alternative course which history might have followed. An equally reasonable answer is, yes, there probably was. A full answer would go beyond the scope of this book, but one only has to look to Italy, to take one example, to imagine a different scenario which might have developed in Britain. In that country, for the entire post-war period, a coachbuilding industry has flourished by providing services which the volume manufacturers cannot provide themselves easily or

Vanden Plas was a captive coachbuilder for Austin and its successors from immediately after World War 2. Its work was confined for many years to building coachbuilt bodies on the top-of-the-range chassis known variously as Sheerline and Princess. This is a Princess IV of 1957.

By 1959 one of Carbodies' major clients was Ford, to whom it was supplying drophead conversions of Consuls, Zephyrs and Zodiacs.

James Young was one of the longest-surviving bespoke coachbuilders, only withdrawing from the business in 1967. This is the James Young version of the S2 Bentley Continental, about 1959. Note that the concept of a true full-width body is only now completely accepted; even so there is a swage-line hinting at a rear wing.

cheaply. These services may be summarised as design innovation, prototype manufacture and small-run production. They capitalise on the strengths of the firms involved - creative flair, technical skill and initiative, flexible production facilities, low overheads and so on. These strengths are exactly those which the pre-war coachbuilding firms in Britain possessed in abundance, and which they could have harnessed to the same ends after the war if they had so chosen.

All that was needed was the vision to see that the integral body was the only route for car manufacture in the long term, and that a support industry such as body-building could only flourish by working within this system rather than with an outdated technology such as separate chassis. The requirement for such support certainly existed in post-war Britain, but it was eventually provided by totally new companies not rooted in the old tradition. Probably the nearest to achieving it was Carbodies, which showed the way with its drophead conversions of Austin, Ford and Hillman pressed-steel bodies during the fifties, and estate-car conversions in the sixties. Even this company lost its way, bled by the needs of the BSA group, but thankfully its Austin-based taxi saved the day and the company is still with us.

THE A-Z OF BRITISH COACHBUILDERS

ABBEY: 1935 MG PB special two-seater (left), with particularly deep door cutaways, and (below) a 1936 Mercedes-Benz two-seater – a rare chassis for any British coachbuilder.

ABBEY COACHWORKS When A P COMPTON moved to Hanwell, West London in 1930 and renamed his firm Arrow Coachworks, his remaining partner W H Terry, together with one D H B Power, remained at the Merton address and formed Abbey Coachworks Ltd. Abbey appears to have eventually outgrown its premises and in 1933 moved to Minerva Road in the new Chase Estate in Acton, London NW10.

The company became well known for attractive open tourer and drophead designs on mainstream chassis. Some of these were adopted by the manufacturers as catalogued models, others were commissioned and marketed by large dealers. One of the earliest commissions was from Eustace Watkins, the London Wolseley dealer, in 1930, for special bodies – sports four-seaters and fixed-head coupés – on the Hornet chassis. Next Abbey produced a four-seater sports version of the Rover Speed Twenty and Speed Meteor, and then went on to body MGs for University Motors, Wolseley Hornets for E C Stearns, Ford 8s for Dagenham Motors and Morris 10-4s for JARVIS (which by this time seems to have given up much of its own coachbuilding activities). Abbey also built a sports 2/4-seater on the Vauxhall Light Six, and a two-door saloon for Railton.

There then followed an unusual series of events. Abbey had got as far as exhibiting at Olympia for one year (1936), but then found that MARTIN WALTER's 'Wingham' cabriolet business was up for sale. Abbey not only bought it but also changed its own name to 'Wingham Martin Walter', and exhibited at Olympia the next year under that name (Daimler and Vauxhall cabriolets and a Delahaye sports saloon). Presumably it felt that the Wingham reputation and folding-head expertise were so highly regarded that they meant more to a buyer than the Abbey name. The whole thing might have paid off for Abbey but for the attentions of Adolf Hitler; as it was, Martin Walter definitely had the better of the deal, and nothing more was heard of either Abbey or Wingham.

ABBOTT After serving as a naval pilot in World War 1, Edward Dixson Abbott became a pupil apprentice at the Wolseley company and then worked in its design office. Thereafter he joined the Surrey coachbuilders PAGE AND HUNT, becoming its 'London salesman and specialised coachwork manager'.

ABBOTT: 1934 Lancia sports saloon (above). The front end is more successful than the back.

1934 Lagonda M45 concealed-head two-seater (right), with high radiator line turned into a feature.

Healey 2.4-litre drophead coupé, c.1950 (below), shows separate front wings now merging into the doors.

This combination of technical and commercial expertise came into its own in 1929 when Page and Hunt went into receivership. Abbott took over the premises and equipment at Wrecclesham, near Farnham, and formed a new company under his own name. It was a brave move at a time when the recession was already beginning to bite but it appears that Abbott had sensed an opportunity in the commercial body market, and he managed to secure some contracts to construct bus bodies. He also developed the car retailing side of the business.

Nevertheless car bodybuilding continued. The new company exhibited at Olympia for the first time in 1931 and would do so every year thereafter until World War 2. As a first move it joined the fashion for putting special bodies on the Austin Seven chassis, producing fixed-head coupés, drophead coupés and saloons. Thereafter, it was no doubt Abbott's previous knowledge of the London scene which helped him develop associations with major

dealers; he was soon bodying Daimlers and Lanchesters for Stratstone and Talbot 105s for Pass and Joyce. The Talbot connection was to develop into a substantial source of business after the Rootes take-over in 1935, and even into 1938 when the marque had become Sunbeam-Talbot, with Abbott constructing various designs of drophead coupé on the 10hp chassis. A measure of the size of the Talbot business can be gained from the effect of a major fire at Farnham in late 1935 (from which happily the firm made a quick recovery): no less than 25 Talbot chassis were destroyed, as well as numerous others.

At the same time (1934) the firm obtained the contract from the Lagonda company for coachwork on the new Rapier. Gerry Maddox, a refugee from the recently expired Huntingdon company of that name, is credited with helping to obtain the order. It involved sports, drophead coupé and sports saloon designs, and must have represented the major part of Abbott's workload during the 1934-35 period. Unfortunately it ended in receivership for Lagonda, and although some Rapier production continued under the new Rapier Cars company very few were bodied by Abbott.

Another useful, although smaller, contract which ran at the same time as the Rapier one was with Frazer Nash-BMW; around 40 chassis were imported from Germany and Abbott clothed them with saloon and coupé bodies. It also had an involvement with Aston-Martin (a sure sign that its prices were keen!), starting with the 1½-litre

saloon in 1934 and going on to drophead coupé bodies for the 2-litre chassis in 1937-38.

After World War 2 Abbott was amongst the few to restart bodybuilding activities. Initially it even picked up its Sunbeam-Talbot connection, once more building drophead coupés. There followed drophead bodies on such chassis as Bentleys and Lanchester LD10s, then the special-bodied Healey Abbott, and even some Bentley saloons. By this time Abbott was owned by Gordon Sutherland, owner of Friary Motors and former owner of the Aston-Martin company. Eventually it found a niche in converting the larger Ford saloons into estate cars. This was good business for the firm in the fifties and early sixties, but then died away; Abbott finally closed in 1972.

ADAMS
Horace Adams (Newcastle) Ltd of Newcastle-on-Tyne is known only for having bodied a Bentley 3-litre tourer in 1925, and also a Bullnose Morris some time in the twenties. The company appears to have survived until the start of World War 2.

AEW
See WRIGHT, A E.

AIRSTREAM
Airstream Ltd was a company formed by a Capt Fitzmaurice to develop coachwork designs (e.g. the Singer Airstream). There is no evidence that it had its own coachbuilding capacity.

AKERS
R D Akers Ltd of Hanwell in West London built a body on an Austin 12/4 in 1933 which was specially designed for an invalid passenger.

AIRSTREAM: 1935 Singer Airstream saloon, designed by Capt Fitzmaurice's company Airstream Ltd.

ALBANY CARRIAGE
Originally located in Kingsbury Avenue, St Albans, Albany Carriage moved in 1924 to a former tram depot at Hanwell, London W7. In 1927 it began exhibiting at the Olympia Show, although this only lasted two years; its motivation could well have been to show off its expertise in constructing Weymann bodies, which it made under contract for Alvis (12/50) and the London dealer Charles Follett (Lancia Lambda), and also in some quantity on Bentley chassis.

The firm's most famous design by far was the 'Airway' saloon on the Lancia Lambda chassis, illustrated on page 26. This was intended to recapture the spirit of air travel at the time; it boasted not only a highly streamlined rear to the body and airliner-style wickerwork seats, but even an air-speed indicator. The rear treatment was unconventional. Since the chassis did not permit sufficient headroom with the 'fastback' treatment, the problem was solved by adding a kind of lantern roof.

Sadly, exactly at the moment (November 1927) when Albany seemed to be riding high, it suffered a terrible blow through the sudden death of its managing director, Capt Norman Wallis. Although the firm put out brave statements about carrying on the business, it seems that his loss – coupled no doubt with the increasingly difficult economic climate – was behind Albany Carriage's demise. Its problems were not helped when, at the beginning of 1928, Alvis cancelled its Weymann body contract, on the grounds that the Alvis-designed 'Alvista' body was so

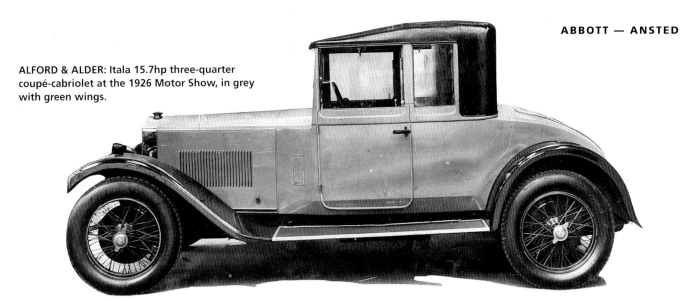

ALFORD & ALDER: Itala 15.7hp three-quarter coupé-cabriolet at the 1926 Motor Show, in grey with green wings.

ALLINGHAM: MG PA Airline coupé (above), designed by Allingham's firm but built by Carbodies, and Ford V-8 81A limousine of 1938 (below) designed by Allingham's Vehicle Developments but built by a sub-contractor – probably Ranalah, or possibly Whittingham & Mitchel.

much cheaper to produce. Albany seems to have given up around 1930, since this is when A P COMPTON moved in to its former premises.

ALFORD AND ALDER

This south-east London firm, established as long ago as the early 1800s, exhibited continuously at London Motor Shows from 1919 to 1926. Its good-quality but otherwise unremarkable designs were shown on the more upmarket chassis such as Armstrong-Siddeley and Delaunay-Belleville. The firm seems to have had a particular affinity with Renault, Peugeot and Crossley. It would appear that the engineering business which it formed into a separate company in 1925 showed more promise than coachbuilding, and the firm eventually became well known as an original equipment supplier to the motor industry. It later relocated to Hemel Hempstead and in 1960 was taken over by Standard-Triumph.

ALLEN AND SIMMONDS

Although this Reading-based firm exhibited at the White City (an annexe of the Olympia Show) in 1920, little else is known. On that occasion it showed a landaulet and an all-weather, both on Talbot 25hp chassis. It is also known to have bodied a Bean coupé the following year.

ALLINGHAM

After the demise of his HOYAL company in 1931, H W Alllingham struck out in an entirely new direction. Instead of setting up another bodybuilding factory, he worked from a central London address as an independent designer, and with considerable success. His Vauxhall Airline and Stratford tourers were made for him by WHITTINGHAM & MITCHEL, Vauxhall Vitesse tourers by OFFORD, Vauxhall 27hp coupé de villes by MOTOR BODIES, MG NA and PA Airline coupés by CARBODIES and the similar MG 2/4-seaters by WHITTINGHAM & MITCHEL.

At the same time (1934) Allingham formed a company called Vehicle Developments, and in cooperation with the Ambi-Budd company of Germany developed a standardised pressed-steel door and pillar for drophead coupés. These were capable of being fitted to a wide range of chassis lengths and led to his 'Sandringham' design being sold on Austin, Ford, Morris, Vauxhall and Wolseley chassis. They were made for him by RANALAH, WHITTINGHAM & MITCHEL and JONES BROS.

Strictly speaking, Allingham was not a coachbuilder and therefore should not qualify for inclusion in this list. Nevertheless his influence was so strong that he deserves to be made an exception.

ALL-WEATHER BODIES

See GILL

ALPE & SAUNDERS

See WYLDER

ANSTED

An obscure bodybuilder from Weybridge, known only to have rebodied a 12/60 Alvis in 1934.

ARNOLD (MANCHESTER): 1936 Alvis Speed 20 SD four-door saloon with the flowing tail typical of this firm.

ARC

Arc Manufacturing of Hyde, Cheshire, was one of the many small firms which decided to offer a special body on the Austin Seven chassis. This design, given the unlovely name of 'coupette' by its makers when announced in 1927, offered slightly more sophisticated all-weather equipment than much of the two-seater competition.

ARCHER HOLMES

This Cowes, Isle of Wight, firm bodied a Rover 8 coupé in 1924.

ARMSTRONG

A Shepherd's Bush, West London, firm known to have built drophead coupé bodies on Austin Sevens.

ARNOLD (LONDON)

W H Arnold was a pioneer motorist and one of the early car bodybuilders. His business in Baker Street, London W1 went back certainly to 1910 and probably earlier. He exhibited continuously at London Motor Shows from 1919 to 1923, showing his firm's work on a variety of chassis, including Rolls-Royce, Bentley, Minerva, Talbot, Alvis, Armstrong-Siddeley, Singer and Crossley. Interestingly, only one of these makes was imported, yet at his bankruptcy examination (he had become personally bankrupt in early 1924) he blamed the McKenna duties on imported cars as the main cause of his plight (doubly sad, as they were abolished only a few months later). He left the industry and worked as a sales manager for the next 10 years until he died in 1934.

ARNOLD (MANCHESTER)

William Arnold of Manchester, although a provincial firm, and although a coachbuilder only as a minor adjunct to its car-dealing business, had the highest credentials. It had been bodying cars since 1910, was at Olympia for every one of the inter-war Shows, and its clients used only the best chassis. Initially after World War 1 it seemed to be Daimlers and Crossleys to which these wealthy Mancunian clients were drawn; then, from 1923, Hispano-Suizas; then a little later Bentleys, Lanchesters and Sunbeams. Many bodies on these chassis

ATCHERLEY: Brough Superior drophead coupé of c.1935, its front wing almost reminiscent of a 'Traction' Citroën.

were 'Arnaulets', Arnold's special style of landaulet.

What is surprising is that no Rolls-Royce apparently passed through the Arnold coachworks until 1931, after which the marque seems to have become quite popular. Yet also in the thirties Arnold managed to widen its appeal by moving down to medium-price chassis, particularly Standard and Humber. The 'Arnaulet' now became the generic name for a sports saloon with a sunshine roof incorporated in the specification, and it was applied to both these makes – Standard until 1933 and Humber until 1936. Thereafter Arnold seems only to have built limousines, together with a design of sports saloon called the 'Slip-Stream', until World War 2 intervened.

Arnold designs tended to be 'safe', never moving ahead of customers' tastes, yet quick to incorporate the latest technical innovations: Weymann, Silent Travel and so on. Occasionally, though, it allowed its decorum to lapse – such as in 1925 when a Bentley landaulet was painted primrose and mauve, or in 1934 when another Bentley was given a streamlined sports saloon body with art deco front wings and a slightly over-bulbous tail. William Arnold tried to restart coachbuilding in a small way after World War 2 but soon gave up that side of the business and concentrated on motor dealing. It was in existence under its own name until very recently.

BARKER: 1921 (Olympia Show) Rolls-Royce 40-50 Silver Ghost 'barrel-bodied' tourer (right), and (below) a beautifully- proportioned 1932 Rolls-Royce Phantom 2 sedanca de ville.

ARROW
See COMPTON, A P

ATCHERLEY
Although W C & R C Atcherley is known to have existed for most of the period between the wars, there are very few records of car bodies constructed by the firm. Those it did produce were on good-quality chassis – Rolls-Royce P1, Bentley, Minerva, Invicta, an early Aston-Martin and so on. Its best-known period was when it was responsible for the bodies on the original Brough Superior cars of the late thirties. It eventually became part of the Bristol Street Motors group.

AUSTER
Auster Engineering Co, of Wembley, North West London, built a coupé body on a 6-litre Bentley chassis in 1927.

AUTO SHEET METAL
A Shepherd's Bush, West London, firm who supplied two- and four-seater bodies for the Deemster car in 1922-24.

AVON
See NEW AVON

BAKER
A Baker of Leamington Spa is known to have bodied a Daimler six-light saloon in 1920.

BAMBER
R Bamber of Southport bodied two 3-litre Bentleys in the early twenties. This is all that is known of the firm's coachbuilding activities, but it went on to become a major car dealer with branches in a number of northern cities.

BARKER
Founded as carriagemaker in 1710, Barker & Co Ltd was already a highly prestigious firm when in the early twentieth century it turned its hand to car bodywork. It achieved virtually instant success when in 1905 it showed the Hon C S Rolls an example of

BARKER: 'sports pullman llmousine' (ie saloon limousine) c.1937.

its work. At that time Rolls had just started distributing cars for Royce Ltd; he is said to have announced that 'all Rolls-Royce cars will be fitted with Barker bodies', and certainly for the next 25 years Barker was viewed as the 'official' coachbuilder to Rolls-Royce. At that time Barker was located in Covent Garden in London's West End, but four years later – no doubt because of the increased business which Rolls had brought – it moved its workshop further west to Shepherds Bush. Before long, however, Barker found it necessary to maintain a set of West End showrooms, and for most of the inter-war period it was synonymous with its address in South Audley Street.

There was never any question about Barker's quality; alongside HOOPER and H J MULLINER it was in the very top rank of British coachbuilders. Moreover it had – initially at least – a lightness of touch in its designs which was not always present in the more formal work of Hooper or even H J Mulliner. Barker produced a series of famous models, starting with what is now the best-known Rolls-Royce of all – the 1907 40/50 'roi-des-belges' with aluminium-painted panels and silver-plated fittings, which was christened the Silver Ghost and thus gave its name to the whole model range. It was also the probable innovator of the barrel-sided tourer, a distinctive shape which became associated with the name of Barker. Although Barker bodied numerous upmarket chassis, it will always be associated with three marques – Rolls-Royce first and foremost, and then Daimler and Bentley. Its Motor Show exhibits bear this out: throughout the period 1919 to 1937 there was always a Rolls-Royce on the stand, and almost every year one or other of the other two – sometimes both. The Bentley connection flourished even more after the Rolls-Royce take-over, Barker claiming to have bodied the first 3½-litre chassis to emerge.

At about this time, however, it became clear that all was not well. Famed initially for the light weight of its bodies, Barker had been putting on middle-aged spread, and Rolls-Royce, for one, did not like it; it would also appear that Barker was not listening to the manufacturer as closely as it once did, and preferred to do things the way it always had. Rolls-Royce's concern, as always, was that coachbuilders were building bodies that were both too heavy and yet not strong enough, thus reducing both the performance and the life of their cars. The upshot was that in developing new bodybuilding techniques it chose to work not with Barker but with Park Ward, whom it found much more flexible and innovative.

Enough of this reputation must have trickled down to Barker's potential clients to have affected sales, for in 1938 it went into receivership; it was bought by HOOPER – one of that company's few misjudgements, for it could do nothing with the Barker name before World War 2 started. During the war Hooper itself, and therefore Barker with it, were bought by the BSA group, which of course included the Daimler company, and this determined the remainder of Barker's history. Moved to Coventry, it became no more than an upmarket trading name for certain Daimler and Lanchester models, although it exhibited under its own name at Earls Court until 1952, always using Daimler or Lanchester chassis. In its last days Barker was probably best associated with the Lanchester LD10 saloon, although the majority of those bodies were an all-steel design from Briggs, the coachbuilt version only being used on the last batch in 1951. The Barker name was last used for the Daimler 2½-litre convertible of 1952-54.

BATLEY COACHWORKS See MOTOR BODIES (NEWCASTLE)

BEADLE John Clayton Beadle is known to have bodied car chassis from as early as 1899. He turned his business into a limited company, John C Beadle Ltd, of Dartford, Kent, in 1915. From its early days the company appears to have been involved in both car and commercial bodybuilding; it exhibited at London Motor Shows continuously from 1920 to 1930, but during the same period it was also at the Commercial Motor Shows, exhibiting its bus and coach bodies.

To judge from Show exhibits, in Beadle's earlier car work it specialised in imported chassis – particularly Packard, Renault and Delage; later on Minerva and Stutz

BEADLE: Delage 40-50hp seven-seater saloon from the 1924 Motor Show.

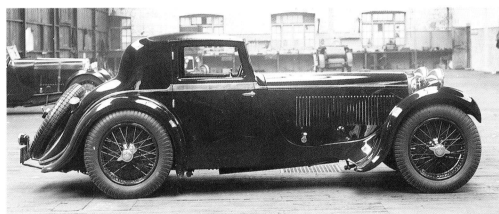

BERTELLI: 1930 Aston-Martin International fixed-head coupé, from the era of long bonnets.

featured. It also bodied some of the bigger chassis from such British manufacturers as Austin, Morris and Talbot. Its work was clearly pitched at the upper end of the market, with beautifully-trimmed limousines and saloons predominating.

Thus when the Depression came it is no surprise that Beadle moved away from the car business and concentrated on the relatively healthy bus and coach market. This it continued until the fifties; it was eventually taken over by the Rootes Group, and concentrated on car dealing. Later, however, it was bought back into private hands and continues today as a major Rover dealer – still in the same premises purpose-built for the firm back in 1911.

BEAL Nothing is known of J B Beal of York before 1921, which also happens to be the first and last year that the firm exhibited at Olympia (White City annexe). Its single exhibit was a saloon on a 24hp Delage chassis ('in an unfinished condition'). The firm survived until 1924 but then appears to have gone out of business.

BEAUMONT Predominantly a commercial body-builder, Beaumont of Pinner justifies an entry purely because it was pressed into service on a sub-contract basis when the Lagonda company was particularly overworked in the early thirties. Its task was to build two 'tiger-hunter' bodies for Indian rajahs. Beaumont still existed in recent times, but no longer connected with bodywork.

BEDDOES MOORE A little-known coachbuilder from Stourbridge, Worcestershire, whose patented 'vanishing head saloon' in the twenties was built on Austin Sixteen and Singer Senior chassis.

BERTELLI Enrico ('Harry') Bertelli was the brother of Augustus Cesare ('Gus') Bertelli of Aston Martin fame. After Gus had taken over the running of that firm he brought in his brother to supervise the body-building side at Feltham, and indeed to act as body designer. In 1929 Harry started E Bertelli as a separate coachwork business, on the same site, incorporating it as E Bertelli Ltd a year later. In this form he was permitted to body other chassis, although in the firm's ten year life probably only a couple of dozen such chassis were involved. They included some Alvises (four or five in total), two six-cylinder Rileys, two MGs, two Lagonda Rapiers,

BLAKE: 1923 Wolseley 15hp 'saloon landaulet' – ie with no division.

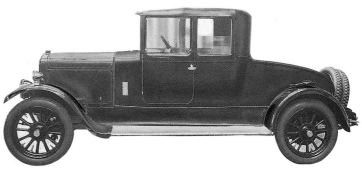

BOTWOOD: Austin 20hp two-seater coupé with dickey at the 1920 Motor Show; blue with black mudguards.

a Type 57 Bugatti, a 3-litre Bentley and an Amilcar racer. Bertelli was also listed as supplying tourer bodies on the Hudson Special for Shaw and Kilburn, but how many were actually constructed is not known. It also supplied bodies for either the Graham British Special or its successor, the Lammas-Graham. There is a suggestion that it was implicated in two GROSVENOR bodies on Vauxhall chassis, possibly supplying panels for Grosvenor to assemble (for some strange reason). There was also a Frazer Nash-BMW drophead coupé for Lionel Martin.

Meanwhile the business of bodying Aston Martins continued. This notably included the prototype Type C, plus modifying seven other chassis to Type C specification. In 1938, the year after his brother had left Aston Martin, Harry Bertelli closed down the bodybuilding business and started making fire-pumps. He did not lose all his motor industry connections, however, as he also acted as a consultant to the Atalanta company.

BIRMINGHAM MOTOR BODY
All that is known about this company is that it bodied a Buick saloon in 1925.

BLACKBURN
Why the Blackburn Aeroplane Co Ltd of Leeds should want to produce even one car body is unknown, unless it was to please a special customer (a Mr Rayne Roberts, who 'suggested' the design to Blackburn in 1920). Let us hope he was satisfied with the resulting all-weather body on his Bianchi.

BLAKE
J Blake and Co Ltd of Liverpool began as a coachbuilder in 1871, and is known to have bodied car chassis from as early as 1907. It was soon a dealer for Wolseley, and was one of the first for Ford, being appointed in 1910; later it became a distributor for Hudson and Essex. Blake appeared regularly at Olympia from 1923 to 1927, exhibiting some quite elegant enclosed coachwork on Lanchester, Wolseley, Bean and Bentley chassis. At the same time, however, it was involved in commercial bodybuilding, particularly buses and coaches, as well as motor dealing. In the end these latter activities must have prospered sufficiently for the firm

to decide to give up the car coachwork side, although it continued with commercial bodybuilding until well after World War 2. Today Blake is still a Ford dealership.

BLIGH BROS
Bligh Brothers was established as carriage-builder in Canterbury as long ago as 1812, when William Bligh started his business. His two sons then took over, and presumably gave the business the name by which it became known. They were very successful, opening showrooms in London's Long Acre and winning prizes at international exhibitions. The firm withdrew back to Canterbury, however, when it hit hard times (there appears to have been a bankruptcy in 1913).

After World War 1, it is known to have bodied a 1924 Hispano-Suiza tourer and re-bodied an early Aston Martin racing-car. Its most famous connection, however, is with Count Zborowski, since it was responsible for bodying all his famous Chitty-Chitty-Bang-Bangs – not surprisingly, since for whatever reason the Count had become the owner of the company. After his death in 1924 it moved from coachbuilding to repair work, and later became a general automobile business with branches throughout East Kent. The company closed in 1974.

BOTWOODS
The forerunner of Botwoods of Ipswich, Bennett & Botwood, is known to have existed before 1861, but it was in 1875 that William Botwood set up on his own account as a carriage-builder. On his death in 1896 his two sons took over, renaming the business W T & S E Botwood. They soon moved into the motor trade, taking an agency for Gobron-Brillié and building bodies on imported chassis.

In 1902 J R ('Reggie') Egerton joined the business. He was the brother of Hubert Egerton who by that time had already formed MANN EGERTON in Norwich. The company formed a separate coachbuilding side, known as Botwood & Egerton; it clearly flourished, at one point producing bodies for Napier on a batch basis. However in 1910, after a major disagreement, Reggie left the firm and set up on his own under the name EGERTON'S (IPSWICH) LTD. The Botwood firm then put its remaining business into a limited company (Botwoods Ltd).

BOWDEN BRAKE: 1923 Morris Cowley saloon with tubular frame and sliding doors.

BOYD-CARPENTER: Wolseley Hornet sports of c.1931. Note louvres at bottom of tail panel.

Soon the company was beset by more problems. In 1914 William Botwood resigned his directorship and left the company. Then in 1918 the other brother, Samuel, died at the early age of 44. It is therefore no surprise that a year later the company was taken over – ironically by Mann Egerton. This was not to be quite the end of the coachbuilding business, though, as Botwoods continued to operate under its own name – and even exhibit at Olympia, in competition with its parent company – until 1923. It was a typical good-quality provincial coachbuilder, bodying the better type of chassis such as Sunbeam and Minerva for the local gentry. Coachbuilding activities seem to have stopped by the mid-twenties.

BOWDEN BRAKE

It comes as a surprise to learn that the Bowden Brake Co of Birmingham was once in the coachbuilding business. It even exhibited at three successive Olympias, from 1922 to 1924, presumably to demonstrate its unique system of frame construction using weldless steel tubing. It is a pity that such an innovation did not succeed since it might have changed the history of car coachbuilding. Certainly it showed sufficient strength as one of its exhibits – a Morris Oxford saloon – was even fitted with a sliding door. No doubt cost killed the concept at the time, and Bowden reverted to its main business.

BOYD-CARPENTER

Originally known when it was started in 1926 as Boyd-Carpenter & Thompson Ltd, the firm became Boyd-Carpenter & Co Ltd from 1930. F H Boyd-Carpenter himself had been previously employed by GORDON ENGLAND, and then set up initially as a tuning specialist, using the former Gordon England service garage in Kilburn, North-West London. He used his own Austin Sevens to good effect at Brooklands. Once it moved into bodybuilding, the company's speciality became a good-looking pointed-tail two-seater body on the Austin Seven chassis. It produced something similar on the Wolseley Hornet, as well as a four-seater fixed-head coupé. It is also known to have bodied a Standard Nine tourer. Sales were handled by the London dealer Normand Garage. As World War 2

BRADBURN & WEDGE: 1925 Rolls-Royce 20hp saloon. Note oval rear window.

approached F H Boyd-Carpenter decided that aviation was the industry to be in and set up the Rumbold company, which specialised in aircraft seats among other things. His sister was left in charge of the Kilburn premises, and no record remains of the company thereafter. Boyd-Carpenter himself had not broken his connection with coachbuilding forever, though, as much later he purchased JONES BROS Ltd.

BRADBURN & WEDGE

Nothing is known of this firm other than the existence of a Rolls-Royce 20 bodied by it in 1925.

BRAINSBY

This Peterborough firm was typical of the provincial coachbuilders of the twenties, producing unexceptional designs on middle-of-the-road chassis such as Crossley, Fiat, Hotchkiss and so on, with the occasional Rolls-Royce to test its skills. It exhibited at Olympia from 1924 to 1929, and then – almost – disappeared. The caveat is because overlapping with Brainsby, in early 1929, there emerged a firm of coachwork suppliers called Brainsby Woollard; this firm seems to have started with three 4½-litre Bentleys and then moved on to limousines on Stutz chassis. It is also known to have supplied bodies on M45 Lagonda and Alvis Speed 20 chassis.

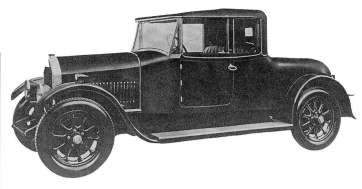

BRIDGES: 20hp Humber three-quarter coupé of c.1925 (above), probably a standard design, and 1925-26 Sunbeam 14/40hp tourer (below).

BRAINSBY: Humber 14/40hp D-back limousine (above). BRAINSBY-WOOLLARD (with Lancefield): 1930 Rolls-Royce 20/25 landaulet (below) presumably built by Lancefield and sold through Brainsby-Woollard.

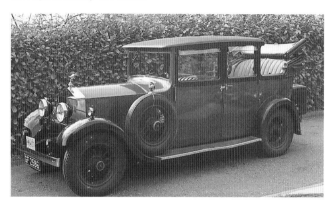

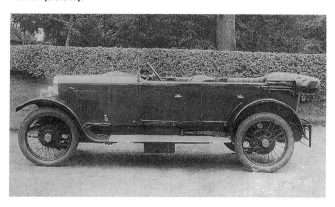

There is no evidence, however, that Brainsby Woollard had any bodybuilding facilities of its own; on the contrary, it sub-contracted everything, either to LANCEFIELD (Stutz, Rolls-Royce, Alvis) or JOHN CHARLES (Stutz, Lagonda, Alvis). It seems likely that the firm was a partnership between the original Brainsby and a salesman by the name of Charles Harry Woollard. Its seems to have ceased operating around 1936.

BRANKSOME
Branksome Carriage & Motor Works – presumably located in the suburb of Bournemouth, Dorset, of the same name – built a coupé body on a 1925 Bentley.

BRIDGE
Bridge of Southport, Lancashire, is known to have bodied a 3-litre Bentley in 1923.

BRIDGES
Bridges Garage of Cirencester was a relatively small provincial firm which at one time had an influence beyond its size. During the twenties it not only bodied significant numbers of Sunbeam chassis but also held the Sunbeam agency for the whole of the western side of England.

Wilfred George Bridges founded the firm known originally as W G Bridges in 1901. When he died in 1919, his two partners formed Bridges Garage Ltd and took over the business. It exhibited at Olympia continuously from 1919 to 1926; the emphasis was obviously on Sunbeam, but the firm also showed its work on Essex and Humber chassis. Thereafter there was a major shift in fortunes; the 1926 show had clearly cost too much money for the business gained, and Sunbeam itself was in trouble. Bridges negotiated an extension to its Morris Commercial agency to cover cars as well, pulled back from the coachbuilding business, and concentrated on being a conventional repairer and retailer.

Interestingly, in spite of the financial vicissitudes of the thirties and forties, Bridges has retained its Morris (now Rover) franchise to this day, operating as Bridges Motor Co Ltd.

BRIGDEN
Brigden of Brighton rebodied two front-wheel drive racing Alvises in 1928-29.

BRIGGS
Briggs Motor Bodies of Dagenham, Essex, is of course best known as a captive supplier of pressed-steel bodies to the adjacent Ford plant; indeed since 1953 it has been owned by Ford. Nevertheless it qualifies for inclusion in a book about traditional coachbuilding by reason of having occasionally built bodies of a composite construction and – it is believed – mounted them on the relevant chassis. One such instance was the Ford Y 8hp, where Briggs built a sporting body, probably a one-off, in competition with the many other coachbuilders who were offering the same thing. Another, and a more serious proposition, involved the 1936 Flying Standard range; although the smaller models had all-steel bodies from Pressed Steel, the larger ones (12, 16 and 20hp) were composite bodies from Briggs, who may or may not have mounted the bodies on the chassis as well.

BRIGGS: 1936 Standard Flying Twenty – a rare composite body from this manufacturer.

BRISTOL AEROPLANE

Originally known as the Bristol & Colonial Aeroplane Co, this company bodied some Armstrong-Siddeley 30hp chassis during 1919.

BRISTOL WAGON

The Bristol Wagon & Carriage Works Co Ltd seemed to have made a successful transition from horse-drawn wagons to car bodywork. It was at the Olympia Shows of 1919 and 1920, with examples of its work on Vulcan, Vauxhall and Morris chassis. The firm's main feature was the 'Condick patent all-weather body', which allowed the car to be used either as an open tourer or with the rear compartment closed.

In 1921 the company was taken over by the Leeds Forge Co, which wanted the whole of its facilities for the manufacture of railway rolling-stock, and car coach-building came to a sudden end.

BROMFORD

The Bromford Body Co of Birmingham took over production of the Trinity body from MEREDITH COACHCRAFT when that company closed down in 1934. It is known to have applied the design to at least one chassis, a Wolseley Hornet, and also produced a saloon on a Lanchester chassis.

BROOM

Victor Broom existed in London NW1 from at least 1924, and exhibited at Olympia from 1926 to 1929. Even during this short history it seems to have had financial troubles, with Victor Broom (1928) Ltd taking over from the original company. It was undoubtedly at the upper end of the market, concentrating on closed bodywork on expensive chassis such as Delage, Hispano-Suiza, Bentley, Minerva and Invicta, and appears to have gone out of business after 1929.

BUCHANAN

J Buchanan of Glasgow exhibited at the 1921 Scottish Motor Show and, unlike some of the exhibitors there, seems to have constructed

BROOM: 1926 Delage 40/50hp limousine, described as 'semi-sporting'.

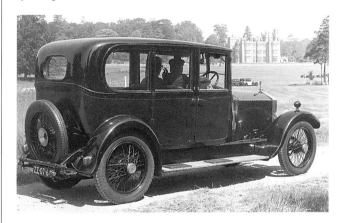

BUCKINGHAM: 1925 Rolls-Royce 20hp saloon.

for itself the coachwork which was on its stand. This was a landaulet on a Wolseley chassis.

BUCKINGHAM

J Buckingham of Bradford Street, Birmingham, was primarily a builder of bus bodies in the twenties, but it is known to have bodied a Rolls-Royce 20hp in 1925.

BURGHLEY

See WILSON (LONDON).

BURLINGTON

The history of the Burlington Carriage Company goes back to before

BURLINGTON: Armstrong-Siddeley's in-house coachbuilder is believed to have bodied this 1935 20hp limousine.

Opposite page: Daimler 25hp saloon, from Abbot's 1930 catalogue (above). Vauxhall DX 14hp 'Stratford' tourer (below) designed by Allingham and built by Whittingham & Mitchel.

CADOGAN: purposeful-looking 1927 Invicta 3-litre drophead coupé.

World War 1, when it was situated in London's Marylebone Road. From 1913 on, when the Siddeley-Deasy company bought Burlington and relocated it to Coventry, it was the in-house coachbuilder to what soon became Armstrong-Siddeley. It gave its name to a part of Armstrong-Siddeley's Parkside site which ever after was known as Burlington Works, and which still exists to this day (but not for much longer, according to latest reports).

Burlington had a brief moment of glory in the thirties, when the Armstrong-Siddeley management decided that its coachbuilding side – still nominally a separate company – should exhibit at Olympia. This it did for three years from 1934 to 1936, but it only showed its parent company's products, and the whole exercise was clearly a device to give more exposure to the group's upmarket brand, the Siddeley Special.

Burlington Works continued to body Armstrong-Siddeley chassis until the end of car production in 1960. Its last work was a contract from Rootes to produce the body for the Sunbeam Alpine; this ended in 1962.

BUTLIN The partners who formed Butlin's of Coventry in 1932 were ex-employees of Charlesworth. James Butlin had been a co-owner of Charlesworth in the late twenties (before the 1931 receivership).The firm acted as a contract coachbuilder for Daimler and Lanchester, and is also known to have bodied at least one Alvis. It did not survive the beginning of World War 2.

CADOGAN Famous for the remark that it was 'a third-class firm producing first-class work', Cadogan was the creation of one S R Moss-Vernon. Located in London's Chelsea, during the early twenties it constructed rather formal closed bodies on

expensive chassis such as Delage but soon it was producing smart, almost racy, open sports or tourer designs on Bentley, Invicta, Packard and OM chassis, and showing a distinct sense of style. Cadogan exhibited at Olympia from 1924 to 1927, but then had to go through a financial reconstruction, coupled with a move further out to Fulham. It continued to provide bodies for Invicta and OM, but disappeared from the scene after 1930.

CAFFYN This Eastbourne-based group still exists as a major car dealer, but in the twenties was at least as well known as a coachbuilder. The company exhibited continuously at Olympia from 1919 to 1930 but never again thereafter. During that period it behaved as a typical leading provincial coachbuilder should, bodying a great variety of chassis as required, but perhaps with an emphasis on Darracq, Wolseley and Sunbeam.

Caffyn purchased another coachbuilding business, ROCK, THORPE & WATSON, but presumably this was more

A SALOON ON THE 25 H.P. DAIMLER CHASSIS.
DRAWING Nº 2819.

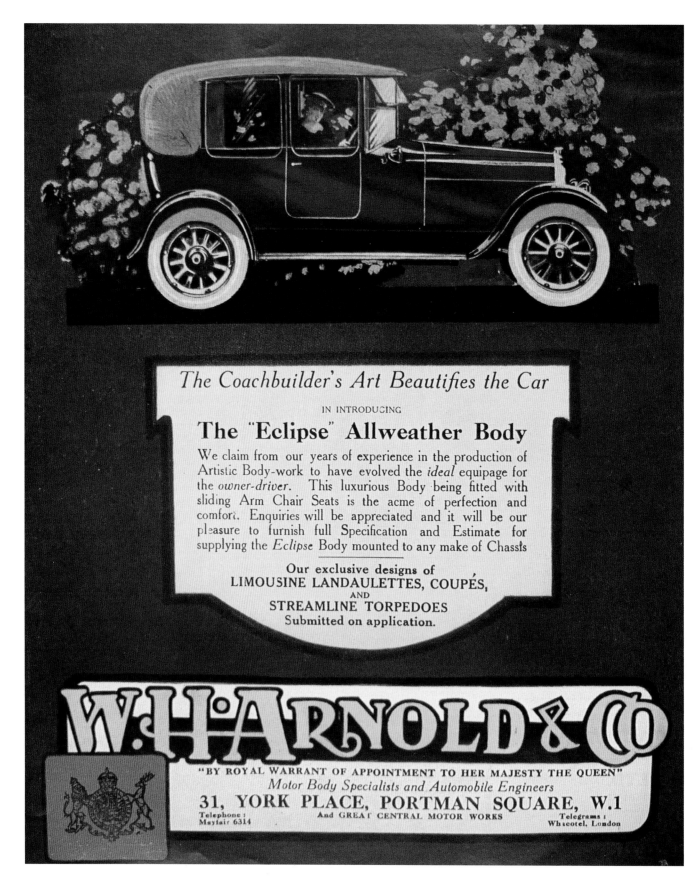

A 1919 colour advertisement for the 'Eclipse' all-weather design
by Arnold (London).

1935 MG Airline fixed-head coupé – another Allingham design
built by Carbodies.

The M.G. Two-litre Tourer
Four-Seater Open Model
by Charlesworth.

Price
£385
Ex works

CAFFYN: 1936 Rolls-Royce 25/30, rebodied as a drophead coupé after World War 2, with faired-in headlamps and no running-boards. Together these features suggest an up-to-date design, but the effect is spoilt by a less than full-width body.

Opposite page: elegant 1938 MG SA tourer by Charlesworth, and Coachcraft's 1938 Railton Fairmile Series 2 drophead coupé.

CARBODIES: the Coventry coachbuilder is believed to have bodied this 1935 Rover 14hp four-door streamline coupé.

in order to expand its motor-dealing coverage. Similarly in the late thirties it bought the MALTBY company, though this time for its premises rather than for its coachbuilding business. Caffyn did, however, build at least one car body after World War 2 – a drophead coupé on a Rolls-Royce chassis (probably a rebodied pre-war one) – apparently to get round restrictions on steel supplies.

CARBODIES

Carbodies has one of the longest continuous existences of any car-related firm in Coventry. Founded in 1919, first in Old Church Road and then in West Orchard, it moved in 1928 to Holyhead Road and is still there today. It owes its birth to what we would nowadays call a management buy-out, when Robert ('Bobby') Jones took over the bodybuilding business of his employers, Gooderham & Co; previously Jones had been works manager at CHARLESWORTH, then general manager at HOLLICK & PRATT.

The company was always more a contract body-builder than a bespoke firm. One of its first customers was Alvis, and Carbodies produced bodies for the 10/30 and many later models. It was also a supplier to MG, and in the early years (1925-30) almost the only one.

Perhaps it was a sign of the times that the company started to exhibit at Olympia in 1929, soon after the PRESSED STEEL COMPANY had started production of all-steel bodies. Those coachbuilding firms which were

looking ahead could see the market for their products diminishing, and none more so than those in the large-volume contract field. It is therefore all the more credit to Carbodies that it survived the difficult Depression years and managed to find volume contracts right up to the war. Its strongest relations were with Rootes for which Carbodies produced special – mainly drophead – bodies on the Minx chassis from its introduction in 1932 right through to the end of the thirties, as well as bodies for Humber. Another long connection in the thirties was with the Rover company, to whom Carbodies was an 'approved supplier' (often with its models incorporated in Rover's own catalogue) from 1932 to 1936; this history is reputed to include the development of a sports saloon from what was originally a CHARLESWORTH design.

From 1935 Carbodies produced contract bodies for Railton – several models of saloon, a drophead coupé and a tourer; again, this work continued right up to World War 2. Later it also did work for Singer and Standard, and became a significant supplier of light steel pressings.

CARBODIES: 1937 Railton tourer (left) in a post-war competition in Malaya and the attractive 1956 Daimler Century roadster (below).

During World War 2 the company bodied military vehicles and also produced aircraft components. Afterwards it returned to contract car work, and also obtained the contract to manufacture London taxis (helped by the number of presses acquired under the wartime 'lease-lend' scheme). During the fifties and sixties it was successful in getting work from many of the major manufacturers, specially noteworthy being its production of convertible bodies for the Ford Consul/Zephyr/Zodiac range and also for the Austin Somerset/Hereford, Hillman Minx and Daimler Conquest. It was also responsible for estate versions of many of the models of the sixties and seventies; most noteworthy was the Triumph 2000 estate, of which Carbodies produced almost 2000. In the meantime, in 1954, Robert Jones had sold the company to the BSA group.

Eventually the car conversion work dried up. Meanwhile, however, taxi production had gone from strength to strength, and this is now Carbodies' main source of business. Today it is part of the Manganese Bronze group, which bought what remained of BSA in 1973.

CARLTON The Carlton Carriage Company originated from a group of coachbuilding firms whose early history is difficult to clarify. The original firm was called MOTOR CAR INDUSTRIES, located in Kilburn Lane, London W10, and was a partnership between two individuals named Halsall and Biddle. It seems that one partner then began trading separately, firstly as Kelvin Carriage and then, around 1925, as Carlton Carriage, from an address in Great Portland Street, while the other set up as the PROGRESSIVE COACH & MOTOR BODY CO (later renamed MAYFAIR CARRIAGE).

Carlton moved soon afterwards, probably in 1926, to Waldo Road in Willesden, NW10. A year later it began exhibiting at Olympia, initially with rather conventional bodies on Chrysler and Hotchkiss chassis, but soon moving to the drophead coupé and coupé-de-ville styles for which it became well known – modern designs with a certain flair which customers appreciated. In 1931 Carlton changed owners when a senior employee named Archibald Neale bought the company outright. One of his first jobs thereafter was bodying the extraordinary Burney Streamliner for his friend Sir Dennistoun Burney. Neale in turn sold Carlton in 1937 to D G C Trench, who remained as chairman and managing director until the mid-sixties.

If the company had any specialities they were, firstly, Talbots – usually for the London agents Pass & Joyce, sometimes directly for the makers – and Humbers, where

CARLTON: 1937 Bentley 4¼-litre pillarless saloon (above), full of Art Deco curves, and a 1932 Rolls-Royce 20/25 drophead coupé (right) with a suggestion of a falling waistline.

some of its styles formed part of the catalogued range. It also bodied numerous American chassis for the importers – Buick, Chrysler, Essex, Hudson, Oldsmobile and Pontiac. The market in which Carlton worked was clearly very competitive, and more than once it had to fall back on sub-contracting. At one stage it appears to have taken a considerable amount of work from OFFORD, especially on Lagonda chassis, and it also built some continental touring saloons and drophead coupés on the Vauxhall 27hp chassis for CONNAUGHT. Nevertheless it also carried out much bespoke work, often drophead coupés, on such prestigious chassis as Rolls-Royce, Bentley and Hispano-Suiza.

Probably the finest design to emerge from Carlton was its Bentley sports saloon of early 1937 (shown above), which had all the trends then fashionable, including separate front wings, no running boards and Art Deco motifs on front and rear wings, all blended together in a stylish whole. This represented Carlton's high point; it produced no more car coachwork after 1939, although it survived as a company until recent times.

CARVILLE A Chalk Farm, North-West London, firm, known only for having rebodied a 1929 3-litre Bentley tourer in 1933 and converting it into a drophead coupé.

CASTLE Castle Motor Co of Kidderminster produced a three-seater body on an Essex chassis which appeared on the Essex stand at the 1922 Olympia Show.

CAVERSHAM Caversham Motors Ltd of Reading is known only for holding a Weymann licence in 1928.

CENTRAL GARAGE Central Garage Ltd, Bradford, bodied a Bentley chassis in 1925.

CHALMER & HOYER (HOYAL) The story of this company runs throughout the inter-war period and encapsulates the history of coachbuilding in those 20 years.

CHALMER & HOYER: 1925 Buick 27hp limousine (above left); 1928 Austin Seven Special two-seater (above), with outsize chassis louvres; 1928 Morris Oxford four-door saloon (left) – a standard design.

Nothing is known of Mr Chalmer, but H Hamilton Hoyer was a force in the industry. As well as (probably) having his own bodybuilding company (see HHH LTD), he joined with Chalmer and H W Allingham in 1921 to set up Chalmer & Hoyer, initially at Hamworthy near Poole in Dorset. Hoyer's speciality was production, while Allingham looked after sales. The company's strategy was clear: it was interested only in volume sales and dealt exclusively with the trade. It was aware of the latent demand for closed bodies, provided they were not too expensive compared with the open alternative, and would therefore concentrate on this form of bodywork. In practice, however, it would achieve its ambitions in two ways: either it would supplement a manufacturer's range with its own variants, under its own name, or it would supply a manufacturer with straight sub-contract bodies.

This policy proved an outstanding success. By 1924 the company had to find additional capacity and purchased a second factory at Weybridge (the former Lang propellor works and then, briefly, Gwynne car factory). A critical factor in this decision was clearly the amount of business it was obtaining from Morris; in that year Morris had decided to add two closed styles to the Oxford range, and to contract out the whole volume to Chalmer & Hoyer. By 1925 it had to dedicate the Hamworthy factory solely to that one customer's production.

Meanwhile, the company shrewdly continued to exhibit at Olympia, which kept its name in front of both the trade and the buying public and also enhanced its reputation for quality. It had started exhibiting in 1922, soon after its formation, and the next year showed a Bentley with a four-door saloon body constructed under the new Weymann patents; Chalmer & Hoyer was the first British coachbuilder to take out a Weymann licence. Its exhibits thereafter tended to reflect the contracts it was gaining – Morris Oxfords, Austin 12s and so on.

The company was by now a significant force in the bodybuilding industry. It was a pioneer in the use of jigging for wood frames, not only for single large-contract designs but even across more than one design; this was achieved by the skilful use of existing parts when developing new designs, possibly without the customer knowing. By the beginning of 1926 the workforce totalled more than 700, split between the two factories, and output was running at 120 bodies a week. It was at the end of that season, however, that the blow fell: the Morris contract was not to be renewed because the new PRESSED STEEL facility was going to come on stream.

One can feel considerable sympathy for Chalmer & Hoyer. Morris had allowed it to build up its capacity and then had suddenly pulled the rug from under it. On reflection, however, this simply does not stand up. Morris's

CHARLES: This 1934 Lancia Augusta fixed-head coupé (above) was a March design. A Stutz 36hp eight-cylinder saloon (below) of c.1934; slightly unhappy rear-end treatment.

plan to form the Pressed Steel Company and build a facility at Cowley was well known to anyone who read a newspaper, much less worked in the industry. Furthermore Allingham had spent some years working in America; indeed, it was his American experience that convinced him to instal a cellulose paint plant at a very early stage. He as much as anyone should therefore have been aware of the trend towards the all-steel body. More likely, Allingham and Hoyer were very aware that their Morris contract was under threat but assumed that they would soon get the business back from somewhere else, for the imminent slump was not yet on people's minds.

Indeed, the company was still set on expansion. In 1925 it had started extending the Weybridge factory with a new panelling shop, and the following year authorised new mounting and finishing shops. At the same time, the two partners decided to change the name of the company. For some years they had been using the brand-name 'Hoyal' (formed from the first letters of their names), and so at the beginning of 1926 the Hoyal Body Corporation came into existence.

When it became clear that new car contracts were not going to fall off trees Hoyal diversified by starting (or rather restarting) the building of bus bodies, a business that it had intended to be in from the beginning until swamped by car body contracts. By 1930, when *The Automobile Engineer* toured the Weybridge factory, there was a large, separate department dealing with bus work. The Hamworthy factory was even more adventurous, moving into the manufacture of motor launches and speedboats.

Even so, a financial squeeze was starting. In 1928 the

Hoyal Bodybuilding Corporation (1928) was formed, apparently in preparation for going public later the same year, but the plan seems to have been aborted. The contracts-only policy went out of the window, and the workforce found themselves bodying a great variety of unfamiliar chassis such as Wolseley Hornets, Austin Sevens and MGs. The company reported losses for both 1929 and 1930, and by August 1931 it was all over; a receiver was appointed and Hoyal ceased business.

There was an epilogue of sorts, or even two. Firstly, two former Hoyal employees, John L Dalrymple and Charles H Livesay, purchased some of the Hoyal equipment from the receiver and started a new coachbuilding business under the name of John Charles & Co (see CHARLES). Secondly, H W Allingham created a new and influential role for himself in the industry during the thirties (see ALLINGHAM).

CHALMERS
John Chalmers & Sons Ltd, of Redhill in Surrey, were licensed to build Weymann bodies in 1928; nothing else is known about the company.

CHARLES
John Charles & Co started in February 1932 at Kew Gardens, south-west of London. Its founders were fugitives from the failed Hoyal business (see CHALMER & HOYER). One of the principals must have been an impressive salesman, for within a year it was producing special bodywork – sports, coupés and saloons, including pillarless saloons – on a range of chassis, mostly sold through major dealers. Examples were Alvis Speed 20s for Charles Follett, Chryslers for Chrysler Motors, Ford 8 tourers for Lambert Motors of Kingston, Morris 10-4 pillarless saloons for Woodcote Motors of Epsom, Morris 10 sports for JARVIS, Singer 9 coupés for Hanson Moore of Eastbourne and Wolseley Hornets for E C Stearns of Fulham Road, London as well as for MARCH. Another design from the same stable which Charles built was the Riley March Special. Some others that were sold directly – or more probably through a number of dealers – were on British Salmson, Lancia Dilambda and Astura, Lagonda M45 and Lagonda Rapier chassis. John Charles also bodied the first Railtons to be produced, in 1933. For many of the designs it used the brand-name 'Ranalah'.

The company exhibited at Olympia in its second and third years of existence, 1933 and 1934. The work shown largely reflected current contracts, but an Essex Terraplane coupé and a Lanchester sports saloon made appearances. John Charles is also known to have bodied some Daimlers. The business built up so quickly that it was soon forced to move to larger premises in January 1934, when it relocated to Brentford on the western edge of London. During 1934 it gained contracts for a full range of catalogued special bodies on both Citroën and Crossley chassis.

In the face of so much success it is surprising how

quickly the company failed. Perhaps it was a measure of its desperation that in 1934 it was accepting business from the 'middleman' firm of BRAINSBY-WOOLLARD; orders for bodies on Stutz, Lagonda and Alvis seem to have arrived via this route. The last news of John Charles was in late 1934, when it was bodying one of the ill-fated Squire sports cars. By early 1935 it was out of business, but a successor was soon in being (see RANALAH).

CHARLESWORTH

Charlesworth Motor Bodies Ltd was located in Much Park Street, Coventry, for the whole of its comparatively long life. Founded in 1907 by three partners named Gray, Hill and Steane – and with a top-class works manager in Robert Jones, who went on to found CARBODIES – it at first concentrated on supplying contract bodies to local manufacturers such as Hillman and Singer. During World War 1 it undertook aircraft work for the Siddeley-Deasy company. The policy of supplying contract bodies continued after the war, when Charlesworth allied itself with the new Dawson company; the Dawson stand at the 1919 Olympia Show held four chassis, all with different designs of body and all by Charlesworth. Much was expected of the Dawson, not least because its founder was the former works manager at Hillman, but the car proved to be too expensive and the company ceased business in 1921.

Charlesworth then turned its attention to the Alvis company and its first car, the 12/30. For a year or two Alvis listed a four-seater by Charlesworth, but the two-seater model proved much more popular and the opportunity for a long-term contract again disappeared. Alvis would not be a customer again until the thirties. At the same time (1921) Charlesworth began exhibiting at Olympia, possibly in search of further contracts or because it had decided to move more into the bespoke business. The result seems to have been the latter, for although no further contract work appeared until 1925, the company was soon bodying a great diversity of chassis: Daimler, Bean, Peugeot, Rolls-Royce, Calcott, Armstrong-Siddeley, Minerva, Bentley, Sunbeam and Talbot were just some of the makes which went through the works within the space of four years. Within this diversity, Minerva and Talbot figure several times, suggesting some sort of favoured arrangement with the importer.

In 1925 Charlesworth gained a contract from Morris for saloon bodies, though maybe only because Hoyal had insufficient capacity. Later on (1929 and 1930) it seems to have been working with Humber (drophead coupés), Hillman (sunshine saloons) and Daimler (Weymann saloons). This workload, however, was not enough; suddenly Charlesworth was absent from the 1931 Motor Show, and in the next month (November) its reconstruction as Charlesworth Bodies (1931) Ltd was reported. James Butlin, principal shareholder until then, left and formed a new company under his own name (see BUTLIN).

The bright spot in this bad news was that it brought in James Reynolds as managing director and major share-

CHARLESWORTH: the ill-fated 1919 Dawson saloon.

holder. One can only deduce that it was his influence that transformed the company. Admittedly his timing was good: the Charlesworth collapse had been late compared with many coachbuilding firms – unluckily so, one might say – and the recovery from the Depression was already starting. Nevertheless, it was under his management that Charlesworth immediately began to secure contract work. In 1931-32 there was the first of two important contracts for Rover (and one presumably carried over from the old company) which was for the 'Pirate' foursome coupé. In 1932-33 – and exhibited at the 1932 Show – came a novel four-door close-coupled pillarless saloon on the Speed Pilot chassis, together with a racy-looking 'super-sports' saloon on the same chassis and an updated Pirate coupé; all three were catalogued Rover models.

Another aspect of the firm's work during the 1930s for which Reynolds must take credit is the quality of its design. We cannot be certain of the identity of the talented individual behind it; quite possibly it was A J Cannell, at various times chief designer and works manager. Whoever he was, he consistently produced work which was not merely graceful but outstandingly stylish. He must have been an important influence in the company gaining the next series of contracts – with Alvis, Lanchester, Daimler and MG – for each of which it produced some magnificent designs. Of these, the predominant customer was undoubtedly Alvis; Charlesworth produced the standard saloon body on the Speed Twenty and its derivatives from 1932 onwards, and followed it up with equally attractive fixed-head and drophead coupés. In 1937-38, out of Charlesworth's annual production running at about 500 bodies, Alvis was taking some 350-400 in each of the two years.

Very much in the same idiom as the Alvis bodies, and highly attractive in their appearance, were the four-seater tourers on the MG SA and WA chassis. Daimler production consisted of saloons and tourers on the Straight Eight chassis, and Charlesworth also produced a good-looking saloon on the 1938 Brough Superior V12 chassis. Its last known bodies before moving to aircraft work in 1940 were the Daimler Dolphin saloon prototype and a Phantom III Rolls-Royce for King Farouk of Egypt (possibly a

CHARLESWORTH: 1937 Alvis 4.3 saloon (above) from Charlesworth's finest era. Elegant Daimler straight-eight saloon (right) of c.1938. 1947 Invicta Black Prince 'Wentworth' saloon prototype (below), showing American influences.

contract picked up from HOOPER).

After World War 2 Charlesworth tried to rebuild its coachbuilding business. It won the contract for the three prototypes of the Invicta Black Prince, but unfortunately this very advanced car proved too expensive for the market in 1947 and Invicta collapsed. The next job proved to be Charlesworth's last: a new six-light saloon from Lea-Francis, its near-neighbours in Much Park Street. Once again, this never went beyond the experimental stage, but this time the outcome was different: Lea-Francis decided it needed its own bodybuilding facilities and obtained them by buying out Charlesworth.

CHARLES CLARK: 1927 Rolls-Royce Phantom 1 'brougham de ville' (see page 34 for picture of interior)

CHELSEA CARRIAGE

Chelsea Carriage Works Ltd existed from 1921 or before until at least 1927. Run by two partners named Middleton and Johnston, it was situated in Lots Road in London SW but also had premises in nearby Danvers Street. The firm showed its car work at Olympia in the three years 1921 to 1923, on Unic, Palladium and Belsize chassis. It was also represented at Commercial Motor Shows during the same period and it is likely that it concentrated on commercial work after 1923.

CLARK, CHARLES

Little is known about the work of Charles Clark & Sons Ltd of Wolverhampton, with one magnificent exception, this being the famous 1927 Phantom I Rolls-Royce brougham de ville, still in existence, with its totally over-the-top Louis XV interior. It was produced, unsurprisingly, 'to the order of a lady'; the design is credited to a Mr J H Barnett.

Otherwise, the firm is known to have bodied Rolls-Royces from 1921 or earlier. It was at one stage bought by Rubery Owen and still exists today as a car dealer.

CLARK, JC

J C Clark of Shepherds Bush, London, apparently had a brief spell in 1921 when it bodied a number of Rolls-Royce chassis, and also a Hudson. Thereafter it seems to have concentrated on building single-deck buses, exhibiting at Commercial Motor Shows, although some car work continued. In 1930 it bodied a Lanchester straight-eight limousine for the playwright George Bernard Shaw.

COACHCRAFT

When ARROW COACHWORKS had finally ceased business, its premises at Hanwell, West London, were taken over in 1934 by a newly-formed company, Coachcraft Ltd. From the outset this was a smaller operation than Arrow as a portion of the building was set aside for use as a service department for the Hupmobile marque. The company was set up and managed by Percy Twigg, an unusual character who had been persuaded by an Oxford friend to enter the coach-building industry, and who then worked at both WINDOVERS and MOTOR BODIES before starting on his own; his partner, who seems to have provided the finance, was Captain O'Neill Butler.

The company concentrated on supplying low-volume, standard bodywork to smaller manufacturers and importers. Its first such contract was with Railton; it seems to have started in parallel with JOHN CHARLES in 1934, making drophead coupés. These were later named the 'Fairmile', and Coachcraft went on producing them until the start of World War 2 (John Charles having gone out of business in early 1935). The company also offered the 'University' saloon ('sponsored' by University Motors) and the slightly cheaper 'Stratton' saloon on Railton chassis in 1935. Coachcraft also took over from CARBODIES the production of the 'Cobham' saloon from 1937 onwards.

Overall, Coachcraft bodied more Railtons than any

COACHCRAFT: 1937 Delage 'Vita' D6-70 sports saloon (right), showing the influence of Paris coachbuilder Chapron, and (below) a 1939 Hudson 'Country Club 8 Riviera Coupé' with superb lines spoilt by a rather ugly set of door-hinges.

other coachbuilder, and this was reflected on its stands at the London Motor Shows, where it exhibited from 1935 to 1938. Some other marques were also shown, including Terraplane, Hudson and Delage, the latter becoming something of a speciality in the late thirties. Coachcraft's designs, under chief designer Geoffrey Durtnal, showed a definite flair; some detected a certain French influence, especially in his work on Delages, after Durtnal was sent on a six-month secondment to Chapron of Paris. Throughout this period the company was apparently on the verge of bankruptcy, and in 1937 even reached the stage of having a receiver appointed.

By 1938, however, Coachcraft was developing another slightly bizarre source of business: working for SOUTHERN COACHWORKS, it would update older chassis – particularly Rolls-Royce – by rebodying them in current style. In at least some cases it was able to hold down its costs (prices of £500 were quoted for a drophead coupé)

by the simple expedient of covering over the existing body and thus avoiding the need for a new framework. This is not to denigrate its quite separate, although small, business bodying new Rolls-Royce chassis under its own name.

There is no doubt that Coachcraft built its bodies down to as low a price as possible – otherwise it would never have retained business from Railton, a company noted for switching its contracts whenever a better price emerged. Nevertheless Coachcraft's products were stylish and much admired. During World War 2 the company was part of a network of former Railton contractors, organised by Noel Macklin, producing gunboats, Coachcraft's contributions being such things as gun covers and cockpit awnings. In 1946 it was bought by University Motors, the London dealer, although Twigg stayed on as a director; he died in 1958, aged 58. The company was renamed UNIVERSITY COACHWORK.

COCKSHOOT: 1923 Rolls-Royce 20hp tourer (left). The early date is given away by the very high scuttle. Interior of a 1929 Rolls-Royce 20/25 limousine (below left) showing occasional seats erected. 1934 Bentley 3½-litre saloon (below) with a tail treatment reminiscent of Gurney Nutting.

COCKSHOOT

Joseph Cockshoot & Co Ltd of Manchester was amongst the oldest and most prestigious of provincial coachbuilders. It could trace its history back to 1724, although the Cockshoot name did not arrive until 1844, and it consistently won awards for carriages throughout the latter part of the nineteenth century. It quickly adapted to the arrival of the motor-car, bodying its first car chassis in 1903 and becoming the major body supplier on imported Renault chassis. Shortly afterwards Cockshoot was appointed one of the first agents for the Rolls-Royce marque (which of course also came from Manchester). By 1906 its first garage was already too small, and it opened new premises at Great Ducie Street. In 1907 it built the 'Pearl of the East', a famous Silver Ghost thought to be the first Rolls-Royce to be exported to India.

Cockshoot started exhibiting at London Motor Shows in 1911, and was to do so continuously (apart from 1919) until the last pre-World War 2 Show in 1938; a Rolls-Royce appeared every year. During World War 1

it turned its skills to making Crossley Air Force tenders and other military vehicles. Many of these were then converted to civilian use after 1918, which provided a useful cushion of work until normal supply of chassis was resumed. Even when this happened Cockshoot was in the happy position of having more work than it could cope with – firstly with Rolls-Royce, where it both supplied the chassis and then bodied it, and then with Armstrong-Siddeley and Morris for which marques it had become agent. The Armstrong-Siddeley connection, one can assume, also generated coachbuilding customers. The level of business required even bigger premises, and in 1928 Cockshoot opened a large showroom in St Ann's Square in the centre of Manchester.

The success of the car dealing side hid a steady decline in coachbuilding work. Cockshoot records reveal a steady drop year by year in the number of new bodies built, from 41 in 1920 to 5 in 1938. Even this does not tell the whole story: in the depths of the Depression, in 1932, it built only one body in the whole year. The pick-

COLE: Daimler 30hp cabriolet on Cole's stand at the 1919 Olympia Show.

up after that date can partly be attributed to the arrival of the Derby Bentley, for which marque Cockshoot naturally became agent as an adjunct to Rolls-Royce. It had a Bentley on its Motor Show stand every year from 1934 onwards, and was seemingly inspired to produce some exceptionally well-proportioned bodies on this chassis. In general a Cockshoot body was attractive in its lines without being a leader of fashion and was finished to the highest standards. One can only surmise that the reason for the company not being better known was its small annual output.

During World War 2 Cockshoot was engaged in the manufacture of aircraft components as well as normal body repair work, but it seems that bodybuilding had effectively ceased in 1939. After the war the company continued as a Rolls-Royce and Bentley dealer and in 1968 became part of the Lex group.

COLE William Cole & Sons of Hammersmith, West London, was active immediately after World War 1, exhibiting at Olympia in both 1919 and 1920, on Daimler, Talbot, Vauxhall and Charron chassis. It then withdrew, and probably hit financial problems, as the next news was the formation of Wm Cole & Sons (1923) Ltd. Thereafter the firm is known to have bodied a 1923 Minerva and a 1925 Rolls-Royce 20hp. It ceased production in 1939.

COLE & SHUTTLEWORTH Located in New Kings Road in the Fulham area of London, Cole & Shuttleworth Ltd was reputedly a partnership involving WM COLE & SONS. It is best known for having produced a smart sports two-seater on the Austin Seven chassis, built between 1926 and 1928, which featured an enclosed spare wheel and a concealed hood. The company also bodied a Bentley in 1926. See also KC.

COMPTON & HERMON Compton & Hermon was a firm located in Thames Ditton, Surrey, known to have produced sports bodies in the twenties including an Aston-Martin and an ABC Super Sports in 1923. This was the first of Arthur P Compton's many ventures in coachbuilding; he went on to be designer and general manager of JARVIS of Wimbledon, then started COMPTON SONS & TERRY, then A P COMPTON, then COMPTON'S (DITTON).

COMPTON, A P Arthur P Compton formed the company bearing his name, and broke away from his partners in COMPTON SONS & TERRY, in early 1930. Later that year he moved to Hanwell, London W7, taking over the premises formerly occupied by ALBANY CARRIAGE. The key to this move seems to have been the Arrow coupé, a two-door fixed-head style first applied to the Austin Seven chassis in 1929 – in other words before Compton's official split from his partners. Whatever the background, Compton clearly believed he was on to a winner: the styling, characterised by helmet-style front wings, no running boards and a low scuttle, was very appealing, and could be applied to open bodies as well. He promptly named his new premises 'Arrow Coachworks', and set to work on a Jowett Arrow, a Standard Arrow (on the Little Nine chassis) and a Morris Minor Arrow. The company also wasted no time in exhibiting at Olympia: the Jowett was present at the 1930 Show alongside a two-seater Morris Minor – unaccount-

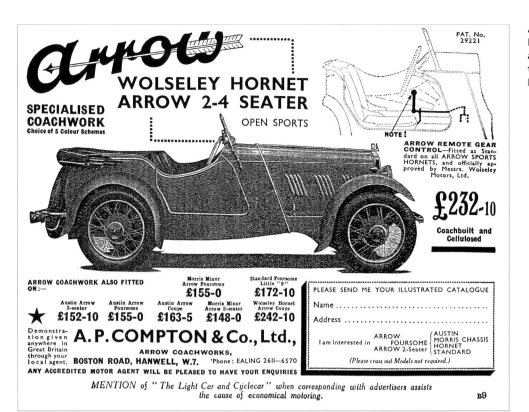

Arrow
WOLSELEY HORNET
ARROW 2-4 SEATER

SPECIALISED
COACHWORK
Choice of 5 Colour Schemes

OPEN SPORTS

PAT. No.
29221

NOTE!

ARROW REMOTE GEAR
CONTROL—Fitted as Stan-
dard on all ARROW SPORTS
HORNETS, and officially ap-
proved by Messrs. Wolseley
Motors, Ltd.

£232-10

Coachbuilt and
Cellulosed

ARROW COACHWORK ALSO FITTED
ON :—

| | Morris Minor Arrow Foursome | Standard Foursome Little "9" |
| | **£155-0** | **£172-10** |

| Austin Arrow 2-seater | Austin Arrow Foursome | Austin Arrow Coupe | Morris Minor Arrow 2-seater | Wolseley Hornet Arrow Coupe |
| **£152-10** | **£155-0** | **£163-5** | **£148-0** | **£242-10** |

Demonstra-
tion given
anywhere in
Great Britain
through your
local agent.

A. P. COMPTON & Co., Ltd.,
ARROW COACHWORKS,
BOSTON ROAD, HANWELL, W.7.   'Phone: EALING 2611—6570
ANY ACCREDITED MOTOR AGENT WILL BE PLEASED TO HAVE YOUR ENQUIRIES

PLEASE SEND ME YOUR ILLUSTRATED CATALOGUE

Name . . . .

Address . . . .

I am interested in   ARROW
FOURSOME
ARROW 2-Seater

AUSTIN
MORRIS CHASSIS
HORNET
STANDARD

(Please cross out Models not required.)

*MENTION of "The Light Car and Cyclecar" when corresponding with advertisers assists
the cause of economical motoring.*   B9

ably named the Dart – and a Talbot.

By the end of 1930 the industry was in the grip of Wolseley Hornet fever, and Compton also contracted the disease, announcing its first Hornet Arrow in the December, while at the following Olympia, 1931, it showed both open and closed Arrow versions. This was to be its last Show, however, as financial problems seem to have struck during 1932 and in August of that year it was announced that a new company, Arrow Coachworks Ltd, would be continuing the business 'without a break'. There was certainly a break in personnel, however, as Arthur Compton left Hanwell and started yet another firm, COMPTON'S (DITTON). Arrow Coachworks, meanwhile, turned to providing special bodies on the less-expensive chassis under contract to manufacturers and dealers, including Hillman Minx convertibles for Rootes, Crossleys for Shrimpton Motors, Ford 8 tourers for W J Reynolds, Ford V-8 fixed-head coupés for W H Perry and Vauxhalls for Shaw & Kilburn. H A Saunders became the distributor for Austin Arrows, replacing Normand Garages.

Even this change of policy was insufficient to save the company and it went out of business in 1934. Some of the remaining Austin Arrow Special bodies were sent to WHITTINGHAM & MITCHEL for finishing, and the Hanwell premises once again had a change of occupant: this time it was COACHCRAFT.

COMPTON'S (DITTON)
This was the last firm with which Arthur Compton is known to have been associated after he left his Arrow Coachworks (A P COMPTON). Located in Long Ditton, Surrey, it began operating in 1932 and was incor-

porated as a limited company in June 1933. Its main work seems to have been in sub-contracting, but it is also believed to have bodied some Wolseley Hornets.

COMPTON SONS & TERRY
Arthur P Compton was for some years in the twenties both designer and manager of JARVIS of Wimbledon. In early 1929 he decided to set up on his own, together with W H Terry, in nearby Merton, South-West London. At the time, the expressed intention was to specialise in 'sports, racing and lightweight bodies'. The partnership was not destined to last long, however, since Compton soon went his own way (see COMPTON, A P) to develop his 'Arrow' designs. In the few months it was operating, the firm is known to have bodied a Bugatti and a Talbot tourer, as well as starting production of the Austin Seven Arrow coupé. After Compton's departure, the remaining partners formed ABBEY COACHWORKS.

COMPTON, JACK
See RANALAH.

CONNAUGHT
The Connaught Motor & Carriage Co was one of the oldest names in the coachbuilding industry, with a history going back to 1770. For a century and a half Connaught was located in Long Acre, London's traditional centre of carriage-building. It successfully made the transition to car coachwork, and exhibited at Olympia continuously from 1919 to 1930. It bodied the finest chassis, from Rolls-Royce through Daimler, Bentley and Minerva to Lanchester and Armstrong-Siddeley.

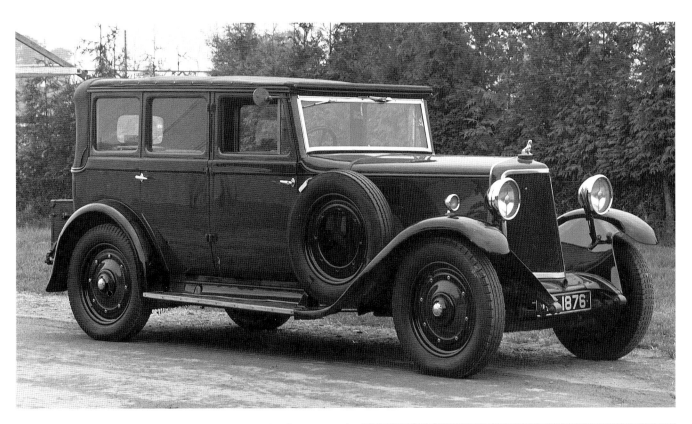

CONNAUGHT: 1931 Armstrong-Siddeley 20hp 'Moorland' (above) – described as an 'all-weather tourer' rather than a sunshine saloon, and (below) 1924 Minerva 'London' limousine; note moulding giving 'brougham' shape to leading edge of front door.

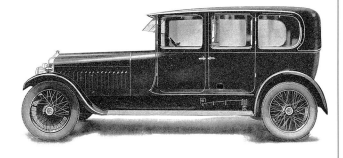

COOPER: 1931 Rolls-Royce 20/25hp chassis bearing a saloon body originally destined for an Austin 20.

Yet behind this superb tradition all was not well. By about 1925 the Long Acre premises had been abandoned and instead there was a succession of addresses in central London – not the area to set up a coachbuilders' workshop. Numerous other coachbuilding firms began to be associated with the Connaught name – particularly PALMERS of Dover, CARLTON and even BERTELLI. The strong suspicion is that from the mid-twenties onwards Connaught was simply a design house, with no production facilities of its own, and that by the thirties there was no point in maintaining a presence at Olympia. Instead, proprietor Howard Godfrey kept his prestigious address in London W1 and did his business from there. By 1934 even the company's name had changed, to Connaught Coachwork Ltd.

During the thirties Connaught was mainly associated with special bodies on Vauxhalls. In 1934-36 it supplied an all-weather and a continental touring saloon on the 27hp Big Six chassis, and in 1936 a drophead coupé on the same chassis. The latter two were made for Connaught by CARLTON; who made the first is not known, but we can be sure it was not Connaught. After that there is no record of any coachwork bearing the Connaught name.

CONSTABLE F Constable, of Cirencester in Gloucestershire, built a coupé body on a Bentley chassis in 1926.

COOPER Cooper Motor Bodies operated originally (in the twenties) from an address in London's Shepherds Bush, but by 1931 had moved a short distance south to Putney Bridge Road. Its speciality was buying end-of-run bodies cheaply from major manufac-

CORSICA: famous low-slung sports design on the 1931 Daimler Double-Six (above), and 1936 British Salmson S4C 12/55 tourer (below); high radiator makes sporting lines difficult to achieve.

turers to mount on other chassis. Some of its known creations involve Austin 20 and Lagonda bodies, both mounted on Rolls-Royce chassis. It is also known to have bought 19 end-of-run Austin Nippy bodies in 1937 and retailed them for £20 each.

Whether this expertise can be described as coachbuilding is debatable, but they certainly mounted bodies on to chassis and hence they qualify for this book.

CORINTHIAN Corinthian Coachwork Ltd took over the former premises of MAYFAIR CARRIAGE in Kilburn Lane, London W10 in late 1934. Its only known achievements are to have bodied two Lagonda Rapiers and a Derby Bentley.

CORSICA Corsica coachworks took its name from the street in north London – the Kings Cross area – where it started in 1920, although it soon moved to nearby Grimaldi Street and later on to Cricklewood. The principals were Charles Stammers and his two brothers-in-law, Joseph and Robert Lee. This was never a large firm, having no more than twenty employees at its peak. One of its claims to fame was that it did not employ a designer, and it certainly never exhibited at Olympia. As a result, no doubt, it managed to keep costs down and allowed customers to indulge in bespoke bodies who otherwise could never have been able to afford such a luxury.

Indeed, Corsica turned this deficiency into a positive advantage, claiming that it was the customers themselves who designed their own bodies.

This is of course simplistic: there was a design process going on, as the succession of sensational-looking cars coming out of the Corsica works confirms. What the firm managed to do was to simplify the process dramatically. Firstly, a customer's ideas would be sent out to a freelance draughtsman. These would then be sketched full-size directly on to wood by the foreman – in effect creating the 'sweeps' or templates which were needed as patterns for the body frame members. Finally – another device to reduce overheads – the milling of the frame members was sub-contracted to an outside firm.

Understandably, this combination of low prices and the ability to reproduce any shape the customer wanted tended to attract the sporting fraternity to Corsica's doors. Little is known of its output in the twenties; those vintage Bentleys which claim Corsica bodywork are more probably the result of rebodying. The first design to attract wide attention, at the beginning of the thirties, was a low-slung sports version of the Double-Twelve Daimler. Corsica attracted another sort of attention when it produced the open two-seater bodywork on Donald Healey's Dolomite of 1935; not only was the car a close copy mechanically of the Type 8C-2300 Alfa Romeos, but so was it in body-style as well (presumably on the customer's instructions).

Later the firm created quite a reputation for bodying Bugatti Type 57s and they are known to have clothed at least 14 of these chassis. Best known of all was a two-seater sports for Malcolm Campbell; once again, it is impossible to tell how much of the design was due to the customer and how much to Corsica's skills in interpreting his wishes, but the result was sensational. Other chassis to go through its hands were Wolseley Hornet, Lea-Francis, Frazer Nash, British Salmson, Humber Snipe, Mercedes-Benz, Alfa Romeo and Rolls-Royce. It also bodied one of the famous Squire sports cars of 1936.

The firm closed down during World War 2 and never reopened, although former employees later started small post-war firms such as Panelcraft and Williams & Pritchard.

COUNTY
The County Motor & Engineering Co Ltd was located at Craven Arms, Shropshire. No doubt its main business was as a provincial garage, but it is known to have bodied several Essex chassis in 1929 and 1930, all of them Weymann designs.

COVENTRY MOTOR & SUNDRIES
Little is known about the activities of this company, based in Spon End, Coventry. From its name one would deduce that it was mainly engaged in supplying components, but it also built some complete bodies around 1930 – sports two-seaters on Morris Minor chassis and at least one Wolseley Hornet.

COVENTRY SUPPLY GARAGE
One of the many small firms in Coventry in the twenties which found work bodying the C-type Lea-Francis.

COWLEY, PEACHEY
A Hillingdon, Middlesex, firm, known only to have bodied a Type 8A Isotta-Fraschini tourer in 1925.

CRIPS
Crips Bros of Sidcup, Kent was started by Walter Crips at the end of the last century as a cycle

CRIPS: Morris Oxford tourer of uncertain mid-twenties date.

CROALL & CROALL: 1926 Daimler 35hp landaulet has rather dated looks.

dealer; in 1906 he was joined by his brother Eddie. The firm expanded into motorcycle manufacture and then, just before World War 1, into motor repairs and coach-building. It became a substantial Morris and then Nuffield agent. The coachbuilding side of the business was clearly peripheral, but it is known to have bodied Humbers before World War 1 and Bullnose Morrises afterwards. During World War 2 the coachworks was employed on converting private vehicles into such things as ambulances. After the death of Eddie Crips in 1951 the business was continued by his widow, but she eventually sold it to the dealer BEADLE of Dartford.

CROALL & CROALL
This high-class Scottish coachbuilding firm retained its own bodybuilding facilities in Edinburgh until well into the twenties: it certainly exhibited its own work at Scottish Motor Shows from 1921 until 1927. The chassis used ranged widely; there seems to have been a close relationship with Fiat, with both the 15-20 and the 20-30 chassis making frequent appearances, and similarly with Daimler and Humber. Other marques bodied were Rolls-Royce, Armstrong-Siddeley, Delaunay-Belleville, Charron-Laycock and even Morris (Oxford). The weight of evidence, however, is that Croall & Croall was no longer making its own bodies after 1927 even though it continued to exhibit at Scottish Motor Shows.

CROALL, JOHN
The relationship between John Croall & Sons on the one hand

JOHN CROALL: This 1933 Rolls-Royce 20/25 saloon, although sold as having a John Croall & Sons body, was actually bodied by its subsidiary company H J Mulliner

CROSBIE & DUNN: 1932 Rolls-Royce Phantom 2 limousine; sloping pillars line up with door shut-lines, but the effect is questionable.

and CROALL & CROALL on the other is unknown, but there must have been one at one time – particularly as both were based in Edinburgh. John Croall was a significant firm in its own right, having a stand at Scottish Motor Shows from 1921 to 1929; equally importantly it was the owner of the much-revered London coachbuilder H J MULLINER, which it purchased in 1914. This acquisition allowed it to become even more prestigious than its namesakes, as witnessed by their long-standing relationship with Rolls-Royce, whose products appeared on its stands almost every year.

It would also seem to be the case that John Croall was innovative by nature. It embraced the Weymann system with enthusiasm, claiming in 1927 that it was the only Scottish maker of genuine Weymann bodies. Then the next year it announced its own fabric-body system, launched as 'Croallight', but later streamlined to 'Krolite'. Soon after this, however, it appears that John Croall gave up its own bodybuilding facility, and from the late twenties on if you ordered a Croall body you had an H J Mulliner by another name. Even this deception seems to have ceased by about 1934.

CROFTS Alban Crofts had worked for Branson of Croydon before setting up on his own in the same town in 1922. The firm bodied a great variety of chassis during the twenties, including Alvis, Daimler, Delage, Fiat, Ford, Lagonda, Rolls-Royce and Trojan. By the end of the decade, however, its largest business was in the building of van bodies, and the firm decided to concentrate solely on commercial work. There was one interesting exception during the thirties, and this was the contract for the original HRG 1500 – some 25 bodies. Crofts did not resume bodybuilding after World War 2, and finally closed in the seventies.

CROSBIE & DUNN A Smethwick, Birmingham, firm started by two former FLEWITT employees in 1927. It bodied some 75 Rolls-Royces during the twenties and early thirties, and two Derby Bentleys, but after 1939 confined itself to repairs only. It was still in existence in the 1970s.

CROSS & ELLIS No one would pretend that the Coventry firm of Cross & Ellis Ltd

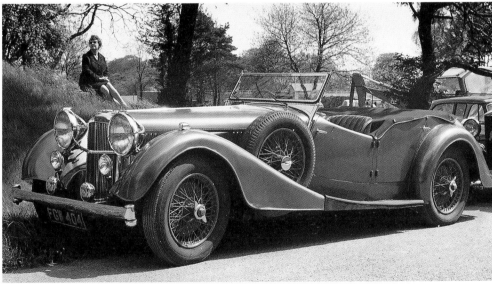

CROSS & ELLIS: 1930 Lea-Francis P-type 12/40 drophead coupé (above) has an eager appearance. 1938 Alvis Speed 25 (right); four-door tourers of sporting appearance were the company's speciality.

produced coachwork of the highest quality. On the other hand it survived for nearly 20 years, supplying good-looking bodies under contract to the Coventry motor industry at what can only have been cut-throat prices. And the matter of survival should not be underrated. During the 20 years between the two World Wars, at least 19 Coventry firms competed in the business of building complete bodies; ignoring the two 'in-house' firms (BURLINGTON and MIDLAND MOTOR BODIES), and SWALLOW who became a car manufacturer, only two – CARBODIES and CHARLESWORTH – survived longer than Cross & Ellis, and one of those two had undergone a financial reconstruction.

Even the matter of quality has to be put into perspec-tive. When Cross & Ellis was supplying bodies to, say, Alvis at £120 each, there was little time available in the costings for a cabinet-maker to fit panels of inlaid walnut, or for the hidden frame joints to be perfectly finished. Yet the company was perfectly able to construct one-off bod-ies to very high standards, as its customer list would attest: Sir William Courtauld, for example, of the textile firm, would not have tolerated any compromise in stan-dards on his 1937 Daimler coupé.

Alf Ellis and Harry Cross first met in the bodyshop at Daimler, where they were both working during World War 1. They went into business together in 1919, starting with motorcycle sidecars and progressing through bodies for lorries and charabancs to car coachwork. Probably their first car contract was with the fledgling Alvis company, in 1921, for its 10/30 model; from then on Cross & Ellis was a major supplier to Alvis, with sports and tourer bodies on all the 10/30's successors including the highly popular 12/50. Its second important customer was Lea-Francis, and for much of the twenties these two manufacturers absorbed the large majority of Cross & Ellis' capacity. C & E products were regularly on show each year at Olympia on the Alvis and Lea-Francis stands, thus enabling the company to avoid the expense of a stand of its own.

This is not to suggest that things went easily, however. In 1924, Alvis' undercapitalisation was stretched too far and it was forced to deal with a receiver; Cross & Ellis found to its horror that it was the largest creditor and petitioned for winding-up. In fact Alvis survived under a scheme of arrangement, but it must have been a tense period for the coachbuilding firm. Then in 1931 it had a not dissimilar experience with Lea-Francis; no doubt this led to a search for new customers and a decision to exhibit at the Motor Show in its own right, which it did between 1934 and 1937. Meanwhile, though, it had restored relations with Alvis, which entrusted C & E with the manufacture of its special design of fabric saloon, the Alvista, introduced in 1927. There followed a succession of Alvis models to be clothed in saloon, drophead coupé and tourer styles, covering virtually all four- and six-cylinder chassis up to 1938.

The drive to widen its customer base soon showed results. On its first Olympia Show stand in 1934 Cross & Ellis showed a 'doctor's coupé' on a Triumph Gloria chassis and as this appeared again in 1935 it would seem to have been a standard – possibly catalogued – design. A similarly named design was available the same year, 1934, on the Vauxhall Light Six chassis. The appearance of four-door saloons on Humber and Hillman chassis during these two years suggests there was also a relationship with the Rootes combine. In 1936 C & E were offering a good-looking four-light drophead coupé for the Wolseley 25hp.

Nevertheless it is with Alvis that the name of Cross & Ellis will always be particularly associated; its four-door tourer on the Speed 25 chassis was its last and arguably its finest design for that customer. Sadly, however, the combination of falling sales and pressure on prices meant that Cross & Ellis could not remain profitable, and in 1938 it had to go into liquidation. It had managed to survive as a company longer than most and – fortunately for us – many of their products have survived to this day.

CUBITT

The name Cubitt is nowadays associated only with civil engineering, being part ot the Tarmac group. Some may be aware that Cubitts Engineering Co Ltd of Aylesbury built cars under its own name from 1920 to 1925, but not many will know that it also built bodies for Alvis for a short time on the 10/30 and 12/40 chassis. The one outstanding quality of a Cubitt body

seems to have been its cheapness: the company could apparently produce a tourer body for as little as £20. Needless to say, the quality was at a similarly low level, which probably explains why Alvis changed supplier. The engineering subsidiary was put into voluntary liquidation in 1925.

CUNARD

The Cunard Motor & Carriage Co Ltd started in 1911, but it was not long before it had become a subsidiary of Napier cars and generally known as 'in-house' coachbuilder for that company. This was not to imply that they were on adjacent sites – far from it; Napier was in Acton, West London, while Cunard was in Lower Richmond Road, London SW15, although driving a bare chassis that sort of distance was a normal occurrence in those days.

After World War 1, to judge from its exhibits at Olympia, Cunard was permitted to branch out occasionally and body other chassis – Sunbeam and Crossley, for example. Napier continued to dominate, however, and in some years was the only marque on the stand – limousines, coupés, landaulets and 'torpedos', all no doubt built to the highest standards to match Napier's cost and prestige. Indeed Cunard was noted at this period for skill in aluminium welding, which allowed it to produce an unbroken surface from front to back. Then in 1925 it all ended. The British WEYMANN company had been looking for premises in which to build bodies, and solved the problem by purchasing the Cunard company outright; this solved a problem for Napier as well, since it had just ceased manufacturing cars.

And that, one might have thought, was the end of Cunard – but it was not. At this point we have to introduce one R I Musselwhite (he was always known by his initials, never his Christian name). Musselwhite had worked for Cunard from 1914 to 1923, latterly as managing director. He was a powerful figure in the industry, having been president of the IBCM (later IBCAM) in 1918. His departure for WINDOVER might have been a surprise at the time, but it was probably connected with the trouble brewing at Napier. In any case he did not stay long at his new employers, moving on after 12 months to BARKER, and then after another couple of years to THRUPP & MABERLY to become works director.

It was in 1930, after four years at Thrupp & Maberley, that he made his biggest move. Quite why he should want to revive Cunard is unknown – maybe he had something to prove, to himself or to others. But 'revive' is exactly the word he used in his announcements to the trade; presumably he bought back the name or the shell company from Weymann. The old Cunard premises were no longer available but this was no obstacle to Musselwhite who constructed a brand-new factory in Acton (and this during the depths of the Depression).

Musselwhite's partner in the new venture was V E Freestone – another name to conjure with in the industry – who by that time was also working at Thrupp &

CUNARD: Napier Type 75 40-50 'all-weather cabriolet' (above) from 1920, when Cunard was Napier's in-house coachbuilder. Morris Ten-Six Special tourer of 1934 (below); by this time Cunard had been 'revived' and then sold on.

Maberly. Freestone was to be responsible for factory layout and production, while Musselwhite was in charge of the 'technical' (whatever that was) and sales departments.

The first body to emerge from the new factory, in early 1931, was a 'false cabriolet de ville' on a Rolls-Royce P2 chassis. This was in no way indicative, however, of what was to be the new Cunard company's normal production, for almost as soon as it had opened for business it was taken over by Stewart & Ardern, the London Morris agent. Just why this should have happened is unclear but the fact that Freestone certainly, and Musselwhite probably, left the company that same year (1931)

suggests that it was a forced takeover rather than a voluntary one. Thus Cunard's output was soon dominated by batch production of special bodies on Morris chassis, particularly drophead coupés and four-seater sports. Similar volume production soon followed for Rover – a four-door saloon for the 1932-33 catalogue. Cunard also, inevitably, bodied Wolseley Hornets.

It seems that Cunard's production gradually switched to commercial vehicles; Stewart & Ardern had previously used WILSON of Kingston for its commercial bodywork. The company's last Olympia appearance was in 1934. Later it changed both name – to The Cunard Commercial Bodybuilding Co – and location, further out of London to Wembley, where it retained a separate identity at least as late as the sixties.

CURTIS Curtis Automobile Coachbuilders Ltd, of London W1, exhibited at the London Motor Show just once, in 1921. As well as a good-looking Bentley landaulet and a Lancia 35hp torpedo, its stand contained an example of its patent disappearing pillars on a Voisin coupé; this was a feature that had so impressed MAYTHORN two year previously that Maythorn used it under licence. It was still in existence in the late twenties, when it is known to have bodied a Hispano-Suiza.

CWS The Cooperative Wholesale Society furniture factory in West London has to be recorded as manufacturing five fabric saloons on Austin Seven chassis in about 1928. Those interested in the reasons for

CURTIS: 1929 Mercedes-Benz fixed-head coupé; a graceful execution of the 'long-bonnet' theme.

DUPLE: 1932 Alvis Speed 20 SA two-door saloon, from a firm better known as builders of motor-coaches.

production not continuing are referred to Bryan Purves' hilarious account in *The Austin Seven Source Book*.

DALKING Dalking Motor Body Works, of Hammersmith, West London, is known to have bodied a Meteorite two-seater in 1924.

DU CROS W & G Du Cros Ltd, based in Acton, West London, was a taxicab operator before World War 1, and later became part of the Sunbeam-Talbot-Darracq combine. At that time it manufactured mainly commercial bodywork, but also bodied some Talbot 14/45 coupés in the late twenties. The company went out of business at the time of the STD collapse in the mid-thirties.

DUPLE The name Duple was first used before World War 1 by Mr Herbert R White, whose business at that time was known as the Bifort company. It described a dual-purpose (hence 'Duple') vehicle which could be quickly changed from a tourer into a goods van, and which proved highly popular amongst farmers. On his return from war service in 1919, White formed Duple Bodies and Motors Ltd, with a factory at Hornsey, North London, and restarted production of his dual-purpose vehicles. They were built on Ford Model T chassis and sold through International Motors.

At the same time the company was moving into other types of bodywork, for both cars and, especially, coaches. The growth so generated caused a move to larger premises at Hendon in West London in 1925. In the same year the company took a stand at the London Motor Show, exhibiting an Essex chassis with combined tourer and shooting-brake coachwork, and another which converted from two seats to four.

Further expansion happened in 1928, when W E Brown, after a split with his partner at STRACHAN & BROWN, joined Duple as a director and brought a considerable number of customers with him. The Brown family was to play an important part in Duple's future, with elder son Reginald becoming sales director and the younger, Denis, technical sales manager.

Duple was at Olympia Shows until 1930, using a variety of chassis but often with 'convertible' bodies in one form or another. Increasingly, though, its main business was in the production of long-distance coaches, and for two years it ceased exhibiting. It then made a comeback for one year, in 1933, perhaps celebrating a contract to supply Vauxhall with special bodies, since the stand contained nothing else. These roadsters, tourers and dropheads formed part of the official Vauxhall catalogues for 1934 and 1935, but not thereafter; it would seem that the volume of sales was not sufficiently attractive compared with the opportunities in the coach-body business.

Duple made no more car bodies after that time but continued to prosper with its coaches until well after World War 2; the firm disappeared some time during the seventies.

EAGLE See NEWNS.

EASTER J H Easter, in the Paddington area of London, was associated with Bentley cars in the immediate post-World War 1 period; links with W O Bentley himself started before then, since it bodied some of the DFP cars which he used to import before the War. Easter is known to have been involved with at least 28 chassis during the period 1921-24, but nothing more is known of them, although the firm was still in existence in the late twenties.

EGERTONS: AC 12hp boat-tailed cloverleaf sports at the 1925 Olympia Show, finished in black and white.

EGERTONS

Egertons (Ipswich) Ltd was started by J R ('Reggie') Egerton in 1910, after falling out with his partners in BOTWOODS, also of Ipswich. He later took a J R Davies into partnership. The firm was at Olympia from 1919 to 1928, using a variety of chassis as would be expected from a provincial coachbuilder. However, Egertons developed a particular relationship with AC and produced an attractive clover-leaf sports three-seater for a number of years. It also specialised in landaulets on Wolseley chassis, and later on in using the Alvis 12/50 and Talbot 14/45 chassis.

Car work seems to have ceased after about 1929, with one exception, but the firm remained in existence and therefore must have moved over to commercial work. The exception was a one-off exercise on the 1938 Vauxhall 25 chassis; it was called a 'sportsman's special', and with good reason – it had a full-length double bed in the back.

ELKINGTON

The origins of the Elkington Carriage Company are uncertain, but probably are from immediately after World War 1. Originally a partnership between Messrs Taneborne and Kendall, Elkington came into Kendall's sole ownership when his partner left in 1922. In that same year the firm is known to have bodied a DFP tourer which was on the manufacturer's stand at Olympia. The next year Elkington took its own stand, and continued to do so until 1931.

Elkington Carriage's first premises were off Chelsea's Kings Road. It moved from there further west to Chiswick in 1928, for reasons not known (GURNEY NUTTING took over the old address). Throughout this time it produced some unexceptional designs on a variety of upmarket chassis, but it clearly had a close arrangement with the Minerva importer, as his wares were never absent at Motor Show time; they were usually limousines or large saloons. Later, Elkington began to specialise in

ELLIOTT: 1950 Healey saloon, from a firm whose main business by then was shopfitting.

the Talbot marque, and eventually produced quite a pretty four-seater three-quarter coupé on the Talbot 75 chassis.

Elkington's last major business was bodying the majority of Frazer-Nash production during the period 1931-34. In 1934, however, Frazer-Nash opened its own bodyshop, and Elkington seems to have gone out of business at about that time.

ELLIOTT

Samuel Elliott & Sons (Reading) Ltd was in the coachbuilding business during the twenties. In 1924 it was appointed sole British concessionaire for Carrosseries Vanden Plas, the Belgian associate of the British firm of the same name, which up to that time was a regular exhibitor at the Olympia shows. It would appear that the arrangement with Elliott replaced the Vanden Plas presence at Olympia, as the Belgian firm did not exhibit the next year. Meanwhile Elliott took a stand there in the two following years, 1925 and 1926, showing saloons and landaulets on imported chassis such as

Voisin and Fiat. The 1926 Voisin saloon was quite striking in appearance, with its low bonnet-line and sloping
windscreen. The arrangement with the Belgian firm, however, must have lapsed, as Carrosseries Vanden Plas was
back at Olympia in 1926 and its London address revealed
that it was now being represented by the importing firm
Lendrum & Hartman.

After Elliott withdrew from Olympia nothing more
was heard of its bodybuilding activities for many years,
and the company moved into the field of joinery and
shopfitting. Suddenly it re-emerged in 1946 as builder of
the Healey Elliott saloon – claimed at the time to be the
'world's fastest closed production car'. This contract
lasted until 1950, after which Elliott seem to have
reverted to shopfitting. The company still exists to this
day as part of the Trafalgar House group.

ENGLAND, GORDON

E C Gordon England,
having undergone an
apprenticeship in a railway workshop, spent his first
dozen years of employment in the aircraft industry. There
he became an unusual combination of test-pilot and
designer, and then during World War 1 an aircraft factory
manager.

After the war, though, he became interested in motor
racing, working with his father George in the latter's
garage business at Walton-on-Thames, Surrey. In 1922 he
became interested in the sporting potential of the new
Austin Seven and persuaded Sir Herbert Austin to pre-
pare a chassis for him which he and his father then bodied.
His success in racing this and later cars encouraged him

GORDON ENGLAND: 1927 Austin Seven fabric two-seater
(above), a typical inexpensive sports car of the period. 1929
Austin Seven Stadium two-seater (below).

to offer his own vehicles based on the Austin Seven chassis to the public.

Although his racers were highly tuned, the models he
started selling to the public were essentially on standard
chassis, the attraction being in the bodywork. England
had strong ideas about this subject, based on his aircraft
experience, believing that the biggest problem with existing coachwork was its weight and therefore inertia, and
he set about designing a light but very strong body. He
achieved this by using plywood extensively; the lower
part consisted of plywood box-girders, and the upper an
ash frame covered with plywood panels from which the
door apertures (and window apertures in the case of
saloons) were cut afterwards. The whole exterior was
then covered in fabric; later, the option of steel panelling
on the exterior was offered.

FLEWITT: 1923 Rolls-Royce 40-50 Silver Ghost limousine; domed roof was an attempt to prevent drumming.

The fundamental difference between England's system and WEYMANN'S was in the matter of rigidity. Whereas the Weymann body was rigidly attached to the chassis and made to flex when the chassis did, a Gordon England body was a rigid structure but attached to the chassis flexibly, via rubber mountings at three points. Both, of course, were very light in weight, and both were claimed to be silent.

The first Gordon England model sold to the public was the Brooklands two-seater in 1924. The next year saw the Cup Model, also a two-seater, and the Fabric Saloon; these two were the first to be sold through Austin dealers. The latter model led directly to the Austin AD saloon of 1926, Austin's first saloon on the Seven chassis, with Gordon England supplying the bodywork under sub-contract.

Such rapid expansion meant that premises had to be found. Initially these were in Felsham Road, Putney, South-West London, and were taken in the name of George England via a newly-formed company George England (Motor Bodies) Ltd. Even so, the early Cup Model bodies had to be contracted out to Weymann before Putney could be established, and the company thereafter expanded into space in Horseferry Road (the former Victoria Coachworks premises). The company also ran a service station in West End Lane, NW6.

It was an obvious step for England to extend his bodybuilding system to other chassis in addition to Austins. As early as 1925 it was used on a Rolls-Royce, by the LONDON IMPROVED company under licence and by 1927 it had been applied to Bentley, MG, Morris Oxford and Wolseley chassis. No doubt it was this further expansion which triggered another move in 1927 when the firm took up residence in the Palace of Industry at Wembley, North-West London – the former site of the famous Wembley Exhibitions. The service station was moved there at the same time (BOYD-CARPENTER took

over the old premises). In the same year the company exhibited at Olympia where a notable entry was a 3-litre Invicta saloon panelled in aluminium rather than fabric.

Gordon England was also at Olympia in 1928 and 1929; an Austin 16 saloon in 1929 struck another blow in the war between fabric and metal panelling, having cellulosed panels inlaid on the outside of the doors 'to relieve the fabric finish'. Meanwhile the company was reformed as Gordon England (1929) Ltd preparatory to going public, and the press was invited inside the Palace of Industry to see how it was living up to its name, producing 35 bodies a day. From then on, however, things went rapidly downhill. Within a year the newly-launched public company was in receivership, production had ceased, and Gordon England himself had moved on to a job outside the motor industry. The combined effects of the Depression and the all-steel saloon had made a mockery of the company's brave production forecasts.

EWART Ewart & Sons of Campden Town, North London, built three two-seater bodies on Bentley 3-litre chassis in 1922.

FAULKNER Faulkner of Chiswick, West London, bodied a 3-litre Bentley chassis in 1924.

FERGUSON A Northern Ireland firm known to have built an open-drive limousine body on a Rolls-Royce 40/50 chassis in 1921.

FLEWITT The Flewitt Co was based in Alma Street, Birmingham, but also had premises at one time in Hednesford, some 20 miles away. Founded in 1905, it is known to have bodied Rolls-Royce and Daimler chassis in the twenties, but in the mid-thirties became associated exclusively with Austin, offering a sports saloon on the mid-range models and a limousine on the

20hp; all these were apparently official catalogued models. The sports saloon in particular was quite distinctive, giving an almost racy look to the marque's otherwise rather staid image.

Flewitt continued in business until at least the mid-sixties, specialising in commercial bodybuilding.

FORTON & BETTENS

A London firm situated in the Victoria area known only for having bodied a Benz in 1921 and a Bentley saloon in 1923. However, a Jimmy Bettens was the London representative for the Silent Travel Lock Company in the thirties, and he was possibly an ex-partner of this firm.

FOUNTAIN

Stanley J Fountain was works manager at Brighton Coach Works from 1909 to 1912, and then secretary and commercial manager at MULLINER's of Birmingham from 1912 to 1913. With experience on both the production and the commercial sides, he clearly felt qualified to set up his own business and in 1913 started Fountain's Auto-Carriage Works at Horsham, Sussex.

After being away on war work during 1914 and 1915 he returned to Horsham and his coachbuilding business. The firm started exhibiting at Olympia in 1921 and continued to do so until 1930. Initially it seems to have concentrated on imported chassis, particularly Buick, Bianchi and Fiat, but later was associated with drophead versions of Hillmans.

In spite of being well occupied during 1930, with 300 drophead coupés alone built during the year, Fountain ceased appearing at Olympia after this date, and nothing more is known of the firm.

FOUNTAIN: Bianchi 15-50hp four-door six-light saloon at the 1925 Motor Show, in a colour described as 'burnt straw'.

FOWLER

John Fowler & Sons of Harrogate, Yorkshire, built an all-weather body on a 3-litre Bentley in 1924. Later it is known to have held a Weymann licence.

FREESTONE & WEBB

For a company which retained a high reputation in the coachwork field over many years Freestone & Webb Ltd underwent a remarkable number of changes. It was founded in 1923 by V E Freestone and A J Webb, and started operating from premises in Willesden, North-West London, which were to remain home to the Freestone & Webb business for the whole of its existence. Both men had apparently been working previously at the nearby Sizaire-Berwick factory.

Initially the company was highly successful. Even in its first year it started bodying Bentleys, and soon tourers, coupés and saloons on the 3-litre chassis were flowing through the F & W works. These were followed in their turn by all the other Cricklewood models, the final tally before Bentley went into receivership being some 230. Rolls-Royces soon followed, and then in 1926 the first of a remarkable number of Mercedes and Mercedes-Benz chassis, a marque which remained a Freestone & Webb speciality until the end of the thirties. The reason for the company's rapidly growing reputation was clearly a combination of superb design and high quality of execution. Technically, too, it was intent on being a pioneer: it was one of the early coachbuilders to take out a Weymann licence and managed to produce some highly attractive designs – not something which every Weymann builder

FREESTONE & WEBB: Mercedes-Benz cars outside workshop, 1928. Saloon on the left is probably the 1928 Motor Show car.

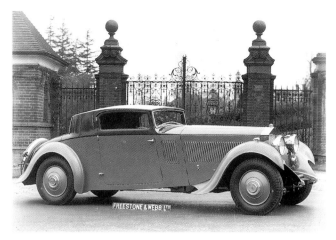

FREESTONE & WEBB: 1933 Rolls-Royce Phantom 2 'sports coupé', a surprisingly late example of the low-windscreen style.

FREESTONE & WEBB: 1933 Alfa-Romeo two-seater sports (above); might have looked better as a four-seater. 1936 Rolls-Royce 25/30 sports saloon (left) in early 'razor-edge' style.

could honestly claim. It was also one of the instigators of the craze for cycle wings and steps instead of running boards.

Financially, though, all was not well and the company went through a series of reconstructions. In one of these, it was temporarily renamed 'Freestone Endura', and in another, Freestone was forced out of the company. (He was later involved in the ill-fated revival of the CUNARD name.) From this time (1930) onwards the feeling grew amongst those in the know that F & W's quality was not quite what it had been; no doubt the accountants were beginning to win against the technical staff and the salesmen. Understandably, too, the company started to widen its customer base by offering standard designs on a num-

GEORGESON: 1936 Rolls-Royce 25/30 fixed-head coupé – an unusual body style on this chassis.

ber of chassis. It took care, however, not to go very far down-market: such names as Alvis, Daimler, Lagonda and Talbot had enough cachet not to frighten off F & W's traditional Rolls-Royce, Bentley and Mercedes-Benz clientele. For the second half of the thirties its production concentrated mostly on saloons and limousines, yet it still found room to innovate: Freestone & Webb's Bentley 'brougham' at the 1935 Motor Show was an absolutely seminal design which single-handedly initiated the style later to become known as 'razor-edge'.

During World War 2 F & W made aircraft components, its speciality being Spitfire wing-tips. After the war it continued to do what it did best – traditional coachwork on Rolls-Royce and Bentley chassis. During this period it maintained and even enhanced its reputation and its elegant, flowing designs were some of the finest to come out of the British coachbuilding industry. It was uphill work, though; when Webb died in 1955 the company was taken over by the London Rolls-Royce dealer H R Owen, and the following year gave up coachwork and became a dealer. In a strange final twist, during the eighties what must by then have been the shell company of Freestone & Webb was bought by the classic car dealers Victoria Carriage.

FULLER
Fuller's of Bath was an old-established firm which had been producing carriages since 1737 and car coachwork from 1906. The last body made, in 1924, was a 'pullman limousine' on a Rolls-Royce Phantom 1 chassis and from then on the firm concentrated on motor distribution.

GAIRN
J Gairn & Co of Edinburgh built a two-seater body on a 3-litre Bentley chassis in 1921.

GAISFORD & WARBOYS
See LANCEFIELD

GARTSIDE
Gordon Gartside of Knaresborough, North Yorkshire, is known only for rebodying an Aston Martin single-seater as a two-seater in 1939.

GEORGE & JOBLING
George & Jobling was a Newcastle upon Tyne firm which started exhibiting at Olympia in 1919 but which had been in business since 1899. It seems to have specialised to an extent in all-weather bodies, especially on Darracq chassis. Its last appearance at Olympia was in 1922, but the firm continued to prosper, converting to a limited company in 1928 and by 1939 occupying three separate premises in Newcastle. However, it seems likely that by then it was only involved in car dealing. It was still in existence in 1965.

GEORGESON
This Aberdeen coachbuilding firm appears to have been in business for most if not all of the inter-war period, but little is known about its work. It certainly bodied two Bentleys in the twenties and exhibited at the 1927 Scottish Motor Show (on the Aberdeen Motors stand). It is also known to have built a two-door fixed-head coupé on a 1936 Rolls-Royce 25/30.

GILL
T H Gill and Son operated from various premises in London's Paddington district. The firm started making car coachwork in 1914, and soon acquired a reputation as a specialist in the all-weather type of body. T H Gill himself retired from the business in 1920 and died only two years later. J J Gill, the son, continued the business in partnership with one W T Vane, but Vane left in 1925. Meanwhile the new management had decided to exhibit at Olympia, and did so continuously from 1921 to 1932 with the exception of a break in 1924-25 (was this connected with Vane's departure?). Exhibits give little indication of any special type of work except a possible link with the Isotta-Fraschini importers.

In 1931 there was a curious development when Gill formed a subsidiary, Gill All-Weather Bodies Ltd, which seems to have been intended to take over the Gill business in this type of bodywork. The two companies certainly operated side-by-side, but while the old Gill business closed down in 1935 All-Weather Bodies continued with its specialised coachwork until 1939 and remained in existence until 1955.

GILL: 1931 Rolls-Royce Phantom 2 all-weather; the firm specialised in this type of body.

GORDON: 1931 Austin 20hp landaulet, its staid appearance not helped by small wheels.

GLASSBROOK

Founded in 1922, this West London firm specialised in servicing Rolls-Royce cars and also built some bodies on R-R chassis – mainly limousines and landaulets. It still exists today under the name Mascot Motors and is run by the son of the founder.

GORDON

Gordon & Co of Sparkbrook, Birmingham, was a faithful exhibitor at London Motor Shows from 1921 to 1938 and for most of that time was equally faithful to the Austin marque. To begin with, though, it was known for bodying Model T Fords and other American imports such as Chevrolet, Overland and Dodge. The first Austin chassis to grace the Olympia stand was a 12hp saloon in 1923; there followed a succession of saloons, sunshine saloons, drophead coupés and (especially) saloon-landaulets on the 12, 16 and 20hp chassis – none of them particularly stylish, but all outstanding value for money.

It is not clear how these models, obviously standard ones, were sold during the earlier years. However, by 1935 they were certainly catalogued models sold through dealers in the normal way. By this time Gordon was following the fashion for giving names to its products; in ascending order of pretentiousness they were: Pixie, Moth, Elf, Comet, Iris, Ambassador, Royal, Regal, and Imperial. The last-named was no less than a D-back limousine or landaulet on the 20hp chassis, priced at £605 in 1933-35 – but still £50 cheaper than the equivalent FLEWITT model.

Around this time (1933) Gordon made some bodies for Vauxhall and Standard, and again for Vauxhall with a 25hp limousine in 1938. Nevertheless, the bulk of its production stayed dedicated to Austin until bodybuilding ceased in 1939.

GORDON ENGLAND

See ENGLAND

GRAHAME-WHITE

Although basically an aircraft company, based at Hendon aerodrome in North-West London, Grahame-White bodied at least two Daimlers in 1919, and at least one Rolls-Royce.

GRANVILLE

This South-West London firm produced its 'Wydor' fixed-head coupé on the Austin Seven chassis in 1927 and in the following year a similarly wide-doored version of the Austin 12.

GREAT WESTERN MOTORS

Based in Reading, this firm exhibited at Olympia Shows from 1922 until 1927. It used a variety of chassis, but seemed to be particularly loyal to the Bean. The firm then appears to have given up bodybuilding, as the following year its premises were being

GROSE: 1923 Alvis 12/50 two-seater sports (left) with dickey in polished aluminium and dark red. 1936 Vauxhall 'Coton' Big Six four-door sports saloon (below). American influence is clear.

used by another coachbuilder (see HARRIS, JOHN). It concentrated on car distribution and still exists in Reading under the Wadham Kenning name.

GRIFFITHS

Griffiths & Co. was a coachbuilder in Pontypridd, South Wales, known only for having bodied a Hampton two-seater in 1922

GROSE

Grose Ltd of Northampton was a substantial family firm of coachbuilders throughout the inter-war period, which developed a recognisable style in its products. Although it could and frequently did produce bespoke bodies, its speciality was selling standard designs, which enabled it to manufacture in batches and keep costs down. Originally, in the twenties, this was via a catalogue of designs, presumably used in conjunction with exhibiting at the London Motor Show, which Grose did most years. Its first such efforts were on the Alvis 12/40 and 12/50 chassis, with a good-looking two-seater sports with a dickey-seat; this was probably the debut of what was to become a Grose trademark – a flap which opened out to form a step. Later (1925) a company catalogue shows a Crossley 20hp saloon, a Buick 'limousine coupé', a Dodge landaulet and a Rover all-weather. The numerous appearances of Talbot and Darracq chassis at Olympia suggest that these marques also were the subject of standard designs.

When the thirties' fashion for special bodies on affordable chassis was at its height, Grose adopted the simpler tactic of becoming an approved supplier, with a place in the manufacturer's catalogue. Its first such contract was with the Rover company in 1931-34, when it built the 'Kingsley' drophead coupé on three sizes of chassis. Then in 1933 came a similar arrangement with Vauxhall, lasting until 1936, where Grose built a range of fixed-head coupés ('Brampton' and 'Alderton'), drophead coupés ('Lamport') and saloons ('Coton'). Many of these designs bore one or both of two further Grose trademarks – a lengthened bonnet, sometimes right up to the windscreen, and a 'brougham door' shape to the rear edge of the bonnet.

From 1935 onwards Grose developed two standard drophead coupé designs on Riley chassis – 'Burcote' and 'Horton'. There was also the 'Sywell' four-door saloon on the Alvis Firefly chassis. These were the last standard designs; the company did not exhibit at the Motor Show after 1936, and soon afterwards coachbuilding ceased altogether. However it still survives as an independent motor dealer.

GROSVENOR

The Grosvenor Carriage Co Ltd was established in Kilburn, North-West London, in about 1910. It became a subsidiary of Shaw & Kilburn, the main Vauxhall dealer in London, although exactly when is not clear; certainly Grosvenor was building predominantly on Vauxhall chassis, to judge from its Olympia exhibits, from at least 1919.

This does not explain why in 1923 Shaw & Kilburn decided to have its own presence in the coachbuilding section at Olympia, but it did, even though from an early date all its exhibits were made by Grosvenor. Presumably this move gave its products – not only Vauxhalls, but also

GROSVENOR: 1931 Vauxhall 'Newmarket' T80 saloon (above); it might have looked better without the 'brougham door' moulding. 1934 Vauxhall Big Six landaulet (above right) from the manufacturer's in-house coachbuilder. 1939 Vauxhall 'Westminster' 25hp limousine (right) – a popular choice for hire-car work.

Essex and Hudson – more exposure, and encouraged sales directly off the stand. Shaw & Kilburn continued this practice up to 1930.

Vauxhall was one of the first manufacturers to realise the advantage of contracting out their lower-volume coachwork styles, and Grosvenor began supplying designs as part of the Vauxhall catalogue from as early as 1929; these were the 'Hurlingham' sports two-seater and 'Melton' coupé on the 20/60 chassis. Then in 1932 came the 'Newmarket' and 'Kimberley' special saloons, models which persisted on various chassis, including the big 25 and 27hp, right up to 1939. In 1934 the 'Hurlingham' name was applied to a fixed-head coupé on the Big 6; later (1935 onwards) there were drophead coupés on the Light 6 and 25hp chassis, and sports saloons including the 'Velox' two-door version on the 25hp. Grosvenor also supplied the 'Westminster' limousine and landaulet on the larger chassis from 1934 on, although the landaulet style was dropped in the later thirties.

Even during this period of close collaboration with Vauxhall, Grosvenor also apparently worked with other manufacturers; it made limousines on the 20 and 25hp chassis for Daimler from 1929 to 1933, and a four-light saloon for Lanchester in 1931 and 1932. Thereafter, though, it acted solely as 'in-house' coachbuilder for Vauxhall. After World War 2 it was invisible until 1956, when it suddenly appeared at the Earls Court Show with an estate conversion of a Vauxhall Velox. Strangely neither this model nor an alternative from MARTIN WALTER were ever properly developed, and it was left to Friary Motors three years later to show that they had missed a

E. B. HALL: 1927 Angus-Sanderson tourer.

market opportunity. Grosvenor seems to have ceased operating under its own name by the early sixties.

GURNEY NUTTING See NUTTING, J GURNEY

HALE
R E Hale of Newcastle upon Tyne bodied a Voisin tourer which appeared on the manufacturer's stand at the 1923 Motor Show. Its construction was unusual, being of plywood panels completely covered with leather. Hale is known to have been still in existence in 1929 but seems to have gone out of business shortly after this time.

HALL E B
E B Hall of Hammersmith, West London, is known to have bodied an Angus-Sanderson tourer in 1927.

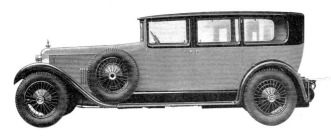

HALL, LEWIS: 1928 Daimler Double-Six 50hp 'Olympia' limousine (above). 1929 Rolls-Royce Phantom 1 limousine de ville (below); conjunction of sloping and straight lines is not entirely happy.

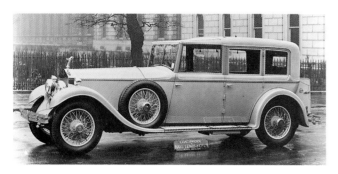

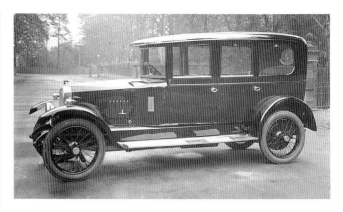

HAMSHAW: Vauxhall 25hp seven-seater limousine (above) for 1921 Olympia Show, in bottle green and black. Humber 14/40 saloon (below) c.1925, with oval rear window and roof peak.

HALL, LEWIS

Hall, Lewis was a firm originally based in South Wales, involved in building railway wagons. It then diversified into the automobile market and became an upmarket coachbuilder, with showrooms in London's prestigious SW1 area and a coachworks in Park Royal, North-West London. This part of its business went back to at least 1923, although it did not exhibit at Olympia until 1926. The firm was particularly known for its work on Rolls-Royce chassis, although it also bodied other prestige marques such as Daimler, Lanchester and Minerva; however, it also had an important business in the manufacture of bus bodies.

After 1926 it ceased exhibiting at Olympia and in 1930 the Hall, Lewis business collapsed. The premises at Park Royal were bought by the Yager family, who formed a new company called Park Royal Coachworks Ltd; from then on output was almost entirely buses (and the occasional railcar). There was, however, one important reversion to car bodybuilding in the post-war period, when Park Royal became the main supplier to Bristol Cars Ltd. From the late fifties on it bodied successively the 406 and 407 saloons and most of the Types 408 to 411.

The Yager family sold Park Royal to the lorry makers AEC and it thus became part of the Leyland group in the late sixties. The Park Royal works closed down in 1980.

HALL W W

W W Hall of Redditch is known to have bodied an early Aston Martin, in 1923.

HAMILTON, CLAUD

Claud Hamilton of Aberdeen was an important Scottish coachbuilder during the twenties. It chose to exhibit at Scottish Motor Shows rather than the London ones, being present from 1921 to at least 1927. It bodied a wide variety of the better sort of chassis including Rolls-Royce, Talbot and Crossley and seems to have had a particularly close affinity with Sunbeam. It is probable that it gave up coachbuilding by the late twenties, and from then on exhibited the work of other firms.

HAMSHAW

The origins of the Leicester firm H A Hamshaw Ltd go back to the middle of the 19th century, when the firm of Parr & Hamshaw was established. In about 1880 Harry Arthur Hamshaw bought out his partner, and from then on created a prestigious business in carriage-building. During the early 1900s the firm began both to sell cars and to body them; it started exhibiting at the Olympia Shows, and was there from 1919 to 1928.

Like most provincial coachbuilders, Hamshaw worked on a wide variety of chassis. The most common ones put on exhibition were Wolseley, Vauxhall, Humber and Sunbeam, for all of which it held agencies; it is also known to have bodied five or six Rolls-Royces. The firm was given a Morris distributorship in 1925 and the business which this brought in was probably a major factor in the decision in 1929 to discontinue bodybuilding.

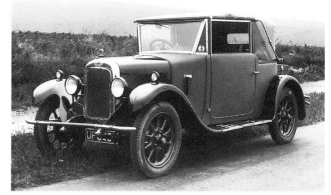

HARRINGTON: Rolls-Royce Phantom 1 tourer (above left) c.1925; note rear screen and side-flaps. Austin 12/4 fabric drophead coupé c.1929 (above right). Beverley-Barnes saloon (above) c.1930, with fussy paint scheme perhaps designed to relieve impact of shallow windows.

Hamshaw retained its independence until 1982, when it was bought by Mann Egerton.

HANBURY

In 1921 Hanbury & Co of Thetford developed its 'DD' system of metal-framed bodywork. This consisted of straight pressed-steel channels into which were slid shaped wood panels. Thus there were no wood-to-wood joints, and the system also gave a claimed 25 per cent saving in both weight and cost. It was tested on a Bean for some 6,000 miles.

HANCOCK & WARMAN

Hancock & Warman was a Coventry firm mainly associated with Rileys. This is supposed to have started in 1923, when it produced a one-off sports three-seater on a Riley chassis which the Riley firm liked so much that it led directly to the Redwing. Hancock & Warman bodied many other marques, however, including Marseal and MG. It got as far as exhibiting at the 1928 and 1929 Olympias, showing Rileys and, the second year, a Daimler 20hp saloon. It is also known to have bodied a Triumph 15 saloon, a Daimler 25 saloon and at least one Double-Six. Then the firm suffered a major fire which was apparently sufficient to put it out of business.

HARDY

R Hardy & Son, with an address in London's Marylebone High Street, offered two special bodies on the Wolseley Hornet chassis in 1933-34 – a sports and a close-coupled saloon.

HARRINGTON

The Brighton firm of Thomas Harrington Ltd was founded in 1897 and is known to have been bodying cars since 1905. Orig-

HARRISON: 1929 Rolls-Royce 20hp coupé with 'British Flexible' body construction.

inally located in Brighton itself, it moved in 1930 to a new factory in nearby Hove. It was also an early producer of motor-coach bodies, and after World War 1 this became its most important area of business. Nevertheless Harrington retained a significant presence as a coachbuilder on car chassis, bodying mainly high-class imported marques such as Lorraine-Dietrich, Austro-Daimler, Peugeot, Panhard, Ballot, Lancia, Minerva, Bugatti, Mercedes-Benz and Delage. British chassis known to have been bodied include Rolls-Royce, Sunbeam, Talbot, Austin and the rare Beverley-Barnes. Numerous bodies were built under the Weymann system.

Harrington exhibited at Olympia from 1924 to 1931 but not thereafter; this latter date seems to have coincided with a decision to concentrate even more on coach production. However it continued to produce car bodies from time to time, notably the advanced Tatra Type 57 commissioned by Capt Fitzmaurice, the Tatra importer, for the 1933 Motor Show.

The company was one of the few to continue to produce special car bodies after World War 2, even though its main business continued to be coaches. Its best-known product was the Harrington Alpine, based on the Sunbeam Alpine sports car and made between 1961 and 1963, but it also built all 50 Dove GTs (a Triumph TR4 variant) and some 230 special bodies on Minis. Harrington finally closed down in 1966.

HARRIS

John Harris (Reading) Ltd took over the coachworks vacated by GREAT WESTERN MOTORS, also of Reading, and immediately (1928) replaced that firm at the Olympia Show – a turn of speed which suggests some kind of management buy-out. There it exhibited a Buick landaulet, a Lagonda two-seater and a Talbot saloon. It would seem, though, that Harris tired of coachbuilding soon afterwards; it made no further appearances at Olympia and by 1930 was describing itself as 'automobile engineers'.

HARRIS & OTHERS

This improbably-named firm is known to have bodied a Rolls-Royce Silver Ghost saloon.

HARRISON

R Harrison & Son was established in 1883 and by the twenties had premises in the NW1 area of London. It seems to have had a dual personality; on the one hand it bodied a succession of top-class chassis such as Rolls-Royce, Bentley and Hispano-Suiza, yet at the same time (1924) it acquired a second factory and advertised it as capable of supplying 'fully-finished car bodies for the trade'. It took no part in Motor Shows under its own name, but its bodies did adorn Bentley chassis at the 1923 Scottish Show and the 1925 Olympia Show. Indeed, Bentley work seems to have predominated, with over 200 chassis passing through its hands during the twenties involving all types of body.

In 1927 Harrison set up a subsidiary, British Flexible Coachworks Ltd, to promote its own patented system of fabric body construction. Unlike Weymann, this used felt between the joints of the wooden frame, and wood-screws encased in rubber bushes. It was offered to other coachbuilders under licence, but few seem to have taken it up.

Harrison closed in 1931, victim presumably not only of the Depression but also of over-dependence on Bentleys. However WOODS, REEVES & CO was apparently at the same address in 1934 and was described as Harrison's 'successors'.

HAWK

See MATCHLESS.

HAWORTH

James Haworth was a Manchester coachbuilder, known only for having bodied a Fiat 501 saloon in 1923.

HAYES

Hayes Auto Bodies Ltd, of Ilford, Essex, exhibited at Olympia once only, in 1920. Its stand contained a Hupmobile landaulet, a Dodge coupé and what would have been a Le Zebre coupé if the strikes that year had so permitted; in the event, it was shown as a chassis with some timber framing mounted on it.

HAYWARD

A mysterious firm, known only to have bodied a Rolls-Royce 40/50 tourer in 1923.

HEATH & WILTSHIRE

Another firm from the small coachbuilding enclave around Farnham, Heath & Wiltshire was small compared with Abbott, but did body some cars in the twenties. It was also a dealer, holding agencies for Wolseley, Bean, Ford, Lagonda and Chevrolet.

HHH LTD

This company, located in Finchley, North-West London, was originally the in-house coachbuilder for De Dion Bouton, bodying all such chassis imported into Britain (bodying them after importation was a way of reducing the duty payable). This business must have been on the decline, however, as

Corsica's 1934 Alfa Romeo 6C 1750GS tourer compares well with Italian-bodied versions.

1933 Alvis Speed 20 SB four-
door tourer by Cross & Ellis.
Note how the cutaway is
carried into the rear door to
maintain the proportions.

Grosvenor 1935 Vauxhall
'Newmarket' B-type Big Six
lwb saloon.

Opposite page: 1928
Minerva AK 32/34 tourer by
Elkington. Typical of the
period with cycle wings and
steps instead of running-
boards.

1928 Triumph 15hp saloon by
Hancock & Warman.

1931 Riley Nine drophead
coupé by Hoyal – good-
looking, but not enough to
save the firm later that year.

HILL & BOLL: advertisement for their all-weather body, c.1924.

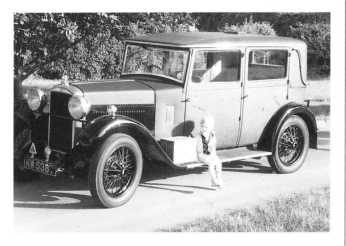

HOLBROOK BODIES (COVENTRY): 1929 Hillman 14hp Weymann saloon believed to be by this coachbuilder.

the De Dion marque lost popularity, and by 1925 HHH were advertising that it could supply all types of body-work to the trade.

Nothing else is known about the firm, and one mystery in particular remains: is the fact that the firm bears the same initials as H Hamilton Hoyer (see CHALMER & HOYER) too much of a coincidence?

HILL & BOLL

Another typical provincial coach-builder, but with a high reputation, was Hill & Boll of Yeovil, Somerset; it was also typical in that the Depression seems to have forced it out of the coachbuilding business. Before that it was a regular attender at Olympia Motor Shows, taking a stand there every year from 1919 until 1930.

Hill & Boll bodied the usual wide range of chassis, but was particularly associated with Delage and was probably a recommended supplier. It also showed a degree of innovation, being one of the first builders to adopt a sloping windscreen.

HILTON

A Rugby, Warwickshire, firm, known only for having built a four-seater sports body on a 1935 Wolseley Hornet chassis.

HOFFMAN

Fred Hoffman of Alperton, West London, was an ex-Bentley service department employee who set up on his own after the Bentley banckruptcy in 1931. Working with H M Bentley & Partners, he would remove heavy and outdated closed bodies from existing Bentley chassis and replace them with open tourer or sports designs. Coupled with other changes such as a shortened chassis and lowered bulkhead and radiator, this resulted in a highly attractive car – as well as providing the only source of 'new' Bentleys during the critical years from 1931 to 1933.

HOLBROOK BODIES (COVENTRY)

A small company called Holbrook existed between 1926 and 1933 in Coventry. It had no connection with the Wolverhampton company, and merely took its name from its address in Holbrook Lane. It is known to have built a two-seater body on a 3½-litre Bentley and some 'Weymann-style' bodies for Hillman before going bankrupt; the premises were taken over by the adjacent Swallow company.

HOLBROOK (WOLVERHAMPTON)

Under its original name of Holbrook & Taylors Ltd, this Wolverhampton company was formed when early in 1930 Sam Holbrook resigned as sales manager of Austin and bought into L & L T TAYLOR LTD. The stated intention was to concentrate on commercial vehicles, as presumably the previous firm had done, but in spite of these words Holbrook took a stand at Olympia the same year, showing a Hillman 'all-weather saloon' and an Invicta sportsman's saloon. The Hillman seems to have marked an early commercial success, since Holbrook supplied Hillman with bodies for a number of years thereafter. The firm continued to exhibit at Olympia and Earls Court until 1937.

In 1933 there was a reorganisation, apparently to allow the Taylor family to take their money out and the Jeffs family (father and son) to invest in their place. Although the name changed to Samuel Holbrook Ltd the firm continued otherwise as before. As well as nurturing the Hillman relationship it struck up a new one with Alvis which was to last for the rest of the company's existence. For Alvis Holbrook supplied a standard design of saloon body for the Silver Eagle, Firefly and Firebird models; under Holbrook's name of the 'Dorchester' this same design was used by Standard on its 16 chassis, while Vauxhall called it the 'Suffolk' on its Light 6, and BSA knew it as the 'Varsity'. The Dorchester design also found its way on to Lanchester 10, Crossley, Hillman Minx and Wolseley chassis. Later Alvis work included (different) saloons on the Crested Eagle, Silver Crest and 4.3 models. Not all Holbrook's bodies were saloons: it produced a drophead coupé on the Singer 11hp chassis for the 1934-35 season.

At the same time the company was urgently seeking

HOLBROOK
(WOLVERHAMPTON): 1933
Standard 16hp 'Dorchester'
saloon (left). This design was
used on a number of chassis.
1935 Alvis Speed 20 SC saloon
(below) with a very modern
front-wing treatment for the
time.

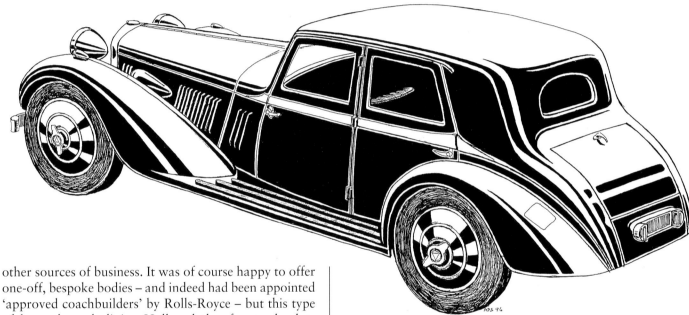

other sources of business. It was of course happy to offer one-off, bespoke bodies – and indeed had been appointed 'approved coachbuilders' by Rolls-Royce – but this type of demand was declining. Holbrook therefore made a late attempt to move into bus and coach bodies (including bodying the AJS motorcycle firm's doomed attack on the same market). It all came to nothing, however, and the company went into receivership in 1938.

HOLLICK & PRATT

The origins of Hollick & Pratt of Coventry go back to at least 1888; this was when Henry Hollick built the body for the Starley electric car – probably the first car made in Coventry. An alternative story is that he made the first car body in Britain, which was then taken to France to be fitted to its chassis. Whatever the truth, Hollick was certainly a pioneer in the car bodybuilding industry. He then found himself with an equally talented son-in-law, in the form of Lancelot Pratt, who also had a coachbuilding business, in partnership with William Fulford. When the two decided in 1922 to merge their businesses, Hollick & Pratt Ltd was the result. One of the two parent firms must already have been supplying Riley, since this was the new company's first contract. In the light of subsequent events,

though, it seems likely that Morris was also a customer.

Once the new company had been formed, things began to happen rapidly. First, in September of the same year, the factory was destroyed in a fire. Then – and perhaps the two events were connected – in January 1923 William Morris bought the company. He immediately started to rebuild the factory, but he seems to have had a more subtle plan: he wanted to concentrate body production at Cowley, and to do this he needed an experienced, talented manager – Lancelot Pratt. The H & P factory, meanwhile, would be used for lower-volume body production.

It has been said that Lancelot Pratt was probably the only true business friend William Morris ever had. Morris trusted him totally, and appointed him 'deputy governing director' – in other words, second-in-command. All the more tragic, then, that Pratt died of cancer in April 1924 at the early age of 43.

In 1926, in connection with the flotation of Morris Motors as a public company, Hollick & Pratt changed its

HOOPER: 1922 Daimler 30hp limousine-landaulet (above), more graceful than some of the period. 1928 Armstrong-Siddeley 30hp limousine-landaulet (right). A rather out-dated design, probably the result of a customer's whim.

name to Morris Motors Ltd (Bodies Branch); William Fulford became a director of Morris Motors.

HOLLINGDRAKE

Hollingdrake Automobile Co (1919) Ltd, of Stockport, exhibited at Olympia just once, in 1927, showing a Daimler 20hp all-weather and a Standard 18 landaulet. Nothing else is known of its coachbuilding activities. The firm still exists as an important car dealer.

HOODS & BODIES

Originally based in the Canonbury area of North London, Hoods & Bodies Ltd is known to have bodied Fords and Gregoires in 1919. It later moved to North Acton, West London, in the late twenties.

HOOPER

Hooper was, quite simply, the best; in any discussion of Britain's top coachbuilders it was not simply on everyone's list, it was at the top – possibly for elegance of line, probably for quality of work-

manship, certainly for an unequalled combination. But as for cost...if you needed to ask, you could not afford it.

The firm was founded as Adams and Hooper as long ago as 1805 in London's Haymarket, to build high class carriages. By 1830 it had received the first of many Royal Warrants; it was coachbuilder to Queen Victoria for 60 years and to her son, later King Edward VII, for 50 years. Indeed it prospered to the extent that by 1896 it had both a showroom in fashionable St James and a factory in the Kings Road.

Naturally, it was amongst the first carriage-builders to build coachwork on a car chassis, and by the beginning of the new century already had a considerable volume of business from this source. The work poured in, to the extent that in 1908 the firm was obliged to open a second factory, in Blackfriars Road, although it later found this arrangement unsatisfactory and instead enlarged the Kings Road works in 1911.

Hooper's designs would never have been described as 'sleek' or 'racy'; the epithets which were most often

HOOPER: 1933 Rolls-Royce Phantom 2 lwb sedanca (left) has both sloping and straight lines, yet they blend perfectly (compare with the Hall Lewis limousine de ville on page 118). 1937 Daimler 32hp 'special landaulet' (below); the purpose of the hinged roof-section can only be guessed at. Daimler DK 400 limousine (bottom) – probably the 1954 Motor Show car.

applied were such words as 'dignified' and 'elegant'. Nothing was too much trouble to satisfy the whims of a customer. Inlaid mahogany cabinetwork, ivory or silver-plated fittings and concealed lighting were everyday items. More unusual requests, such as an electrically-operated, remote-controlled scent spray, were accommodated with hardly a flicker of an eyebrow.

During World War 1 Hooper had turned to aircraft manufacture, producing complete planes such as the Sopwith Camel at an eventual rate of three a day. In 1919 it resumed coachbuilding, and with just as much success, turning out limousines, landaulets, broughams and sedancas on mainly Rolls-Royce, Daimler and, later, Bentley chassis. Demand was such that in 1933 the firm felt it necessary to build a second factory, on Western Avenue at Acton in West London. This allowed it virtually to double output, so that in the peak year of 1936 well over 300 bodies were produced. A production rate of six bodies a week may not sound very much to our ears today, but as bespoke coachbuilding went – and particularly bearing in mind the high value of a Hooper body – this was big business.

As war approached, the company again showed great business acumen by joining in the shadow aircraft factory scheme. It built yet another factory at Elveden Road in Willesden which was opened in 1937, so that by the outbreak of war Hooper was fully prepared for aircraft manufacture. This time it produced major sections for Oxfords and Mosquitos and gliders – an appropriate use of skills since these were mainly made of wood. In 1938 it had showed perhaps less prescience by purchasing the prestigious firm of Barkers from the receivers for by the time the war was over there was insufficient work to justify keeping the Barker name going for more than a few years. It was during the war, too, that Hooper itself changed ownership, being bought by the BSA combine, which included Daimler cars.

There now followed a period in Hooper's history which was even more glamorous, although perhaps slightly less dignified. At successive London Motor Shows in the early fifties, one of the star attractions would be the latest Hooper creation on a Daimler chassis – usually a drophead coupé – designed for Lady Docker, wife of BSA

chairman Sir Bernard Docker. The coachwork was sure to contain some outrageous feature, such as gold-plated fittings, destined to attract maximum coverage from the popular press at a time when post-war austerity had not totally disappeared.

In technical matters the company was not being left behind. Before the War it had experimented with aluminium framing, and from 1949 onwards its bodywork was produced almost entirely in light alloy – fabricated extrusions with some alloy castings and occasional steel components for the frame, and hand-formed aluminium panelling. One thing which had not changed, however, was the need for a separate chassis, and when Hooper learned from Rolls-Royce in 1959 that the successor to the Silver Cloud would not have a chassis, it realised that coachbuilding had come to an end, though it was still concerned to provide a repair and restoration service to former clients. A possible sale of the business was discussed with both H J Mulliner and Jack Barclay (who owned James Young) but it came to nothing. Before BSA closed Hooper down, therefore, it transferred the servic-

HOWES: 1928 Armstong-Siddeley 20hp drophead coupé was a '2/6-seater' – there were two enclosed occasional seats as well as a dickey.

JARVIS (PADDINGTON): Rolls-Royce 20hp tourer – a 1923 chassis rebodied in 1926.

ing and spares to a new, independent company called Hooper (Motor Services) Ltd. The service which the old Hooper company had always provided to the Royal Mews was not included in the deal, and went instead to Park Ward.

Thereafter there was something of a rebirth in the new Hooper firm. In 1970 it was appointed a Rolls-Royce distributor, and in 1981 an officially approved Rolls-Royce coachbuilder. Most recently it merged with the old-established dealer Jack Alpe to form Hooper Alpe Ltd.

HORA
E & H Hora were located in the Peckham area of South-East London. Originally a supplier of coachbuilding components, it then extended into coachbuilding itself, exhibiting once at Olympia, in 1920, where it showed two bodies on Guy chassis and one on a Calcott. Even at this stage, however, Hora's main output seems to have been bus bodies, and the assumption is that the firm concentrated on this side thereafter. It is known to have been still in existence in 1928.

HOWES
The Norwich firm of Howes & Sons was originally a carriage-maker, having been founded in 1784. In the 19th century they sold carriages to the Royal Family at nearby Sandringham and to many members of the German aristocracy. At the beginning of the 20th century it decided to move into the motor trade and became the first Wolseley agent in Norfolk. It also started to body car chassis, and specialised in Wolseleys.

This connection continued after World War 1; Howes

was represented at every Olympia Show from 1919 to 1929, and had a Wolseley on the stand each time. It also specialised in bodying Armstrong-Siddeleys; otherwise its output was on typical better-quality chassis of the times such as Napier and Lagonda.

After Howes withdrew from Olympia it concentrated on commercial bodybuilding, and gave up even this activity after World War 2. The company continues today as a motor engineer and filling-station operator.

HOYAL See CHALMER & HOYER

HUGHES
Thomas Hughes & Son of Birmingham was normally a manufacturer of motorcycle sidecars but decided to be amongst the first (1924) to produce a sporting two-seater body on the Austin Seven chassis.

HULL
Hull City Garage Ltd was at Olympia (White City annexe) for one year only, 1920, and showed a Bianchi 20hp cabriolet 'to the special order of Mr C Wade of Beverley'.

JAQUEST-TAYLOR
This Coventry firm seems to have been related to the Taylor Sidecar Co, which existed for a very short time in the early twenties. The one body it is known to have made was for a 10/30 racing Alvis which took part in the 1921 200 Mile race at Brooklands.

JARVIS (PADDINGTON)
Jarvis Ltd of Paddington, in West London, began business in 1885 as a cycle manufacturer and dealer, but moved up to car dealing at the turn of the century. Coachbuilding facilities in nearby Kilburn were added in 1920, and the company built mainly open style bodies as well as vans until 1940. Unfortunately these premises were totally destroyed during World War 2. Jarvis concentrated on repair business thereafter, and apart from an Alvis TA14 rebodying project is not known to have been involved in any new work. It ceased business in 1975.

JARVIS (WIMBLEDON): Darracq 16hp skiff-type four-seater at the 1927 Show, with tulipwood 'gunwales' and mahogany 'decks' fixed with copper rivets.

JARVIS (WIMBLEDON)

Jarvis & Sons Ltd of Wimbledon, in South-West London was renowned during the twenties for its sporting and racing-car bodies. A particular speciality during the middle of the decade was boat-tailed designs, which were much in vogue at that period. The chief designer (and manager) at the time was Arthur Compton, who later left to set up as COMPTON SONS & TERRY and then as A P COMPTON/ARROW.

The firm is known to have been in existence in 1921 and exhibited at Olympia in 1926 and 1927. It built its racy bodies on such sporting chassis as Aston Martin, Bentley, Bugatti, Itala and OM, but also on more middle-of-the- road ones such as Talbot and Darracq – and often on Rolls-Royce as well. Jarvis was amongst those offering sporting bodies on the Austin Seven chassis and announced its smart two-seater in 1927. It did construct the occasional non-sporting body, such as a Bentley limousine and a Daimler 30hp saloon, both in 1926.

By the early thirties Jarvis seems to have substantially reduced its own bodybuilding facilities and instead was commissioning work from other coachbuilders. For example, in 1933 it offered sports and drophead coupé designs on the Morris Ten chassis, but these were produced by JOHN CHARLES and ABBEY COACHWORKS. In the meantime the company had become a well-known Morris dealer, a business which continued after World War 2 and which led to its last connection with coachbuilding. In 1949 Jarvis announced a 'tourer to coupé' conversion on the Morris Minor, whereby with the addition of a pair of rear sidescreens and a new hood the original convertible could be made more like a drophead coupé. The company was eventually bought by the Mann Egerton group.

JENKINS

P W Jenkins, of Enfield, Middlesex, is known to have bodied at least two Rolls-Royces in about 1920, and also some Calcotts at around the same time.

JENNINGS

J H Jennings & Son Ltd started as wheelwrights in the village of Little Warford in

JENKINS: Rolls-Royce 40-50 two-seater c.1920.

JENNINGS: Ford V-8 91 'woody' estate c.1947.

Cheshire, but at about the turn of the century bought up an existing coachbuilding business in nearby Sandbach. From then on the firm built mainly commercial bodies, and later caravans. However, it qualifies as a builder of private car bodies not only because of a rear-door conversion on the Ford 8 saloon which it marketed in the thirties, but also because it built a 'woody' estate car on a Ford V8 chassis, probably just after World War 2. It eventually became a subsidiary of the ERF lorry company.

JENSEN

Jensen became better known, of course, as a make of car, but the company started life as a

JENSEN: 1936 Morris Eight special tourer (right) with longer lines than the factory body but less legroom at the rear. 1952 Austin A40 Sports (below right).

coachbuilder. It all began in 1928, when the two Jensen brothers, Richard and Alan, built a body to their own design on an Austin Seven chassis. The story goes that the chief engineer of the Standard Motor Company saw the car, liked its lines, and thought that a similar design would look well on a Standard chassis. Since the brothers at that time had no bodybuilding facilities of their own they could only fabricate a prototype so the production contract went to the NEW AVON company and the result was the well-known Avon Standard of 1929 onwards.

The Jensen's next move involved Patrick Motors, the Birmingham dealer. Together they formed Patrick-Jensen Motors in 1930 with the objective of manufacturing special bodies on the Wolseley Hornet chassis. For whatever reason, however, this alliance broke up soon afterwards, and in 1931 the Jensens bought into the West Bromwich coachbuilder W J Smith & Sons, changing its name to Jensen Motors.

The brothers then started to apply their designing skills to bodying a number of chassis. In their first year they made the bodies for the McEvoy Hornet Special and then decided to body that marque under their own name. Their 1932 Wolseley Hornet fixed-head coupé was distinctive – low-built, with triangular quarter-lights under the dummy hood-irons. Even the Morris Minor, given the Jensen treatment the same year with an occasional four-seater open body, was made to look quite sporty. Other 'production' designs followed, all open sports or drop-head coupé, models: Morris 8, 10 and 12, Wolseley 14, and a range of Fords for Bristol Street Motors – 8s, 10s, and V8s.

The company was also involved in bespoke work, including commissions on Delage and Star chassis and the body for Horton's record-breaking single-seater MG. Their most famous commission, though, was a Ford V8 for Clark Gable, the film star, in 1934; it could well have been this car which led to the 1935 meeting with Edsel Ford, when the brothers showed him two prototypes which were to become the 1936 Jensen-Ford.

From this point on the Jensen company must be regarded as primarily a manufacturer rather than a

coachbuilder, and that part of its history is outside the scope of this book. Nevertheless it must be recorded that Jensen resumed some coachbuilding after World War 2, with some Lea-Francis 12hp 'woody' estates, the Austin A40 Sports of the early fifties and later the Austin-Healey 3000.

JONES Jones Brothers of Bayswater, West London, is known to have been in business as early as 1928, specialising in Austin 12/4 taxis rather than private car work. However, it built a streamlined two-door saloon on a Lanchester Ten chassis in 1934 (designed by R A S PHILLIPS), and the next year managed to secure a contract to manufacture a range of ALLINGHAM designs – the 'Sandringham' cabriolets for the various Austin 12 chassis. Jones also bodied a Salmson for the manufacturer's stand at Olympia in 1936. After World War 2 it appears to have been bought by F H BOYD-CARPENTER and together with his Rumbold company moved to Willesden, North-West London. It continued to body cars occasionally – a batch of Ford V8 Pilot six-light saloons in 1950, and the Bristol 405 saloon in 1955. This last contract, however, seems to have ended in tears, the company having gone bankrupt before completing it.

KC K C Bodies, of New Kings Road, London SW3, had an identical address to COLE & SHUTTLEWORTH, and presumably took over the premises from that firm (one even wonders whether the 'C' in the name stood for Cole?). Like its predecessor, KC made a sporting body on the Austin Seven chassis in 1928 and is also known to have bodied at least one Riley, an Invicta and a Talbot (a four-seater tourer for Warwick Wright in 1931).

KELLY DAVIES Kelly Davies & Co Ltd, of Cheetham in Manchester, was licensed by the Weymann company during 1928.

KEVILL-DAVIES & MARCH See MARCH

KINROSS William Kinross & Sons of Stirling exhibited at one Scottish Motor Show in December 1924 (there was also one in March of that year) where it showed an example of its work on a Standard 14 chassis. Thereafter, although the company continued to exhibit, it had other firms' work on its stand, including in 1927 a Willys-Knight bodied by MORGANS of Leighton Buzzard.

KNIBBS Located in the Ardwick area of Manchester, W H Knibbs & Sons Ltd changed its name in the early thirties to Knibbs & Parkyn; its history goes back to the 1850s. Car-bodying activities during the twenties are not well-documented, but the firm advertised itself as a Weymann specialist and is known to have bodied four Bentley chassis and at least one Daimler. In the thirties, under the revised name, it began offering special bodies on Fords – both the small Y (8hp) model and the V8. Another special body, although sold through Colmore Depot rather than directly, was on the 1½-litre Frazer Nash. During this period, up to 1938, Knibbs is also known to have bodied a number of Rolls-Royces and at least one 4¼-litre Bentley.

After World War 2 the company continued with a small amount of bodybuilding, for example six drophead coupés on the Alvis TA14 chassis, but it soon concentrated solely on motor dealing and still exists as a dealer to the present day under the name Knibbs of Salford.

KNIBBS & PARKYN See KNIBBS.

KNOWLES Knowles Motors, in London's West End, is known to have built a fabric saloon body on a Bean Six 18/50hp chassis in 1927.

LANCEFIELD The company was founded in 1922 under the name of Gaisford & Warboys, being made up of three Gaisford brothers and George Warboys; two of the Gaisfords had previously worked for the Grosvenor Carriage Company. The first premises were in Lancefield Street, in the W10 area of London. Later, in 1927, the company moved a short distance to Beethoven Street, but liked the old address so much that it was incorporated into a new name, The Lancefield Coachworks.

Most of the early work was components, or later complete bodies, under sub-contract from other better-known coachbuilders. Gradually, though, Lancefield began to gain orders on its own account, including some Rolls-Royces, a dozen or more Bentleys and several Isotta-Fraschinis. By 1929 it felt confident enough to start exhibiting at the Olympia Show, a practice which was continued right up to the last pre-war show (by then at Earls Court) in 1938. The sole exhibit that first year was a Stutz fabric coupé, which must have led to some special relationship with the importers, as the next year found not only a Stutz on the Lancefield stand once again but also three more, bodied by Lancefield, on the Stutz stand. Also in 1929 the firm was honoured with an order from HRH Prince George (later the Duke of Kent) for a saloon body on an Alvis Silver Eagle.

Lancefield was by now beginning to make a name for the quality and modernity of its designs. These were the work of Jock Betteridge, another fugitive from the Grosvenor company who came into his own in the 'streamlining' period of the mid-thirties, and the later 'art deco' craze. Probably his most dramatic designs were those he did for Michael Haworth-Booth under the latter's 'Parallite' patent. The first of these was a streamlined sports saloon on a Siddeley Special chassis in early-1934; this had a full-width body and faired-in headlamps, both major innovations at the time. The car went on to win its class in the concours d'elegance at that year's RAC Rally. A similar treatment on a Speed Twenty Alvis (confusingly labelled 'Aero Eagle' by Lancefield) had the additional feature of a spare-wheel concealed in each of the front wings. Then in 1935 came the Hudson Transcontinental saloon, also in streamlined, full-width style, but now making such good use of its width that it seated four passengers abreast on the front seat (one being on the outside of the driver!), as well as another three in the rear.

Some of these streamlined creations look ugly to modern eyes, but Lancefield was also quite capable of producing designs which are as stunning now as the day they first emerged from the works. Supreme amongst these must be the concealed-head coupé of 1937-38, first shown on a Speed Twenty-Five Alvis at the 1937 Earls Court Show and subsequently applied to Bentley, Mercedes-Benz, Lagonda and Hotchkiss chassis. Its fluted waistline and louvred wheel spats were 'art deco' touches which still excite the eye today. Another striking design – one of the last before the war stopped coachwork production – was a streamlined V12 Lagonda saloon.

After World War 2 Lancefield resumed coachbuilding for a time. At the first Earls Court Show in 1948 it exhibited two invalid limousines on Humber and Daimler chassis – a type of body which it had been developing

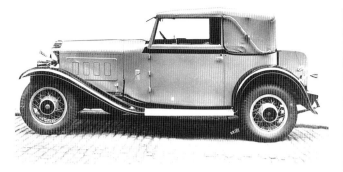

KNIBBS: Willys drophead coupé of c.1931, with unusual pattern of bonnet louvres.

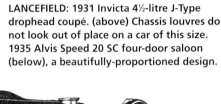

LANCEFIELD: 1931 Invicta 4½-litre J-Type drophead coupé. (above) Chassis louvres do not look out of place on a car of this size. 1935 Alvis Speed 20 SC four-door saloon (below), a beautifully-proportioned design.

before the war. Thereafter the company was not seen at Earls Court, and it eventually withdrew from coach-building around 1960, although it continued in business for some time longer making aircraft components.

LANCHESTER
Although the Lanchester Motor Co of Birmingham was of course a car manufacturer of high repute, its coachwork department – most unusually – was allowed to undertake commissions from private clients on other makes of chassis. Marques known to have been bodied in this way, all during the mid-twenties, were Austin, Daimler, Rolls-Royce and Sunbeam.

LAWRENCE
After World War 1 William Lawrence & Co Ltd of Nottingham started to build a business supplying bodies to the trade, specialising in coupés. It obtained a contract for Ford bodies and then another for four-seaters on the Fiat 10/15 chassis, both running during 1921; the brand-name was 'Lawrencia'. No doubt the decision to exhibit at Olympia in 1920 was also aimed at trade buyers, with coupé bodies priced very competitively at £200 for the Ford and £250 for the Bean. By 1922, however, the contract-only policy was under review, with the announcement that Lawrencia bodies were 'now available in single units'. Nothing more is known of the firm.

LAWTON-GOODMAN
J A Lawton was an important carriage-builders in Liverpool in the 19th century. Jo Lawton's nephew, William Lawton-Goodman, became London manager for the firm and achieved some prominence in the industry, becoming President of the IBCM in 1910 (and again in 1923-24). However, he appears to have quarrelled with his uncle, and thus did not receive preferment when Jo died in 1913. William had previously set up his own company, Lawton-Goodman Ltd, and used this to buy the Whitlock car company and also to acquire premises at Cricklewood, North-West London. From then on he sold cars under both the Whitlock and Lawton names, as well as continuing with the coachbuilding business which had come as part of the Whitlock company; this he moved more to commercial work, especially ambulances, but the firm is known to have bodied Daimler, Rolls-Royce and

Beardmore chassis. Naturally the Whitlock cars also carried Lawton-Goodman coachwork, which thus appeared on the Whitlock stand at Olympia Shows between 1922 and 1929.

William Lawton-Goodman died in 1932; his sons carried on with the coachbuilding business but with increasing emphasis on commercial work. The Liverpool premises were sold in the thirties to the Armstrong-Siddeley company but in London commercial bodybuilding continued until the early eighties. The company eventually closed down in 1991.

LINCOLNSHIRE
Lincolnshire and District Motor Body Works was also known at various times as 'LL Motor Body Works' and 'Thompson & Co'. While the main premises were at Louth, in a former roller-skating rink, it also had an address in nearby Grimsby. It is known to have bodied a Bentley saloon, a Daimler and a Hispano-Suiza at various times. A tale is told about the Hispano, which was bodied in 1921 for a well-known Grimsby family: the son of the house is supposed to have taken delivery and then crashed it on the way home, thus requiring the car to be returned to the coachbuilder forthwith.

Lincolnshire was primarily a bus bodybuilder, but moved to being a bus operator and in the late twenties was bought out by a larger bus group.

LITCHFIELD
Based in West London's Paddington area, Litchfield is only known to have built a four-seater tourer body on a Bentley in 1929.

LOCKWOOD & CLARKSON
This Leeds firm was responsible for bodying Day-Leeds cars – with open two-seaters and coupés; production ceased in 1924.

LAWTON-GOODMAN: Rolls-Royce Phantom 2 limousine of c.1931; superb lines, although the oval window was by then a little dated.

LINCOLNSHIRE: Daimler limousine c.1925.

LOCKWOOD & CLARKSON: 1920 Day-Leeds coupé.

LONDON IMPROVED
The London Improved Motor Coach-Builders (Belgravia) Ltd was memorable more for the length of its name than anything else. The company exhibited its 'Belgravia' coachwork at Olympia from 1919 to 1926, using

LONDON IMPROVED: 1925
Rolls-Royce Phantom 1 saloon
– workmanlike rather than
pretty.

MADDOX: 1933 Morris Minor
fixed-head coupé

a varied assortment of chassis among which only Renault and Crossley featured with any frequency. In 1925 it seems to have taken out a licence from the GORDON ENGLAND firm in order to rebody a 1920 Rolls-Royce 40/50; presumably it wanted to use merely the subframe system with its three-point mounting as the resulting limousine certainly does not look as if it was made out of plywood.

London Improved was still in its premises at Lupus Street, Westminster, in 1927, but by the beginning of 1928 the address was claimed by WESTMINSTER CARRIAGE. Nothing more was heard of London Improved.

LOTHIAN Lothian Coachworks is known to have bodied a Fiat 501 doctor's coupé in 1922.

LOVE Love's of Kingston-on-Thames, Surrey, bodied an early Frazer-Nash tourer in 1923.

LUCAS F W Lucas Ltd, of Brixton, South-West London, exhibited a Bianchi limousine at the 1919 Olympia Show. It then seems to have undergone a finan-

cial reconstruction, emerging as F W Lucas (1922) Ltd and was still trading under this name in 1928.

MADDOX George Maddox, born in 1863 in a village near Huntingdon, was apprenticed as a wheelwright and at the age of 19 moved to Windover's in Huntingdon, eventually becoming general foreman. In 1899 he decided to start his own coachbuilding firm, initially acting as a sub-contractor to Windover's, but later becoming involved in car coachwork. By the early part of the new century he had over a hundred employees.

The firm was a regular exhibitor at Olympia both before and after World War 1, from 1920 to 1934. The list of exhibits during the twenties reveals the usual mixture of marques to be expected from a quality provincial coachbuilder – Armstrong-Siddeley, Bentley, Daimler, Humber, Minerva, Napier, Bianchi, Fiat, Sunbeam, Alvis, Talbot and many others with Fiat and Minerva the most frequently represented. It was during this period that the firm suffered two major blows. Firstly, George Maddox died an early death from pneumonia in 1921; his elder

MALTBY: 1934 advertisement (left) for the company's Humber 12hp and Lagonda Rapier drophead coupés. The hydraulic head in action on an Armstrong-Siddeley 17hp Redfern tourer (below). SS Jaguar 2½-litre drophead coupé (bottom) – the 1938 Show car, in black with silver-grey hood.

son Archie, then 29, took over. Then in early 1924 there was a disastrous fire which completely destroyed the factory (but not the timber stocks); the firm nevertheless still managed to be at Olympia in October the same year.

From the late twenties onward it is clear that Maddox was trying to widen its business by bodying cheaper chassis. In 1929, and the two subsequent years, Morris Minors appeared; in 1930 an MG Midget fixed-head coupé; and also in 1931, although not at the Motor Show, came an Austin Seven coupé. The firm also produced a Wolseley Hornet design, by then mandatory for any coachbuilder. Then in 1932 it obtained 'approved supplier' status from Rover, which meant that its 'Ranee' drophead coupé could be sold by Rover dealers across the whole range of chassis; the arrangement continued, in modified form, for the 1933-34 season.

In spite of these efforts all was not well. The firm had converted to limited company status in 1931 (George Maddox & Sons Ltd) and appeared as such at the 1931 Motor Show, but it was not present at the following year's Show – and this in spite of the Rover business gained. Then in 1933 a new firm appeared – Archie Maddox – using the same address as the previous company. The probability is that it was Archie Maddox which had been awarded the Rover contract, but the firm was too new to gain recognition in time for the 1932 Show.

Archie Maddox's exhibits at the 1933 Olympia Show

were a Hillman Minx coupé and a Standard 9 open two-seater, both possibly factory-approved designs. In 1934 he showed both Rover and Railton drophead coupés; the latter probably represented an attempt to obtain a contract from the new manufacturer. However, it was all too late and nothing more was heard of the Archie Maddox firm, the presumption being that it moved out of the coachbuilding business early in 1935. A Gerry Maddox – presumably Archie's younger brother – became a salesman for Abbott in that year, and a related company, a garage named Maddox & Kirby, continued on the same site as the original Maddox coachworks until very recently.

MAFFRE Louis Maffre was in partnership with Samuel Day in Chiswick, West London at the beginning of the twenties, but then seems to have bought his partner out. The firm is known to have bodied a Motobloc tourer in 1923.

MALTBY Maltby's Motor Works came into existence in 1902 when John Hugh Maltby decided to extend his interests beyond the blacksmith business he had started three years earlier in Sandgate, Kent. Soon afterwards he was joined by his brother Herbert Charles. The firm became a dealer and repairer, even a car manufacturer for a time, and then – in 1912 – a bus manufacturer. At the same time or earlier, one assumes, it started a coachbuilding department. After World War 1 the emphasis continued to be on commercial vehicles, particularly the manufacture of lorries and coaches, although the firm was also a substantial dealer with agencies for Morris, Minerva, Humber, Crossley and Buick, and with three branches in Kent in addition to Sandgate. Then in 1926 John Maltby decided to sell up; the buyer was a Mr Redfern, chairman of the Johnnie Walker whisky company, who installed his two sons to run it (with their sister in charge of reception). Herbert Maltby remained with the firm for a time but left in 1929.

The character of the firm now changed. The manufacture of commercial vehicles ceased, and although car dealing would remain the prime business there was now an emphasis on coachwork for car chassis, underlined by the decision to start exhibiting at Olympia Motor Shows. The first such Show was in 1929, with a Minerva limousine as the sole exhibit. The company – now called Maltby's Motor Works & Garage Ltd – followed a dual policy in respect of coachbuilding: it continued to offer 'bespoke' (but probably modified standard) designs on chassis for which it had agencies, but it also pursued contracts with manufacturers for catalogued designs which would be sold through all dealers for the marque. On the dealing side, Maltby took up further agencies – for Wolseley, Riley, BSA, Daimler, Armstrong-Siddeley, Lanchester and Standard – and in turn exploited them for coachbuilding opportunities.

Thus in 1930 we find three different designs – two sports and a drophead coupé – being exhibited on Morris chassis, Maltby's most important dealership; at a later stage this range would be exclusive to Stewart & Ardern. There followed similar design ranges on Armstrong-Siddeley, Wolseley Hornet, Standard 12, Humber, Wolseley 14 and 25, and Buick chassis; other marques bodied included Alvis, Austin, Hillman and Lagonda Rapier. Increasingly these were drophead versions, although Maltby produced a particularly attractive pillarless saloon for their Wolseley Hornet range. By the mid-thirties dropheads were the speciality, known by the brand-name 'Redfern'. Maltby had developed a smart method of folding the hood, and applied it to both 'saloon-tourers' (four-door, pillarless) and 'coupé-tourers' (two-door). Moreover it was the first British coachbuilder to automate the action of folding or unfolding the hood. Initially, in 1935, its solution was to use the hydraulic pump of the 'Jackall' jacking system but by the next year it had fitted a dedicated electric motor and pump.

The Maltby company, judged as either car dealer or coachbuilder, must be regarded as one of the more successful of the troubled thirties. It is all the sadder, therefore, to record the manner of its end. Francis Redfern, the elder son (and driving force?) was killed in a road accident; his brother Dicky decided to leave the business and sold it to CAFFYN'S. This firm was only interested in the garage side, and coachbuilding ceased.

MANN EGERTON: 1921 Rolls-Royce 40-50 Silver Ghost limousine (above), an impressive design for such an early year. Sunbeam 16hp coupé-cabriolet (below), as shown at Olympia in 1927, with two occasional seats behind the two main ones.

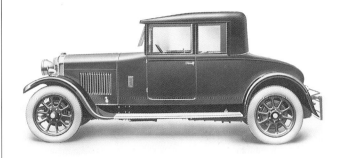

MANN EGERTON

Gerard Mann was by training an electrical engineer. He moved to Norwich in 1899 to take over an existing electrical contractors' business and the firm has remained based in Norwich, in various locations as it expanded, until the present day. Hubert Egerton, a keen early motorist, joined Mann in 1900. Egerton had previously been sales manager for the De Dion company in Britain, and it seems likely that Mann was thinking of entering the motor industry in some form. Egerton had other motoring connections: his brother Reggie was already a well-known character in motoring circles in East Anglia, and was shortly to give his name to two coachbuilding firms in Ipswich – BOTWOOD & EGERTON, and EGERTONS. Sure enough, soon afterwards the two made their move, becoming agents and then (1901) coachbuilders. Mann Egerton and Company Ltd was formed in 1905. In 1909 it was appointed agent for Rolls-Royce, and in the same year mounted its first body, a landaulet, on a Rolls-Royce chassis. This was the start of a long association with the marque; the company regularly exhibited bodies on RR chassis at the London Motor Shows both before and after World War 1. Indeed, of the 20 Shows between the wars there was not one where Mann Egerton was not represented, each time with a Rolls-Royce on the stand.

The company grew enormously both before and after World War 1, not only in the motor trade but also in electrical contracting and even educational furniture. By 1913 it held agencies for nine different makes of car. During the First War it manufactured De Havilland and other planes under licence, and also set up an agricultural department, which later grew rapidly. It went public in 1919 and by 1920 had branches in four East Anglian

MARCH: 1933 Hillman Aero Minx, designed by March but made by (probably) Carbodies.

MARSH: 1921 Rolls-Royce 40-50 Silver Ghost landaulet could almost be a pre-World War 1 design.

MARSHALSEA: Vauxhall 23-60 limousine at the 1924 Olympia Show, in dark blue with grey Bedford cord upholstery in the rear.

towns as well as London. Coachbuilding was thus a minor, though prestigious, activity; besides Rolls-Royce, the other marques which Mann Egerton liked to be seen to body were Daimler, Sunbeam, Minerva, Armstrong-Siddeley, Vauxhall (but not after the General Motors takeover), Bentley (but only after the Rolls-Royce takeover) and Humber. An early association with Austin was allowed to continue. The designs which clothed such chassis had above all to be acceptable to the local clientele, which tended to mean safe and even boring, not adventurous. Quality, however, was never in question and was up to the best London standards.

Such an upmarket approach inevitably meant shrinking volumes for Mann Egerton's coachworks, and car bodybuilding ceased in 1939. After the World War 2 the company continued to expand and became one of the country's leading motor distributors. It had one final fling at coachbuilding, producing a limousine on the long-wheelbase Austin Sheerline and even showing it at the 1951 Motor Show. In 1973 the company was acquired by the Inchcape Group.

MARCH Freddy March, heir to the Duke of Richmond and Gordon, was a talented designer. Through his firm Kevill-Davies and March he commissioned a number of outstanding body designs in the first half of the thirties. However he cannot be regarded as a coachbuilder since neither he nor his firm had coachworks of their own. March bodies are therefore covered in this book under the names of the firms which built them.

MARCHANT H Marchant & Sons, of Croydon in Surrey, bodied a Minerva coupé in 1924.

MARKHAM The Reading firm eventually known as H Markham Ltd was founded in the early twenties by Arthur Markham and later opened branches in High Wycombe and Windsor. It is best known for having bodied one of the famous Squire short-chassis two-seater sports cars (which were manufactured

in nearby Henley-on-Thames) in 1935. The company still exists in Reading as a body repairer, the Markham family connection having been broken only in the 1990s.

MARROWS & ANGELL This firm built a four-seater sports body on a Rover chassis in 1931.

MARSH A mysterious coachbuilder named Marsh exists only in an early official Rolls-Royce photograph, having bodied a 40/50 chassis of around 1921 with an attractive landaulet design.

MARSHALL & BROWN A Manchester firm known to have bodied a Beardmore open two-seater in 1925.

MARSHALSEA Marshalsea Brothers Ltd was a Taunton firm which exhibited regularly at Olympia throughout the twenties and also appeared at the British Empire Exhibition at Wembley in 1924. The types of chassis bodied reveal little other than the versatility required of a provincial coachbuilder in those days; the only affiliation seems to have been with the Fiat importers, whose products appeared on the stand most years. Sunbeam and Talbot chassis also appeared

MARTIN &YOUNG: Talbot 25/50 limousine c.1921; low bonnet line gives away the early date.

more than once. At the 1926 Show Marshalsea announced proudly that, although its products wcrc still hand-painted, it was now going to install a cellulose-painting plant for the following year; this goes to show how long it took for ideas to become accepted in a rather conservative trade, since such equipment had been advertised and available since early 1925.

Strangely, Marshalsea ceased exhibiting at Olympia Shows after 1930, and then made a single reappearance in 1934 with a Daimler 25hp straight-eight limousine. After this, the presumption is that it ceased its coach-building activities. The Marshalsea company still exists in Taunton, as Marshalsea Hydraulics Ltd, but its car interests were sold off in the early eighties.

MARSTON John Marston's Carriage Works of Birmingham was primarily a commercial body-builder, but is known to have bodied Daimler and Rolls-Royce chassis at the beginning of the twenties.

MARTIN & YOUNG This Cheltenham firm produced some fine work at the beginning of the twenties, including bodies on Talbot and Vauxhall chassis, but nothing more is known.

MARTIN WALTER See WALTER.

MATCHLESS Matchless Motorcycles (Colliers) Ltd, of Plumstead, South-West London, was very well known for its motorcycles but not at all for car bodies until it decided to manufacture the 'Hawk' two-seater sports version of the Austin Seven. This was produced in a section of the Matchless sidecar factory in 1930 and 1931.

MAULE The history of Maule & Son of Stockton-on-Tees goes back to 1825 when it began as a carriage builder. At what point it made the transition to

car chassis is not recorded but it is known to have bodied a Mincrva saloon in early 1923, two Bentleys in the twenties, and a Dodge in 1930. It was also a Weymann licensee during the twenties.

MAY & JACOBS Little is on record about this Guildford, Surrey, firm, yet it is known to have bodied cars in the Edwardian period and in the twenties (a Bentley), and again in the thirties when it was responsible for a Bugatti saloon.

MAYFAIR This firm is one of two (the other being CARLTON) to have emerged from a third, original firm named MOTOR CAR INDUSTRIES. The partners in the latter, Messrs Halsall & Biddle, split up in about 1925; one went off to form Carlton Carriage, and the other remained at the Kilburn, North-West London, premises of the former partnership. The Kilburn firm then started trading as the 'Progressive Coach & Motor Body Co', though this mouthful was thankfully changed in 1929 to 'Mayfair Carriage Co Ltd'.

Progressive/Mayfair started exhibiting at Olympia two years later, in 1927. Initially its associations were with Buick and Minerva but from 1930 on it seems to have remained loyal to British marques only, beginning with Humber and Wolseley. It was in 1931, however, that it formed its most important link, with the Alvis company. Starting with a Silver Eagle sports saloon in 1931, Mayfair began to specialise in saloons, limousines and drophead coupés on such chassis as Crested Eagle and Speed Twenty, and then on the Speed Twenty's successors – 3½-Litre, Speed Twenty-Five and 4.3-Litre.

Mayfair's designs of the thirties, particularly on Alvises, had a great deal of elegance about them. Even D-back limousines, normally a style which could look rather heavy, had an appearance of grace and lightness. As for less formal designs, Mayfair's 3½-Litre Alvis sports saloon of 1935 was simply sensational, as was its 1936 coupé-de-ville on the 4½-litre Lagonda. Later on – 1935

MAYFAIR: 1938 Rolls-Royce 25/30 limousine (left); not every firm managed to make the smaller Rolls-Royce chassis look so graceful. Interior of a 1935 Alvis Crested Eagle 20hp lwb limousine (below). Note speaking-tube by chauffeur's ear.

to 1937 – the company bodied a number of Siddeley Special and Armstrong-Siddeley chassis, all apparently limousines; one in particular, in 1937, was a very fine example of the then-fashionable razor-edge style, combining all the formality required of a limousine but with lightness in appearance.

The company moved from its Kilburn premises to a new building in Edgware Road, NW9, in 1934 and the old building was taken over by CORINTHIAN. Mayfair virtually gave up car coachbuilding in 1939; after World War 2 it was involved almost entirely in commercial bodybuilding, although it was persuaded to body two HRGs in the early post-war period. By 1959 the business was only servicing and repairs. It ceased trading in the seventies.

MAYS R Mays of Queens Park, West London, bodied three Bentley chassis during the twenties.

MAYTHORN Maythorn & Son Ltd, of Biggleswade, Bedfordshire, was founded as a carriage-builder in 1842, moving into car coachbuilding in the early part of the twentieth century. For a provincial firm it had an impressive customer list, including the Prince of Wales and the Nizam of Hyderabad. It exhibited at every Olympia from 1919 to 1931 – and that includes 1923 when it had a major fire and had to rebuild the works from the ground up. By then (1918) Fred Maythorn had retired and one Jimmy George had taken over as managing director.

The main association was with the Daimler company, on whose chassis Maythorn built bodies from 1920 to 1931, while links with Fiat and Minerva were of an almost equal duration. Some of the other chassis bodied during the twenties were Rolls-Royce, Bentley, Packard, Crossley, Buick, Voisin, Delaunay-Belville and Armstrong-Siddeley. During this period Maythorn came under common ownership with the HOOPER company, although the two companies traded entirely separately.

The last Maythorn product to gain publicity was a streamlined Daimler Double-Six for Laurence Pomeroy,

MAYTHORN: 1927 Daimler 20/70 limousine. Not an advanced design for its date.

the Daimler managing director, in 1931. The company went bankrupt later the same year.

McEVOY Michael McEvoy was responsible for a number of interesting cars on Wolseley Hornet and Morris Minor chassis but was not a coachbuilder, bodies being built for him by JENSEN.

McMULLEN McMullen & Co of Hertford built an open four-seater body on a 3-litre Bentley chassis in 1925.

Belgravia Bodies

OLYMPIA SHOW
STAND 132

London
Improved
Motor Coachbuilders
Limited

149 Lupus Street
S.W.1

Telephone 3543 Victoria

A 1919 Talbot 25-50 all-weather by London Improved, in a contemporary colour advertisement.

This 1934 Lagonda M45 drophead coupé by Lancefield has a pronounced falling waistline. A 1930 coachbuilder's plate (below right) shows that the relationship with Brainsby Woollard was a close one.

1936 Armstrong-Siddeley 17hp lwb Redfern tourer by Maltby.

1934 Riley Nine Monaco saloon from Riley's in-house coachbuilder Midland Motor Bodies.

Wolseley Hornet Special with 'Trinity' three-in-one body by Meredith c.1932.

A 1939 Alvis 12/70 drophead coupé by Mulliners (Birmingham), with the then-fashionable two-tone paint scheme.

MELHUISH John Melhuish & Co was located in London's Camden Town area and was a faithful exhibitor at all the post-World War 1 Olympia Shows up to and including 1929. Specialities were Delage and Hotchkiss chassis and Melhuish bodied these and others (Beardmore, Talbot, Bianchi, Humber and many more) with restrained designs of limousines, landaulets and coupés. Nothing more is known of the Melhuish company after it ceased exhibiting.

MEREDITH Meredith Coachcraft Ltd of Birmingham was started in the early thirties by F W Mead and the two Smith brothers, Fred and Stan. Its sole product was an ingenious design of body known as the Trinity because it was three in one: open four- or two-seater with disappearing head, or closed four-seater. This was achieved by combining drop-down windows with cutaway doors, and also arranging for the rear squab to lift up to form the two-seater.

Meredith applied this design to 17 Rileys, nine Wolseley Hornets and five BSAs. The business closed down in 1934 and the rights to the Trinity body passed to the BROMFORD concern.

MIDLAND LIGHT BODIES This Coventry firm is known to have existed in the city between 1921 and 1936 but there is very little evidence of its activities. Probably for most of that time it was acting as a sub-contractor, supplying parts and assemblies to other coachbuilders. The firm is also known to have been a body repairer and to have built bodies for commercial vehicles, but it undoubtedly built complete bodies at one point, in 1933-34. For that season at least it was supplying under its own name sports saloons on the Rover 10 and Pilot chassis, and six-light saloons on the Speed Meteor chassis. Both these designs were in the Rover catalogue, and therefore sold through that company's dealers.

MIDLAND MOTOR BODIES The origins of this Coventry firm are obscure, although not its main function in life, which was to supply bodies for Riley cars. In this capacity it became a Riley subsidiary, but just when is unclear. Certainly Riley's requirement for such a source of supply can be dated to the time – January 1923 – when Morris bought HOLLICK & PRATT, which had been Riley's supplier. Midland Motor Bodies had certainly been in existence previously, as the firm supplied bodies to Alvis in the early twenties; it had also bodied Calthorpe, Charron-Laycock, Cluley and Morris chassis. Even afterwards it was not exclusively Riley to begin with, since – for example – it bodied the Westwood two-seater which appeared at the 1924 Olympia Show.

Legally there seem to have been two such companies. The first had existed, before a name change after World War 1, as the Riley Motor Manufacturing Co Ltd, having

MORGAN: Crossley tourer of c.1920 showing the 'Zephyr' all-metal construction.

been formed in 1912; this company was subsumed into Riley (Coventry) in 1931. Then in 1932 a second Midland Motor Bodies Ltd was formed, with two Rileys as directors but apparently independent of the main company. No doubt there were compelling reasons at the time for this complicated manoeuvre.

The only known example of a non-Riley body escaping from MMB thereafter is a single Frazer Nash-BMW.

MILLS W Mills & Sons Ltd, Cheltenham – see WILLIAMS & BAYLISS.

MOORE The unlikely-sounding Moore's Presto Motor Works of Croydon produced a fabric-bodied version of the Morris Oxford in 1928.

MORGAN Morgan & Co of Leighton Buzzard, Bedfordshire, was one of the old names in carriage-building, going back to 1795 when it was located in London's Long Acre, the trade's traditional home. Then in 1886 it bought the business of Mr William King in Leighton Buzzard; quite why this should have become Morgan's home is unknown. After producing Vickers Vimy aircraft during World War 1, Morgan was at the 1919 and 1920 Olympia Shows, exhibiting its work on a range of British chassis. During these two years, Morgan used a unique, patented all-metal system of body construction named 'Zephyr'; it consisted of a framework of high-tensile tubing with steel tie-rods, which was then panelled in aluminium. It appears to have been developed by James, Talbot & Davidson Ltd of Lowestoft for their planned Zephyr car, which never went beyond the prototype stage. The initial customers for such bodies were Crossley, followed the next year by Alvis with the new 10/30.

There then seems to have been a financial crisis. Morgan was bought by R E Jones Ltd of Swansea, which amongst other things was an Alvis distributor, and did not appear at Olympia in 1921. It reappeared the following year, however, showing work on three imported makes – Renault, Hudson and Studebaker. Thereafter, apart from maintaining the Renault connection, the firm reverted to using a range of British chassis, with Bean being especially prominent. Morgan also produced a catalogued body for Vauxhall, the 1926 Melton two-seater roadster.

Morgan ceased exhibiting at Olympia Shows after 1928. It was then associated with an address in Westminster which had been used by the LONDON IMPROVED company, but which by that time was occupied by the newly formed WESTMINSTER CARRIAGE. Whether Morgan was bought by either of these two firms is a matter of speculation.

MORGAN HASTINGS
This firm is known to have built a fabric body on a 1929 T-type Lea-Francis 14/40.

MORRIS RUSSELL
Based in the Shoreditch area of East London, this firm exhibited at Olympia in 1919 and 1920, showing work on a range of chassis – Brazier, Crossley, Hampton and Ruston-Hornsby. Nothing else is known.

MOSS
Sydney Moss, of London's Fulham Road, produced clover-leaf tourer bodies for Aston Martin in 1923 – 'the nearest Aston Martin came to a standard body'.

MOTOR BODIES
The Motor Bodies & Engineering Co Ltd operated in the Holloway area of North London. Other than a similarly-named company bodying a Lea-Francis C-type in 1923, little is known of Motor Bodies before it emerged, complete with Silent Travel licence, at Olympia in 1933. There it showed sports saloon and drophead coupé bodies on Chrysler, Daimler and Terraplane chassis; the Chrysler, and an Essex drophead, were being offered as standard bodies at about this time. The next year it showed two Hudsons – a sports saloon and a limousine – and also a coupé de ville on, of all things, a Vauxhall 27hp chassis. Known as the St James, this was an ALLINGHAM design, and not one of his most successful. In fact it was downright ugly, with a huge trunk grafted on to what

MOTOR BODIES: 1934 Railton 'Berkeley' saloon in pre-restoration state.

looked like a conventional D-back limousine.

Motor Bodies is known to have produced a saloon during 1934 on a Railton chassis, since it appeared on the company's Olympia stand that year. It even had a name – 'Berkeley' – suggesting either that Railton had designed it or that Motor Bodies was putting it forward for series production. Late in 1934, however, the Berkeley was given instead to CARBODIES to produce, which could mean simply that the Carbodies price was better, or possibly that Motor Bodies was starting to get into financial trouble. The 1934 Show cars, and the sports four/five-seater on the Vauxhall Big 6, presumably remained in production into 1935, but Motor Bodies was not at the 1935 Show and nothing more was heard of the firm.

MOTOR BODIES (NEWCASTLE)
This firm was sometimes known by the name of its works, Batley Coachworks. It is only known to have bodied a Sunbeam 16hp drophead coupé in 1930 and a 12/60 Alvis tourer in 1931. The firm then appears to have concentrated on commercial bodybuilding and repair work; it was still in existence in 1965.

MOTOR CAR INDUSTRIES
Based in Kilburn, West London, this firm is believed to have started in 1920 as a partnership between a Mr Biddle and a Mr Halsall, aiming at sales to the trade (for example in early-1921 it was advertising landaulet bodies for Fords in a trade journal). It started exhibiting at the annual Olympia Show in 1921, and appeared to specialise in American imports such as Buick, Chevrolet and Hupmobile, and also the French Le Zebre. The frequency with which Buick and Chevrolet, in particular, were present on the stand suggests that there was a contract with the importer.

By 1925 there was some sort of split between the partners, with one of them going off to start up CARLTON CARRIAGE. The other remained with Motor Car Industries, but renamed it the Progressive Motor Coach & Body Co and exhibited under that name in 1927-28 (after which, to everyone's relief, the name was changed once again, to MAYFAIR CARRIAGE).

ARTHUR MULLINER: 1937 Autovia sports saloon (above), the upmarket V8 from Riley. 1936 Rolls-Royce 25/30 sportsman's coupé (right); note sharply-falling waistline. 1927 Daimler 25/85 cabriolet de ville (below), an early version of the 'three-position' body.

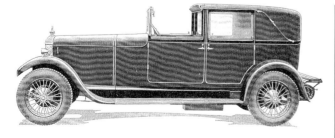

MULLINER, ARTHUR

The different Mulliner firms have histories so intertwined that they are difficult to separate. Nevertheless Arthur Mulliner of Northampton must be regarded as the senior firm, since it was in Northampton that the first F Mulliner set up his carriage-making business in 1760, secured by a contract with the Royal Mail for building and maintaining mail coaches. His son, Arthur H, took over the firm on his father's death.

By this time another branch of the family, with Liverpool connections, had opened a London showroom in Mayfair's Brook Street, run by a nephew of Arthur's. In about 1882 Arthur and the nephew formed a company called Mulliner (London) Ltd to run the showroom jointly; this showroom appears eventually to have gone to H J MULLINER. Meanwhile, the Northampton business passed to the care of Arthur H's son, Arthur Felton Mulliner, born 1859. It was Arthur Felton who moved the company into the construction of motor car bodies. By 1899 it had built 150 bodies, mostly on Daimler chassis, and by 1907 had ceased the manufacture of carriages altogether.

In that same year, 1907, Arthur Mulliner embarked on a two-fold expansion programme. Firstly, it massively enlarged its Northampton works, doubling the frontage and adding two new floors, while the workforce increased from 220 to 350. Secondly, and at literally the same time, it opened a new works and office in London's

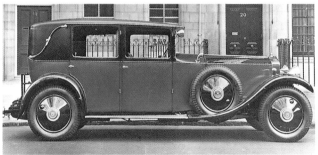

Long Acre, starting it up with 50 men transferred from Northampton (a number which soon increased to 150). The breathtaking self-confidence implied by these moves, which were apparently accomplished with total success, speaks volumes about both the rate of growth in the industry and the quality of Arthur Mulliner's management.

After World War 1, when the company was engaged on manufacturing both military vehicles and shell-cases, Arthur Mulliner resumed exhibiting at Olympia (although not until the second post-war Show, in 1920). There it showed examples of work on Armstrong-Siddeley and Vauxhall chassis. Both these manufacturers were using Arthur Mulliner as a producer of 'standard' coachwork, and later on Rolls-Royce and Daimler would do likewise. With accolades such as these one does not need to ask about quality: Arthur Mulliner won the first ever IBCAM prize at Olympia in 1926 for a Rolls-Royce 40-50 limousine, and repeated the feat the next year with a Daimler 50hp limousine. Yet despite the glamour and ornamentation associated with Arthur Mulliner coachwork – particularly where certain customers such as Indian princes were concerned – the external lines were some of the best in the business, always clean and uncluttered.

During the thirties even a firm like Arthur Mulliner had to fight for orders. Naturally there were still plenty of Rolls-Royce, Daimler and Bentley orders, but fewer than before, and the Armstrong-Siddeley contract had finished in 1927. The company therefore turned to the more moderately priced manufacturers, starting with Lanchester, for which it produced sports saloons, tourers and limousines. Next was Rover: limousine and landaulet bodies by Arthur Mulliner appeared in the Rover catalogue for 1933-34, available on the Meteor chassis only.

Although this extra business must have been welcome, it could not last forever in an environment where any special coachwork was expensive compared with the factory-produced all-steel version. In 1939 Arthur Mulliner sold out to Henlys, the car distributor, which immediately closed down the coachbuilding side; the company itself closed in 1976.

MULLINER, HJ

The Mulliner dynasty can be confusing, but the H J Mulliner who founded this company in 1900 was only a distant relation

H. J. MULLINER: 1952 Bentley Continental two-door sports saloon (above) – an all-time classic design. 1959 Bentley S2 Continental sports saloon (right). Could the rear roof-line be criticised for slight weakness?

of the original Northampton family. Importantly, he should not be confused with the H J who at one time started a Mulliner company in Liverpool – that was in 1854. Nevertheless, this H J did have a closer connection with the main family, as he worked with Mulliner (London) Ltd for four years before setting up on his own.

The fact that H J Mulliner's first address was in Brook Street, in Mayfair, London, suggests that he bought out the existing showroom of Mulliner (London). H J must have attracted work quickly; certainly he caught the attention of C S Rolls, building him for his personal use a two-seater roadster on an early Silver Ghost chassis. The coachworks moved from central London to Chiswick, West London in 1906. At the time just preceding World War 1 H J's business had reached such a size that he was able to sell out to John CROALL of Edinburgh and retire.

After World War 1 Croall maintained continuity by employing Frank Piesse, H J's brother-in-law, to manage the firm; he proved outstandingly successful. Within ten years, H J Mulliner came to be regarded as the best of the 'new' firms and was being spoken of in the same breath as the finest traditional firms such as Hooper and Barker. There was no one secret to the company's achievement; it seems simply to have got everything right – elegant designs, exciting technical innovations, and above all

superb quality and craftsmanship.

Naturally it took a certain amount of time for H J Mulliner to reach this exalted position. Although it exhibited continuously at the Olympia Shows from 1919 onwards, it was not until 1923 that it started to show work on Bentley chassis, and much later – 1928 – before a Rolls-Royce chassis graced the stand; thereafter there would always be at least one Rolls-Royce. The Bentley connection, in particular, became a strong one: during the twenties HJM bodied over 240 such chassis. The firm was probably the finest practitioner of the Weymann system – few others could make a fabric body look so 'right' – and when it moved on to the semi-panelled Weymann variant it again showed everyone else how the job should be done. One of the firm's finest designs of all was a streamlined Bentley drophead coupé, shown at the 1934 Olympia; with its full-width body, concealed hood, parabolic front wings and rear-wheel spats it was literally years ahead of its time.

For the remainder of the thirties H J Mulliner bodied little other than Rolls-Royce and Bentley, with the occasional Daimler, Siddeley Special, Humber and Lagonda. It was one of the few coachbuilders to restart car coachwork after World War 2, and unsurprisingly confined itself for the rest of its days to Rolls-Royce and Bentley

chassis. Throughout the forties and fifties HJM once again produced superb designs – limousines, sedancas, saloons and convertibles – of the highest quality, but in ever decreasing numbers. It gradually moved away from traditional wood-frame coachbuilding techniques, instead using a 'stressed skin' method not unlike PARK WARD's all-steel system. The company's eventual purchase in 1959 by Rolls-Royce was probably no more than an attempt to retain the necessary skills in a declining industry. Two years later H J Mulliner was merged with PARK WARD, which Rolls-Royce already owned, and moved to Park Ward's premises in Willesden to form Mulliner Park Ward. The combined company moved again to nearby Harlesden in 1982, but finally closed down in 1991.

MULLINERS (BIRMINGHAM)

Of all the three Mulliner companies involved in car coachwork, Mulliners Ltd of Birmingham has the least recorded history. Its original members are known to be descended from the same founding family in Northampton, but the firm next appears in 1896, making bodies for the Daimler company. It soon moved from carriage-making to being fully employed on car coachwork. One of its major customers was Calthorpe, now nearly forgotten but at that time a significant producer of light cars. Eventually, in 1913, Calthorpe decided that it needed its own bodymaking facility, and there began a close connection – physical and financial – between the two companies; for the next eleven years (except, presumably, for war work) Mulliners made nothing but Calthorpe bodies.

In the years immediately after World War 1 conditions in the economy in general, and in the motor industry in particular, were chaotic: boom, inflation, slump, and all the time new firms springing up to compete in car manufacturing. As a result many of the older-established firms got into difficulties, Calthorpe among them. In 1924 the Calthorpe company called in the receivers; the car business itself was bought by Colmore Depot, the Birmingham car dealers, but the Mulliner company was treated separately. The then managing director, Louis Antweiler, who was also a Calthorpe director, organised what we would term today a management buy-out, forming a new company – Mulliners Ltd – to buy the assets.

MULLINERS (BIRMINGHAM): 1935 Lanchester Ten sports saloon (above left); coachbuilt bodies at near mass-production quantities. 1948 Alvis TA14 saloon (above), the company's first post-war contract.

Antweiler seems to have had good connections; clearly raising the capital to buy the company was not a problem for him. Equally, he appears to have decided to exploit his connections in order to generate work for his new company. In other words, his policy from the outset was to supply contract bodies to chassis manufacturers rather than to enter the bespoke end of the trade. The opportunities for a coachbuilding firm which could build cheaply and in substantial volume were considerable: it could supply either small to medium manufacturers who had no bodymaking facilities of their own, or else major manufacturers who wanted to sub-contract their lower-volume body styles.

Antweiler's first such order was from Clyno, the Wolverhampton company, for a range of saloon, tourer and two-seater sports bodies. Soon after there began what was to be a long connection with the Austin company which started with the production of open two-seaters, but soon moved on to fabric saloons. Mulliners was an early adherent of the Weymann system for its fabric bodies, but before long the name Weymann disappeared when such bodies were mentioned, and Mulliners is believed to have developed its own rival system. Later, when the 'semi-Weymann' system of mixed fabric and steel panels was introduced, Mulliners became a major user – almost certainly the largest single user in the country. It was the Seven, however, with which Mulliners' name will always be associated where Austin is concerned. From 1927 the company produced numerous varieties of saloons, sunshine saloons, coupés and open sports bodies on the Seven chassis, mostly fabric-covered in their construction.

Mulliners decided in 1926 to start exhibiting at the annual Olympia Shows, and the contents of its stand reflect the work the company was engaged on at the time. For the first five years (with a strange gap in 1928) there was nothing but Austins; Sevens predominated, but 12 and 16hp models were also there. Thereafter, from 1931 onwards, Hillman, Humber, Lanchester and Daimler were the only makes represented, with the exception of a

NEW AVON: 1930 Standard
Special two-seater – Jensen
influence in the design.

sole Standard 20 in 1932. In 1929 the company decided to go public, but whether this was to finance a planned expansion or because of financial constraints (hence the absence from Olympia in 1928?) we cannot tell.

The change from Austin contracts to ones with Rootes and Daimler/Lanchester could well be to do with fabric bodies going out of fashion. Once the bulk of demand was for conventional steel-panelled bodies, Austin was in a much better position to handle body-building either in-house or via the PRESSED STEEL COMPANY, and any remaining crumbs went to the company's traditional supplier Gordon. In fact the first Rootes contract, which seems to have been for Hillman Minx and Humber Snipe special saloons and Minx tourers, only lasted a year; the Minx work went to Carbodies after that.

Mulliners did occasional work for Rootes later in the thirties, on Humber and the larger Hillman chassis, but from 1932 until World War 2 its main association was with the Daimler-Lanchester combine, for which Mulliners became in effect in-house coachbuilder for the cheaper end of the range (interestingly it was namesake, Arthur Mulliner, which provided standard bodies for some of the more expensive Daimlers). These two marques represented the ideal type of customer for Mulliners, requiring coachbuilt bodies in volumes which were substantial but not sufficient to justify the manufacturer setting up a dedicated department.

In the period 1937-39 Mulliners added Alvis to its customer list, producing saloons, drophead coupés and tourers on the 12/70 chassis. Then came the war, during which the company produced military vehicles, aircraft fuselages and gliders. Afterwards, the first body contract was again for Alvis – the TA14, which was based on the pre-war 12/70. There followed work for both small and large manufacturers – Standard (8 and 12 drophead coupés, Vanguard estate), Aston Martin (DB2 and DB2/4), Armstrong-Siddeley Lancaster, Daimler Consort, Triumph Renown, and so on. Sub-contract panelwork

was a problem, which Mulliners eventually solved by taking over one of its contractors, Forward Radiator. This in turn made the company an attractive proposition for Standard-Triumph, which was concerned about the body supply situation and decided to buy Mulliners. This it did in 1958, and from about 1962 Mulliners ceased to exist as a separate entity.

MULLION This London, West End, firm of carriage-makers only just survived into the automobile era but it is known to have bodied one Rolls-Royce 20hp coupé.

NEW AVON The Avon company of Warwick started in 1919 and after some changes of ownership and financial reconstruction became the New Avon Body Co Ltd in 1922. For its first eight years it built primarily for Lea-Francis, and also for the Hampton marque. Then in 1927 it joined the ranks of firms offering special bodies on the Austin Seven chassis. It started with an open two-seater, then a year later moved on to a fixed-head coupé which it named the 'Swan', and then in 1929 brought out a so-called sportsman's two-seater.

The Swan was a JENSEN design and was the second result of New Avon's relationship with the Jensen brothers. The connection had started when the brothers brought to Avon a prototype, commissioned by Standard on a Nine chassis, which they wanted Avon to put into production. There is no doubt that the Jensen flair brought something to Avon which had been lacking, and as a result Avon's special coachwork on Austin Seven and Standard chassis transformed the company. By this time the Lea-Francis business had disappeared with the failure of that company (Avon was paid the balance of its account in finished cars!).

The Standard connection, in particular, was probably the company's salvation; for eight years Avon's output was dominated by special bodies on Standard chassis – 'Swan' fixed-head coupés, 'Wayfarer' pillarless saloons,

NEW AVON: 1934 Standard 16hp two-door saloon (above); drawing by C F Beauvais, the designer. 1934 Standard Ten sports (left), another Beauvais design. 1936 Standard Light Twenty pillarless four-door saloon (below).

and drophead coupés. Soon after, Avon moved on to the Wolseley Hornet, exhibiting a fixed-head coupé at the 1930 Scottish Motor Show which was also probably a Jensen design. At an early stage the Jensen influence dropped out, but the company seems to have had a talented replacement in C F Beauvais, its designer during the early thirties. He made his mark with his first design, a striking sports four-seater on the Standard Little Twelve chassis with parabolic wings and a two-tone colour scheme. The one problem he could not solve was to make his designs look as low as the rival SS cars from SWAL-LOW, which was supplied with a special lowered chassis while he had to make do with the normal one.

Apart from Austin, Standard and Wolseley, Avon built a fixed-head coupé on a Lanchester chassis, exhibited at Olympia in 1933 and 1934. The Standard business dried up overnight, however, when in 1937 Avon was unable to pay the monthly bill for chassis. Standard cut off supplies and foreclosed, New Avon went bankrupt, and a new company named Avon Bodies took over the business. The new company's first job was to adapt the stock of Standard bodies to fit the Triumph Dolomite

chassis. By this time Beauvais had left the company and had been replaced by Arthur Meredith, previously foreman of the experimental bodyshop. Meredith was responsible for the 'Waymaker' saloon, which was supplied to the revived Lea-Francis company.

During the later thirties Avon also entered the commercial bodybuilding field. In World War 2 it was engaged on aircraft refurbishment and after the war tried to resume car work, and bodied some Hillman Minx drophead coupés. No similar contracts came up, however, and thereafter the company concentrated on body

NEWNS: 1929 Wolseley 21/60 straight-eight drophead coupé (top). Who would have thought that the streamlining craze was only three years away? Railton coupé de ville (above), thought to be the 1935 Olympia Show car.

repair work together with some hearse manufacture. And there the Avon story might have ended, but it did not. Having become part of Ladbroke Bodies in 1973, and renamed Ladbroke Avon, the company returned to coachbuilding in 1980 in the form of specialist conversion work, offering a Jaguar XJS convertible, to which a Jaguar XJ6 estate car was added two years later. The business (but not the Avon name) was eventually sold in 1985.

NEWDIGATE The Newdigate Motor Body Co of Nuneaton, Warwickshire, built a two-door sporting coupé body on a Riley Nine chassis in 1930.

NEWNS E J Newns is known to have been in existence in the Surbiton area of Surrey since 1924, and probably earlier – originally at Long Ditton, and then from 1926 at Thames Ditton. It bodied ACs during the twenties, and was bodying fabric saloons of unknown make, probably under sub-contract, in 1928. However, its best-known days were in the three years 1934-36, when it exhibited its wares at Olympia each year – often using the brand-name 'Eagle'. During that period the firm seems to have been working primarily for British Salmson, producing drophead coupé, four-door saloon and two-seater sports versions. In 1934 it also bodied some 11 Lagonda Rapiers, in both pillarless and two-seater sports designs (the latter sold through dealers Warwick Wright) as well as a Brooklands racing-car.

In 1935 an association with Railton began. Newns is best known for having provided the two Light Sports Tourers, fastest of all the Railtons, with their ultra-light aluminium bodies; it was probably one of these two which was on Newn's stand at Olympia that year. Inter-

estingly, they were designed by Frank Feeley in a short break from his employment with Lagonda while that company went through a receivership. In addition, though, Newns produced at least one each of a coupé de ville and a three-position drophead coupé, their last Railton effort being a drophead with disappearing hood in 1939. Nothing more is known about the firm.

NEWSUM Newsum, Sons & Co was a firm of timber specialists rather than coachbuilders. It nevertheless entered the market in 1934 by demonstrating a Morris Six prototype, the body frame of which was made from bent-wood components instead of the usual jointed straight pieces. The process involved steaming the ash members and then bending them round jigs; it was claimed that body weight could be reduced by one third. Nothing more was heard of the system.

NICHOLLS Nicholls & Sons of Bedford was founded in the 1860s by William Henry Nicholls as a carriage-builder, and moved into car coachbuilding during the 1900s. In 1910 William Henry died and his son, also William, took over. The firm expanded throughout the twenties, but the coachbuilding side apparently did not, and although it is known to have bodied Buick, Essex and Armstrong-Siddeley chassis during this period, coachbuilding ceased around 1928. The firm continued as a dealer and repairer until 1961, and then sold out to the Dutton-Forshaw group; a member of the Nicholls family was still on the board at that date.

NORTH OF ENGLAND The North of England Motor Trading Co of Newcastle upon Tyne built a doctor's coupé on a Daimler TT420 chassis in 1922. The firm appears not to have survived beyond the twenties.

NUTTING, J GURNEY Unusually amongst the ranks of coachbuilders, where so many had long experience in the industry, J Gurney Nutting was a novice when he decided to compete in 1919; his firm, incredibly, were builders and joiners. Nevertheless he found premises in Croydon, South London, and began to build car bodies. His success was breathtaking. Although he had a setback when his Croydon works burnt down in 1924, he turned even that to advantage by moving into the fashionable Chelsea area of London. At that same time, too, he was fortunate enough to recruit the great A F McNeil as his designer. Why McNeil should have wanted to join such an upstart firm is a mystery, but we can make a guess: CUNARD, where McNeil was formerly employed as chief designer, was going through a bad patch under its struggling owners, the Napier car company, and perhaps Nutting's position was the only one on offer at the time.

From the outset the Gurney Nutting firm concentrated on coachwork with a sporting flavour, and it was

GURNEY NUTTING: (from the top) 1933 Bentley Owen sedanca coupé commissioned by London dealers H. R. Owen. 1934 Lagonda Rapide saloon displays a skilful combination of falling waistline and high boot. Bentley pillarless two-door saloon of c.1935 with unusual rear-quarter treatment. 1947 Bentley Mk 6 sedanca coupé; a similar model, shown at Earls Court that year, was the firm's last-ever Motor Show exhibit.

particularly associated with the Bentley marque. It had built its first Bentley body even before the move to London; thereafter Gurney Nutting became, after Vanden Plas, the Cricklewood firm's next biggest supplier of bodies, reaching a total of 360 by 1931 (plus no less than 13 chassis lost in the 1924 fire!). Its growing reputation ensured that it was increasingly asked to body the more expensive chassis – Daimlers from 1921, Rolls-Royce from 1925, and so on. McNeil's designs soon attracted the attention of London's smart set, and Gurney Nutting was able to claim both the Prince of Wales and the Duke

of York as clients; needless to say, the Royal Warrant followed in the early thirties.

In 1930 the firm moved to nearby Lacland Place, to premises formerly occupied by ELKINGTON CARRIAGE. The next year it was given the prestigious contract for bodying Sir Malcolm Campbells 'Bluebird' land speed record car, and soon afterwards the Bentley connection was resumed when the new 3½-litre model started rolling out of Rolls-Royce's Derby factory. From then until the end of the thirties Gurney Nutting produced some mouth-watering designs on Bentley chassis, the most famous of all being their series of 'Owen sedanca coupés' made for the London Bentley and Rolls-Royce dealer H R Owen; this style was subsequently claimed to be the model of what we would now call a three-position drop-head coupé. Needless to say, many other quality marques received the Gurney Nutting treatment during this period – among them Alvis, Armstrong-Siddeley, Daimler, Delage, Lagonda and Talbot.

In 1939 all coachbuilding ceased and McNeil moved to the De Havilland aircraft company; when he returned to coachbuilding in 1945 it was not to Gurney Nutting but to rivals JAMES YOUNG, part of Jack Barclay Ltd the Rolls-Royce dealer. This apparently surprising move was made more explicable when it was announced that Jack Barclay was also to take over Gurney Nutting, as a result of J Gurney Nutting being seriously ill; he died early in 1946. Thus McNeil found himself in effect designer to both companies. During the next two years there was an understandable rationalisation of facilities amongst the various Jack Barclay companies. Both Gurney Nutting and the Jack Barclay service department moved out to Merton in South-West London – into the former RANALAH premises – and all timber-machining was concentrated at the Bromley works of James Young. Gurney Nutting exhibited at the first post-war Motor Show, showing a Mk VI Bentley with, inevitably, a sedanca coupé body. From then on, however, the writing was on the wall for this famous firm: the Jack Barclay group found that post-war sales were insufficient to support two coachbuilding operations, and work under the Gurney Nutting name was gradually run down. When the Barclay service department moved back into Central London in 1954, Gurney Nutting coachbuilding had ceased.

OFFORD

Offord & Sons had a history going back to 1791 and was the holder of Royal Warrants for carriage-building. It was involved with car coachwork from as early as 1895, when it exhibited at the Horseless Carriage Exhibition at Crystal Palace. Throughout this time, and right until the firm's end, it was managed by members of the Offord family; it also had responsibility for maintaining the carriages in the Royal Mews.

In the early twenties Offord seems to have made a speciality of its 'featherweight' all-weather bodies, which it even began to make on a batch basis for fitting to Ford and Chevrolet chassis. Through the remainder of the

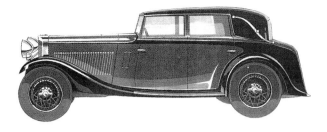

OFFORD: 1933 Talbot 'Antibes' convertible four-door saloon (above), an unusual style which only a year or two earlier might have been described as an all-weather. 1937 Bentley 4¼-litre (above right), another four-door convertible design.

OLIVER: 1925 Rolls-Royce 20hp saloon; a typical, safe design from a provincial coachbuilder.

decade, even though Offord was offering more of a bespoke body service, the American connection remained, judging by their exhibits at Olympia – where it was present for every one of the inter-war years. As well as bodying Buick, Packard and Chrysler, the firm was one of the first to use the exciting Stutz chassis.

A pronounced change of policy came in 1930. Instead of being a general bespoke house, albeit of high quality, Offord now sought to produce standard designs on the better sort of chassis, preferably to be included in the manufacturer's catalogue. The first such connection, and the longest-running, was with Talbot, whose products appeared on Offord's Olympia stand every year from 1930 to 1937 (1938 if Sunbeam-Talbot is included). On this firm's chassis Offord made drophead coupé, continental tourer and sports two-seater bodies with attractive lines.

The next tie-up was with Vauxhall, when for the 1933-34 season Offord made the Vitesse two/four-seater sports tourer. Although not in the catalogue as such it was a standard model which could be ordered through dealers. The most interesting point is that it was designed not by Offord but by ALLINGHAM; in fact, at about this time some clues arise which call into question just how much coachbuilding capacity Offord had at all. It is known that CARLTON built many Offord bodies under sub-contract including at least one Talbot in 1930 (possibly the Motor Show two-seater), some Lagondas and numerous Alivises; by the late thirties only the most unusual bodies were coming out of Offord's own workshops.

Offord's final standard designs were its drophead coupés on the larger Alvis chassis. Starting with the Speed 25 in 1936, it moved on to the new 4.3 model and bodied some 16 examples. The Alvis 4.3 drophead is probably the best-looking design the firm ever produced, and a fitting end to a long history. Offord closed its car coachwork business in 1939, although retaining its workshop and its responsibilities at the Royal Mews.

OLIVER

Oliver of York is known to have bodied a Rolls-Royce 20hp in 1925.

OSBORNE, RW

R W Osborne & Son Ltd of Saffron Walden, Essex, was primarily a commercial coachbuilder, but is known to have bodied a Rolls-Royce 20/25 saloon in 1934. It was still in business in the sixties.

OSBORNE, WILLIAM

William Osborne & Co Ltd advertised as having addresses in both London's Long Acre and Littlehampton, Sussex. It exhibited at Olympia in 1920 and 1921, using Buick and Oldsmobile chassis.

PAGE & HUNT

This Farnham, Surrey firm was formed in 1920 by Arthur Page, a coachpainter and former partner in another coachbuilding business, and Oliver Hunt, who provided the finance. By 1922 the firm was already showing its work at Olympia, built on Bianchi, Packard and Talbot chassis.

By the time of the next show it had obtained a contract with the Buick importers Lendrum & Hartman, and then proceeded to exhibit each year until 1928, showing limousines, coupés and a racy-looking coupé-cabriolet.

Other makes which Page & Hunt bodied during these years included Bentley, Cadillac, Daimler, Delage, Fiat, Talbot and Wolseley. The firm expanded into motor engineering and dealing, and opened a second branch in Guildford. In about 1927 it took on the Armstrong-Siddeley agency for Surrey, and the products of that firm duly started to appear on the Page & Hunt Olympia stand.

Then disaster struck: in September 1929 the firm went into voluntary liquidation. Fortunately the firm's London sales manager was able to step in to save something – see ABBOTT.

PALMERS Palmers (Dover) Ltd was only really heard of in the thirties, when it exhibited just once – 1936 – at Olympia. The motive seems to have been to call attention to the CONNAUGHT continental touring saloons which it was now building on the big 25hp Vauxhall chassis – a contract which the company had just stolen from CARLTON and which it would retain until 1938. Palmers had certainly been in existence some three years before this.

The Connaught connection, however, draws attention to a 'Connaught Coach Works' which existed in Dover in 1926. If this were the same firm as Palmers, it would suggest that Connaught was using Palmers virtually as its in-house coachbuilder.

PARK ROYAL See HALL, LEWIS

PARK WARD William MacDonald Park and Charles W Ward had both been working at F W Berwick Ltd, the producer of Sizaire-Berwick cars, in Highgate, North London. Park was works superintendent there after having been works man-

ager at Brown, Hughes & Strachan. The two decided in 1919 to set up on their own as coachbuilders; they were well fitted by experience, and Park by training, having been apprenticed in the trade before employment at the Argyll car factory and then at Lacre, the London carriage-maker. Ward's training was as a mechanical engineer.

The new Park Ward firm started up in Willesden, North-West London, and seems to have done well from the start. Although there was no doubt the usual sub-contract work to begin with, by the following year – 1920 – it was already exhibiting its own coachwork at Olympia. As one might expect there was a large variety of chassis which the firm was asked to body in the first few years: Crossley, Delage, Fiat, Sunbeam and many others. Then in 1923 began what was to be a long association with Bentley which would continue even after that firm's failure and subsequent purchase by Rolls-Royce. Park Ward was one of the first coachbuilders to use the Bentley's length of bonnet to full effect, by extending the wings into a sweeping curve before they met the running boards, this feature being evident on a Park Ward Bentley saloon body as early as 1924.

The firm had already built its first Rolls-Royce body in 1920, and in 1922 was invited to participate in a scheme set up by Rolls-Royce to produce standardised body types for the 20hp model. The scheme came to nothing, but it was a remarkable vote of confidence in such a young firm. In 1924 there is the first record of Park Ward exhibiting a Rolls-Royce chassis, when it showed a 40-50 limousine at the British Empire Exhibition at Wembley. Now the picture of the future Park Ward is beginning to emerge: an already high reputation was growing rapidly, based on not only the highest-quality workmanship but also a flair for design and innovation. Increasingly the firm was able to concentrate on two makes of chassis – Rolls-Royce and Bentley – commissioned by customers who were drawn by this reputation. One of their early landmark designs was a 1929 6½-litre Bentley sports two/four-seater design, which used the concept of stream-

PARK WARD: 1921 Rolls-Royce 40-50 Silver Ghost salamanca (above), a very early product from this famous firm. 1931 Bentley 8-litre limousine (right), huge but well-proportioned. Rolls-Royce Phantom 2 Continental sports saloon (below) c.1932. Two-tone colour scheme is unusual but effective.

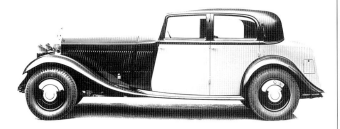

lining long before it became a fashion: its side elevation was a series of parabolas, with separate front and rear wings linked by 'float'-type running boards. Both hood and spare wheels were concealed in the tail, and the finished effect was sensational. Altogether Park Ward bodied more than 140 Bentley chassis during the twenties.

During this period Park Ward was producing about 150 bodies a year. Although this was a commendable output for a bespoke shop the trend was downward, and worryingly so. Of course Park Ward was not alone – very few coachbuilders were experiencing anything else – but it must have feared for its survival, especially in 1931 when it only made some 80 bodies. It must have been such considerations which persuaded the two partners in 1933 to accept an injection of capital from Rolls-Royce which bought the car-maker a minority stake in the business. Rolls-Royce's motives we can only guess at, but it was apparently concerned about the ability of other coachbuilders to adopt new methods and thus wanted its own facility to use as a 'test-bed'.

The results of this new cooperation were soon in evidence. The Bentley connection, in particular, proved most rewarding: Park Ward eventually bodied more Derby

PARK WARD: Rolls-Royce Phantom 3 sports limousine (left) c.1938. Another example of good design concealing the sheer size of the car. 1960 S2 Bentley Continental drophead coupé (below). A power hood was standard.

Bentleys than the next nine coachbuilders put together. A streamlined Bentley two-door saloon in early 1934 was claimed to have greatly reduced air-resistance as 'a result of actual tests on models', and a Rolls-Royce later the same year had been given full-size wind-tunnel tests. Meanwhile, the company was working on its 'all-steel' body, which was announced in 1936 but had been under test on the road for a year previously. If anything was going to justify Rolls-Royce's investment, this development was going to be it, and Park Ward gave it maximum publicity.

One corollary of the all-steel development was that a certain amount of jigging was involved, so it was necessary to start thinking of standardisation, with bodies being built in batches. This cut across Park Ward's instinct to innovate in matters of styling, which implied individual, bespoke designs. The effect was that produc-

tion of all-steel bodies lagged somewhat, while the company continued to produce much-admired new styles. These were not confined to Rolls-Royce and Bentley chassis; Daimlers were seen more frequently, and Lagondas also appeared. It is inconceivable that this downgrading of the all-steel system's importance could have happened without the agreement of Rolls-Royce, and it cannot be unconnected with what followed.

In 1939 Rolls-Royce bought out the remaining shares in Park Ward, and the company became a wholly-owned subsidiary. What could have been Rolls-Royce's strategy behind this move? Possibly it was no more than eventually emerged after World War 2, with the manufacturer producing a standard all-steel model while Park Ward concentrated on more expensive coachbuilt products. Yet this overlooks the matter of the Park Ward all-steel frame, on which both companies had spent considerable money

PATRICK: Wolseley Hornet fixed-head coupé at 1932 Olympia Show.

and publicity, and which was one of the major assets to come with the purchase; was it just to be thrown away? An alternative hypothesis is that Park Ward would retain its flexibility to produce bespoke designs, while the steel-frame system would be the basis of a standard Rolls-Royce body – but in the event the war, tilted the economics away from the steel frame and towards pressed-steel construction.

After the war Park Ward resumed its intended role as 'in-house' supplier of bespoke bodies for the Rolls-Royce and Bentley marques. It also continued with the all-steel frame, although by 1954, borrowing from aircraft techniques, it had changed to extruded alloy. There was absolutely no skimping on quality, but the number of buyers for such expensive products was reducing year by year. There was one interesting departure, presumably to try to keep the order-book full, when Park Ward undertook a contract to supply bodies for Alvis; this lasted until 1967. Rolls-Royce protected the supply of trained craftsmen through the purchase of H J MULLINER in 1959, but then bowed to the inevitable and merged it with Park Ward in 1961 to form Mulliner Park Ward, located in Park Ward's Willesden works. By this time the available chassis had been reduced to the Silver Cloud and Phantom Rolls-Royces and the Bentley Continental. Nevertheless in 1971, at the launch of the Corniche (built by MPW), Rolls-Royce announced that it would in future use special-bodied cars as 'styling leaders' for future production models. The first fruit of this policy was the Carmargue, but although this was built by MPW the gilt was taken off the gingerbread somewhat by the fact that it had been designed by Pininfarina. In 1982 MPW moved to new premises in nearby Harlesden, but in 1991 it was all over: Rolls-Royce decided to produce its own coachwork in future, and Mulliner Park Ward was therefore closed down.

PARSONS

John Parsons & Sons, believed to have been located in the Manchester area, built a fixed-head coupé on a Standard 15hp chassis in 1929.

PASS

Thomas Pass & Son of Coventry had a history going back to the 1850s. By 1919, however, it seems to have been in difficulties, as in that year its premises in West Orchard were taken over by the new CARBODIES firm. Nevertheless Pass remained in existence, and apparently moved to Little Park Street. What it did there is less clear; in all probability it was mainly engaged on sub-contract work, but it is known to have bodied a Morris Oxford in 1923. The firm appears to have gone out of business in about 1929.

PATRICK MOTORS

The Birmingham car distributor Patrick Motors made a first attempt to enter the coachbuilding trade in late 1930, when it formed a joint company with the JENSEN brothers, Patrick-Jensen Motors Ltd, with the stated object of supplying sporting coachwork for Wolseley Hornet chassis. However this venture broke up, apparently acrimoniously, and Patrick Motors decided to go it alone; who it then used as a designer is not known.

The company's first product was, unsurprisingly, on the Wolseley Hornet chassis, announced in the spring of 1931. Whether or not this was a Jensen design is impossible to say with any certainty, but it seems likely. The Hornet chassis was also used at the 1932 Olympia Show, in fixed-head coupé form, but also on show were two examples of the Triumph Southern Cross and a four-door tourer on the Rover Meteor chassis. This last exhibit became an 'approved' design in 1933, being included in Rover's 1933-34 catalogue.

Early the following year Patrick Motors announced a foursome coupé on the Austin 10-4 chassis, and a *Buyers' Guide* later that same year (1933) showed it as an official catalogued design. The same guide, however, made no mention of Patrick Motors amongst the nine different firms producing special bodies on the Wolseley Hornet chassis. Thus it would appear that the Austin coupé, or some Standards which it is known to have bodied, were Patrick's last offerings; it was not present at the 1933 or future Motor Shows, and we can only presume that it reverted to being a dealer.

PENMAN

A C Penman of Dumfries was founded in 1887 when Mr Penman bought the business of Edward Hotson. The company built its first car body in 1902 and exhibited at the Crystal Palace the same year. During World War 1 it built lorries.

Penman was the only Scottish coachbuilding firm to exhibit at Olympia between the wars, doing so continuously from 1919 to 1929. It most frequently showed its work on Armstrong-Siddeley, Wolseley, Austin and Lanchester chassis, and it is probable that Penman held agencies for all these makes. Other marques to appear were Arrol-Johnston, Swift, Daimler, Aster and Citroën. Penman also attended every Scottish Motor Show from 1921 to 1929.

PENMAN: 1923 Sunbeam 24/60 drophead coupé (left) shows unusually racy lines for the time. Wolseley fabric sunshine saloon c.1929 (below left).

PLAXTON: 1927 Crossley 14hp three-quarter coupé, from another firm which became better known for motor-coaches.

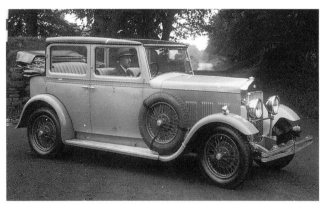

A C Penman died in 1926 at the age of 69. His son, J B Penman, succeeded him, and became President of IBCAM in 1928. After 1929 there is no news of any car coachbuilding activity by the firm, but it continued to prosper as both a motor agent and a commercial body-builder, and is still in existence today.

PETTY D & E Petty of Cheshunt was primarily a builder of bus bodies. However, for reasons unknown, in 1935 it offered a sports saloon body on the Vauxhall Big Six chassis. Production finished some time in 1936, which is the year the firm is believed to have gone out of business.

PHILLIPS R A S (Reginald) Phillips, of Edgware, Middlesex, was an unusual person to become a coachbuilder. From a well-to-do family, and possessing a degree from Cambridge University, he nevertheless decided that he wanted to start his own coachworks, which he did in 1929. The motoring journals were soon lauding both his design and his workmanship, which appeared on Bentley, Isotta-Fraschini and Rolls-Royce chassis, but sadly the perfectionism which produced this level of quality also ensured that he was working at a loss.

His business closed in 1931 after only some seven bodies had been produced.

Phillips had another short spell in the coachbuilding industry in 1934, when he worked for JONES BROS designing bodies for the Lanchester Ten.

PILMORE BEDFORD F Pilmore Bedford & Sons Ltd, of London, built a saloon body on a Bentley chassis in 1928.

PLAXTON F W Plaxton of Scarborough was founded in 1919 by Frederick William Plaxton. Although thought of these days as a builder of motor-coaches, the firm was involved in car coachbuilding during the twenties. It exhibited at three successive Olympia Shows, from 1925 to 1927, and since it showed nothing but Crossleys, we can assume that Plaxton had some sort of contractual arrangement with that firm. Plaxton did body other chassis, though, including Rolls-Royce and at least one Derby Bentley. It also took out a Weymann licence during the twenties. Plaxton is still in existence today, building motor-coaches. After being an independent public company it was very recently bought by the Henly group.

1930 Standard Big Nine
sportsman's two-seater by
New Avon.

1924 Bentley 3-litre tourer,
one of many bodied by Park
Ward.

Gurney Nutting's 1930
Bentley Speed Six coupé (the
'Blue Train' car). Good
proportions belie the car's
sheer size.

1937 Alvis Speed 25 SB
drophead coupé by Offord;
one of the classic designs of
the thirties.

1936 Railton two-door saloon
by Ranalah; another example
of the swage-line used to
separate two paint colours.

There's Nothing

now to hinder your ordering a
body for your new car (no
matter the make), that will
reflect credit on your choice
in any company.

THE REGENT CARRIAGE
Company bodies are built for
the discriminating, those who
require distinction without
freakishness, comfort without
complication, and sterling
quality at an honest price.

Send for particulars of the
latest Regent bodies.

THE REGENT
CARRIAGE Cₒ Lᵗᵈ
126-132 NEW KING'S ROAD
FULHAM, LONDON, S.W. 6.
Telegrams: "Carbodis London"
Telephone: Putney 2240-1.

1919 Fiat saloon by Regent, from a colour advertisement.

R.E.A.L: 1932 Hillman Minx two/four-seater sports coupé (right) – possibly the Motor Show car that year. 1934 Lagonda M45 four-door saloon (below), a well-proportioned design which manages to conceal this marque's normally high radiator. 1936 British Salmson 20/90 two-seater sports (below right).

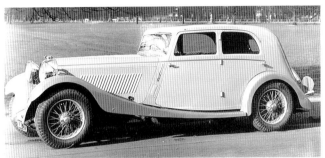

PRESSED STEEL

The Pressed Steel Company of Great Britain Ltd was set up at Cowley, near Oxford, as a joint venture between the Nuffield organisation and the Budd Company of America to produce the first all-steel bodies in Britain. It started production in 1927, working exclusively for Nuffield, but by 1930 the Nuffield interest had been sold, and the company announced that it had the freedom to supply any manufacturer.

Although such a company would seem to have little place in a directory of traditional coachbuilders, it qualifies by reason of having initially supplied 'composite' bodies as well as the all-steel welded variety. These it manufactured in a separate department away from the main production lines; the first, and probably only, user of this facility was the Rover company, whose Light Twenty appeared on the Pressed Steel stand at Olympia in 1930. Thereafter the only bodies shown by the company were of the all-steel type, the major customers being Hillman, Humber, Austin, Morris, Standard, Rover and Vauxhall.

PROGRESSIVE See MAYFAIR

PYTCHLEY

Pytchley Autocar was a Northampton firm, although presumably originating from the nearby village of Pytchley. At the end of World War 1 it was well established as a dealer and coachbuilder and it exhibited at Olympia continuously from 1920 to 1931, showing work on a varied selection of chassis as might be expected of a provincial coachbuilder.

The firm's one loyalty was to Standard – presumably it held an agency for the marque – and it was on a Standard four-door saloon in 1925 that Pytchley Autocar revealed the innovation that was going to transform the firm. This was its design of sliding roof, soon dubbed a 'sunshine roof'. The design appears to have been well thought out, with such features as rainwater guttering included from the beginning. The idea caught the imagination of the both the industry and the car-buying public and within two years the provision of a sunshine roof was commonplace. Most of these were supplied by Pytchley, who had the product well covered by patents.

Pytchley continued to develop the sunshine roof, and in 1929 announced a new model which lay flush with its surround. Meanwhile, in spite of the patents some competitors had appeared on the scene, particularly the Weathershields company. By this time Pytchley could see that there was a much rosier future in manufacturing sunshine roofs than in general coachbuilding, and therefore decided to build a factory on the new Slough Trading Estate devoted to roof manufacture; this opened in 1930. Pytchley continued to exhibit at Olympia until 1931, though more as a means of publicising the sunshine roof than to sell coachwork.

Eventually – apparently about 1934 – Pytchley sold its sunshine roof business to Weathershields. The Northampton end continued as a motor dealer, becoming a Ford agency under the Henry Oliver, and then Alexander, names. Meanwhile the Slough business continued in name until the 1960s, latterly being part of ML Holdings.

QUEENS & BRIGHTON

A Southport firm known only to have bodied a Bentley 3-litre four-seater in 1922.

R.E.A.L.

R.E.A.L. Carriage Works Ltd took its name from its principal, R E Alman. Originally situated in the Chiswick area of West London, where its main product was bus bodies, the company moved in

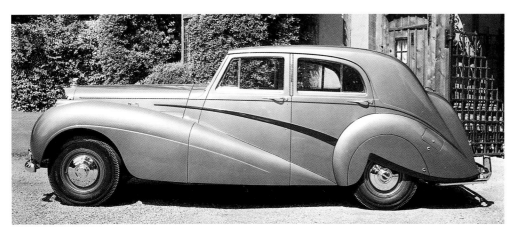

HAROLD RADFORD: 1951
Bentley Countryman (left) –
a special coachbuilt design.
Fitted equipment in 1954
Rolls-Royce Silver Dawn
Countryman (below), by now
a modified standard saloon.

1929 further west to Ealing. While continuing with commercial bodybuilding, it also began an intensive campaign to sell series-produced bodies to car manufacturers and major dealers, and achieved some success. First to sign up was Rover, which included in its 1933-34 catalogue a 'salonette' on the Speed Pilot chassis which had been an exhibit on R.E.A.L.'s stand at the 1932 Olympia Show, its first year there. Later in 1933 R.E.A.L. supplied Charles Follett with a continental tourer design on the Alvis Crested Eagle chassis, Pass & Joyce with a special fixed-head coupé on the Talbot 65 chassis, and the Hudson-Essex importer with a four-seater sports body; all three were exhibited at that year's Olympia.

The 1934 Show saw a continental coupé British Salmson and a two-seater, three-position drophead on the Singer Nine chassis, both being series-production models for the coming season. Also shown was a Railton sports tourer, marking the start of a two-year association with this up-and-coming marque. In 1935 R.E.A.L. formed three new alliances, with Chrysler (tourers), Hudson (tourers) and Vauxhall (roadster and tourer on the Light Six chassis). However, this seems to have marked the high-water mark of the company's achievements as far as cars were concerned for after 1935 it was no longer at Olympia and seems to have produced no more contract bodies after 1936. The last known pre-war car job carried out was in 1938, when R.E.A.L. took over from Bertelli the bodying of a Raymond Mays Special. The company survived after World War 2, having moved to Slough and continued with commercial bodybuilding, but its only known car work was on a 1947 HRG 1500. It was still in business in the sixties.

RADFORD, HAROLD The firm of Harold Radford (Coachbuilders) Ltd is probably unique in having started as a traditional coachbuilder after World War 2. Harold Radford himself had already had a colourful career as a West London motor dealer specialising in Rolls-Royce and Bentley, and then, in the war, as a supplier of highly modified vehicles to His Majesty's more secret forces. With this background it was perhaps understandable that his thoughts should turn to modifying Bentleys, and in 1948 he designed a form of

upmarket estate car on the Mark VI Bentley chassis. Having as yet no coachbuilding facilities of his own, he sub-contracted its building to a small firm called Seary & McReady. The design was an immediate success, winning that year's Cannes concours d'elegance, and led to the formation of the coachbuilding company bearing his name. Three years later he was exhibiting at the Earls Court Show.

The Countryman was originally a specially-constructed wooden body, but it soon changed to become a modified saloon. The rear opening was widened by fitting two lids, the back seat squab folded down electrically, and the backs of the front seats could also fold to form a bed. The car was lavishly equipped, with picnic tables, cocktail and refreshment cabinets, even electric kettle and razor. All the work was of course done to the highest standards, using ash-framing and aluminium panels, and was officially approved by Rolls-Royce. The concept was later extended to the Rolls-Royce Silver Dawn and Silver Cloud and the Bentley R-type, and also to a Mark VIII Jaguar, an Armstrong-Siddeley Sapphire and a Humber Super Snipe.

Radford also carried out other coachbuilding jobs, including constructing two drophead coupés on pre-war Railton chassis and a woody estate on a long-wheelbase Austin Sheerline; it also bodied at least one Jowett Jupiter. The company later became well known for luxurious

RANALAH: 1935 Railton 8-cylinder two-door saloon (above); the high bonnet line was a challenge to coachwork designers. Buick 30hp two-door drophead coupé (below) at the 1938 Earls Court Show.

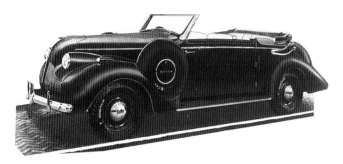

conversions of Minis. In the early-sixties Harold Radford sold his business to H R Owen, although the coachbuilding side was later sold on.

RAMELL
The Folkestone coachbuilding firm of Ramell & Son could trace its history back to 1853, when Frederick Ramell started the business. It is known to have bodied cars up to the early 1920s, but the firm closed in 1927.

RANALAH
It is too much to assume that Ranalah Ltd, of Merton in South-West London, could start up in the same year as JOHN CHARLES – who used the Ranalah brand-name – went out of business, without there being a connection between the two. Indeed Ranalah Coachworks Ltd was formed 'to take over the assets and continue the business of John Charles'. Just how much else was common between the two companies we can only guess at: the premises changed, but probably much of the equipment was relocated there, and presumably the key personnel were the same. Even the contracts were the same to begin with; John Charles was bodying Railtons during 1934, and suddenly so was Ranalah in the following year.

The first contract we know Ranalah received – in late 1935, soon after the company started – was for 'Sandringham' cabriolets. This was an ALLINGHAM design,

which is again significant as it amounted to a reunion of ex-HOYAL personnel., Through his company Vehicle Developments Ltd Allingham had sold the Sandringham to Ford, Morris, Vauxhall, Austin and Wolseley; Ranalah produced bodies for the first three of these makes. Then the company resurrected another former connection, with Lanchester, and produced an attractive drophead coupé which was in production for some three years. Yet another former John Charles connection was revived when Ranalah was given the contract for bodies by Rapier Cars Ltd (which had taken over production of the Rapier from the old Lagonda company).

As well as Olympia in 1936, Ranalah was at the two pre-war Earls Court Shows in 1937-38. The company was also involved, along with COACHCRAFT, in supplying Southern Motor Co with replacement bodies for older Rolls-Royces, and supplied the same service to Jack Compton. In 1939 Ranalah switched to sheet-metal work for the aircraft industry and never restarted coachbuilding. After World War 2 the premises were taken over by Jack Barclay, the London Rolls-Royce dealer, to house both the Jack Barclay service department and the coachbuilder GURNEY NUTTING which had become part of the Jack Barclay group.

RATCLIFFE
Ratcliffe Bros, claiming to be based at both Frinton-on-Sea and London, advertised a special-bodied Triumph Nine in 1932.

RAWORTH
C H Raworth & Son Ltd was one of William Morris's original suppliers, building the body for the Morris Oxford. Even after Morris had set up a bodybuilding department at Cowley, Raworth continued to supply special types of body, but by 1919 this was a very small proportion of the total, especially as HOLLICK & PRATT, and later HOYAL, were also involved. Even so, Raworth is known to have been building Oxford saloons as late as 1926 and was eventually brought into the Nuffield group in 1944 when it was purchased by The Morris Garages Ltd, although the trading name was still in use in the sixties.

REGENT CARRIAGE
The Regent Carriage Co Ltd, of Fulham in South-West London, was a prestigious company bodying the better class of chassis in the early twenties. The managing director, F M Charles, had been head of the coachwork department at Daimler, which no doubt helps to explain Regent's association with Daimler, a marque in which it seems to have specialised. Other frequently bodied chassis were Crossley and Renault.

Regent exhibited at Olympia from 1919 to 1925 and then stopped. Its premises were taken over by an unrelated firm at the beginning of 1927, and one must assume that the company ceased business some time in 1926. Later on these same premises became home to WHITTINGHAM & MITCHEL.

RIPPON: Rolls-Royce 20/25 sportsman's saloon (left) at the 1935 Olympia Show. The firm's liking for low rear wing lines sometimes gave a slightly dumpy appearance. 1939 Rolls-Royce Wraith limousine (below). Users still demanded that they could enter while wearing their top-hats.

RELIANCE Reliance Motor Works Ltd of Hammersmith, West London, is known to have bodied an Austro-Daimler in 1922 and an SPA in 1923.

RIPPON Without doubt Britain's oldest coachbuilder, and one of the highest quality builders of bodies on car chassis, Rippon's name ought to be better known. Only the fact that the company was based in Huddersfield rather than in a fashionable part of London can explain why today we know the names of, say, Barker, Hooper or Park Ward so much better.

The company's history goes back, incredibly, to 1555, when Walter Rippon made the first carriage in Britain, for the Earl of Rutland; apparently several other royal commissions followed. As far as car coachwork is concerned,

the company started in 1905 yet strangely seems not to have begun exhibiting at Olympia until 1925, after which it continued to do so until the last pre-war Show (at Earls Court) in 1938. As to quality, in the thirties a Rippon body could only be compared with those of a very few other coachbuilders – Hooper, Barker, H J Mulliner, Park Ward and Mann Egerton come to mind.

A Rippon body was correspondingly expensive, and the company therefore tended to build on only the best chassis. Amongst its Motor Show exhibits Rolls-Royce, Bentley (post-1931), Daimler and Delage abound, Minerva and Lanchester occur a couple of times each and Invicta once. Rippon bodies tended to be 'luxurious' and 'graceful' rather than sleek and exciting, although those latter words could certainly be applied to its fast-back,

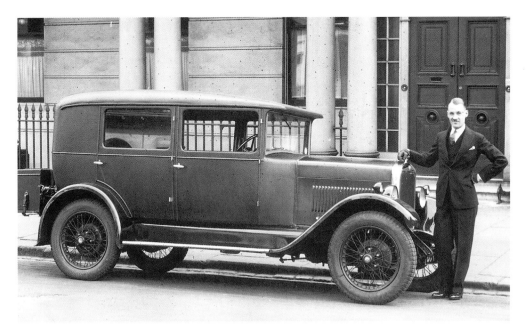

SALMONS: 1928 Hillman 14hp fabric saloon. Huge roof-peaks contributed nothing to aerodynamics.

close-coupled saloon on a 3½-litre Bentley chassis at the 1934 Show. Later on in the thirties, while the luxury was present in just as great a degree, there was a tendency for Rippon saloons and limousines to develop a somewhat hunch-backed look, with thick rear quarters and bulbous curves. Nevertheless the customers must have liked it, especially the one who used the height of his 25/30 sportsman's saloon to good effect by including fishing-rod lockers between the floor and the running board.

One exception to the string of Rolls-Royces and Bentleys was, surprisingly, a Railton limousine, built for none other than Colonel Rippon himself. He used it to win numerous prizes at concours d'elegance events before World War 2. The Rippon company resumed some coachbuilding after the war but ceased in 1958 and concentrated on its car dealing. It later became part of the Appleyard group.

ROBERTSON
John Robertson & Co of Glasgow exhibited at three Scottish Motor Shows from 1923 to 1925 but did not take a stand of its own and instead used the stand of the Clyde Automobile Co. A Rolls-Royce featured in each of the three years, and Sunbeam and Charron Laycock chassis were also used.

ROBINSON
A firm based in Coventry which is known only for having bodied a C-type Lea-Francis in 1923.

ROCK, THORPE & WATSON
This Tunbridge Wells, Kent, firm was known under a number of names. Founded in Hastings, Sussex in 1822 as Rock & Co, it became Rock, Hawkins & Thorpe and then Rock, Thorpe & Co before changing yet again to the name that heads this entry. The firm moved from Hastings to Tunbridge Wells in 1893. Its first appearance at motor shows came in 1926, at both

Olympia and the Scottish Show, in the latter case on the stand of R Y Dickson & Co. At both places the firm exhibited work on Renault chassis, and at Olympia also used an Armstrong-Siddeley chassis. The Armstrong-Siddeley connection was clearly a strong one, as the marque appeared on the stand in the next three years; that was the end, however, and after 1929 the firm apparently ceased coachbuilding. Later it was purchased by CAFFYN.

SALMONS & SONS
The firm of Salmons & Sons, later known by the brand-name 'Tickford', must be counted amongst the most commercially successful of all the pre-war coachbuilders. Not only did it survive the Depression years but it was still building 30 bodies a week even as World War 2 approached.

Salmons was founded in 1820 by Joseph Salmons at Newport Pagnell, Buckinghamshire, where it has remained to this day and the company stayed in the control of the Salmons family until 1939. Originally carriage-makers, Salmons began motor bodybuilding as long ago as 1898. It was at London Motor Shows from before World War 1, including every one between the wars, and had a London showroom for most of this time. From an early period the firm described itself as 'all-weather specialists', and was generally regarded as the pioneer of that type of body. Show exhibits back up the claim: all-weathers, landaulets, cabriolets and coupés filled its stands during the first part of the twenties – and this was before the famous 'Tickford saloon' appeared.

When the 'Tickford' was first announced in 1925, it was understandably described as an 'all-weather', since this was the style it most closely resembled. Such bodies had previously demanded a certain amount of skill, not to mention strength, to fold down the hood. The Tickford method added a gear mechanism, worked by inserting a cranked winding-handle, which made the whole process

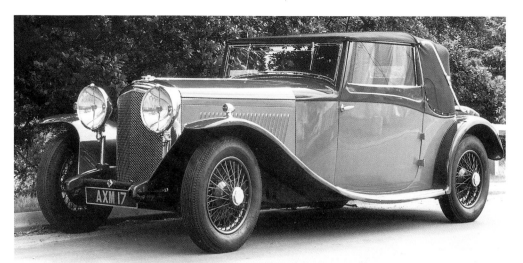

SALMONS: 1934 Bentley 3½-litre drophead coupé (left) – probably designed to look at its best with the hood down. 1938 MG WA drophead coupé (below), one of this firm's finest designs.

far easier. It was in part a coincidence that the Tickford head and the Pytchley sliding roof were announced in the same year, yet not wholly so, as both reflected the motoring public's desire to enjoy fresh air without discomfort or inconvenience. Tickford's solution was the only one of the two to offer the possibility of a completely open car; the Pytchley version, on the other hand, was ideal for the steel-panelled saloons becoming increasingly popular. It was possibly because Salmons perceived this as a threat that from 1926 on, it referred to its body as an 'all-weather saloon'.

The Tickford system immediately became very popular, and for some years bodies built with it were the only ones which Salmons would put on its Show stands. Not all of these were all-weather types, however; the term used by 1928 was 'sunshine saloon', which meant that the side-windows and cant-rails remained fixed while the roof wound down in the normal way. Initially Salmons built the Tickfords as bespoke commissions on any chassis. However, when times became harder in the late twenties the firm was forced, like many other coachbuilders, to seek contracts from the manufacturers, or at least to offer standard bodies on certain chassis. Salmons went even further during the difficult 1929-32 period, and offered sunshine saloon conversions on customers'

own Austin Seven saloons. This became a normal service for the rest of the thirties, whereby a customer could have his saloon converted regardless of make or model.

The first standard offering was on the Talbot 14/45 chassis in about 1929 or 1930, and appears to have been officially approved by the manufacturer. Then in 1931 came two more: the 20hp Armstrong-Siddeley, and the 'Abbey' body on the Vauxhall Cadet, both these being sunshine saloons. Both connections proved to be long ones, the Vauxhall one particularly, with the Tickford body moving on to the Light Six as a catalogued model in 1933 and remaining there until 1938. There were also Tickford offerings on the Big Six of 1934-36 and the 25hp of 1937-38. The next significant contract, in 1932-33, was with Rover, who catalogued a sunshine saloon design across their whole range of chassis.

In 1932 Salmons started to offer an alternative Tickford design, the foursome coupé which still used a winding-handle but was in effect a three-position drophead coupé. The design was applied that year to the Hillman Minx, Wolseley Hornet and Lea-Francis chassis, and later to many others including the Vauxhall Light Six mentioned above; it also appeared in the Rover 1933-34 catalogue.

The year 1936 saw the beginning of the end of the famous Tickford mechanism, when Salmons contracted

TICKFORD: early Healey 2.4-litre saloon c.1951.

with MG to supply drophead bodies on the VA and SA chassis. Probably for reasons of cost, the winding mechanism was omitted and a simple spring-head system fitted instead. This work lasted until the end of the thirties, as did a last contract from Rover for drophead coupés, which ran during 1939 and 1940.

After World War 2, and renamed Tickford Ltd, the company continued for a time with traditional coachbuilding methods. First contracts were for drophead coupé bodies on the Daimler DB18, and on the TA14 Alvis (to be followed later by a similar one for the TA/TC21 range). There were also the inevitable 'woody' estate bodies, on Land-Rover and Humber Pullman chassis, some Humber Super Snipe dropheads, and then the Healey prototype (together with some early production versions). From 1952 on, however, Tickford was increasingly occupied with both drophead and saloon bodies on the 3-litre Lagonda. In 1955 it was acquired by David Brown, all outside bodybuilding ceased and the company was confined to Aston Martin and Lagonda production.

Tickford has experienced an eventful history since, including losing and then regaining its coachbuilding skills, and is now an independent company operating throughout the world.

SANKEY

Joseph Sankey & Sons Ltd, of Wellington, Shropshire, is of course best known as a supplier of steel stampings and components to the motor industry, particularly wheels and chassis. Yet there was a period, around 1921-22, when the company set itself up as a supplier of standard bodies in large quantities. It was clearly aiming at supplying the trade, but the sales literature suggests that it would also supply the complete car with the body ready mounted, and hence Sankey qualifies – just – as part of the coachbuilding trade. Bodies on offer at the time were Ford T saloons, Austin landaulets and Armstrong-Siddeley limousines. The whole venture seems to have fizzled out quickly, presumably because it proved unprofitable, and Sankey contented itself thereafter with supplying individual body panels such as wings. If it had persisted with complete bodies, however, it might have turned itself into a formidable competitor to the PRESSED STEEL COMPANY.

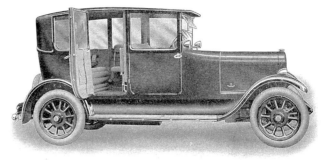

SANKEY: Austin 20hp landaulet c.1921, from a firm better known as a component supplier.

SAUNDERS, CECIL

Cecil Saunders Ltd of Letchworth is known to have existed in the late twenties, since it was responsible for producing the bodies on Sir Henry Birkin's racing cars. By 1933 it was bodying Talbots, Fiat Balillas and an Isotta-Fraschini, and the next year one of its Talbot designs won an award at the Ramsgate concours d'elegance.

Nothing more is known of the company's work in the car field, although it was still undertaking commercial bodywork in 1965.

SAUNDERS, SAMUEL

Samuel E Saunders Ltd of Cowes, Isle of Wight, was the forerunner of the Saunders-Roe aircraft company. In 1924 it built the bodies of the Heron light car, using a highly unconventional 'stitched plywood' construction.

SHAW & KILBURN

Shaw & Kilburn Ltd came into being after World War 1 when the motor-dealing firm of Drysdale Kilburn was joined by Captain H O N Shaw. It had previously acquired premises in Central London through the purchase of another dealer, Mitchells Garage. Shaw & Kilburn was the Vauxhall agent for London, and also an importer, handling Essex and Hudson. It exhibited at Olympia from 1923 to 1929, showing just these three marques and in 1930 showing Vauxhalls only.

The unknown factor in this firm's story concerns GROSVENOR CARRIAGE. It is certain that Grosvenor became a subsidiary of S & K, and from then on built all

its bodies. Just when this happened, though, is not known, nor where S & K's coachbuilding facilities were previously.

The company still exists today as a major chain of Vauxhall agents.

SHINNIE R & J Shinnie of Aberdeen was active in the early twenties. The firm had been founded in 1866 by two brothers, who at one stage had built up (it was said) 'the largest private carriage construction works in Great Britain'. It exhibited at Scottish shows under its own name in 1921 and 1922, and there is also some evidence of its attendance in 1923-24. Robert Shinnie, one of the two brothers – and apparently the one in charge of design – died in early 1924.

SHORT Short Brothers, of Rochester, Kent, was better known as a seaplane manufacturer, but was also involved in coachbuilding during the twenties. In 1921 it was reported as building a new factory 'for quantity production', and the next year it became clear that the production envisaged was for the Salmson 10 body. This contract ran for some time, as Short exhibited at Olympia in 1925 and a Salmson 10 two-seater appeared on the stand, accompanied by a Chrysler all-weather and a Fiat coupé.

At the same time Short was heavily involved in building bus bodies, certainly before 1925, and this activity seems eventually to have taken over from car bodybuilding. Short did not exhibit at Olympia again but was still building buses in 1934.

SIEVWRIGHT The Wolverhampton firm of Sievwright produced some car bodies between the wars, including a Bentley four-seater in 1924, but was more interested in selling its caravans. After World War 2 it confined itself to commercial and repair work; it ceased business in the eighties.

SHAW & KILBURN: Vauxhall 20-60hp 'fabric chummy saloon', in two tones of brown, exhibited at Olympia in 1928.

SIMS & WILSON: 1920 Gilchrist 12hp tourer.

SIMS & WILSON This Glasgow firm was responsible for bodying the Gilchrist light car in 1920.

SINCLAIR Sinclair & Co of St-Annes-on-Sea, Lancashire, bodied at least two Bentleys in the twenties.

SMITH (ABERDEEN) T C Smith of Aberdeen showed a Fiat 10-15 coupé at the 1921 Scottish Motor Show.

SMITH (MANCHESTER) Smith Bros (Motors) of Manchester is known to have bodied a Crossley saloon in 1923.

SOUTHERN Southern Motor Co, London SW4, had no coachbuilding facilities of its own but nevertheless advertised 'Rolls-Royce replicas' in the later thirties; these were new bodies built on older chassis. One

STARTIN: 1931 Rolls-Royce 20/25 limousine; nice proportions, but the usual problems integrating the narrow bonnet into the design.

SOUTHERN: Rolls-Royce 20hp of uncertain age rebodied c.1936 by one or other of Southern's sub-contractors, Coachcraft or Ranalah.

STRACHAN & BROWN: 1923 Aberdonia 16/20 – the chassis was also made by this firm.

of the daughters of the May family, who owned Southern, married Sydney Allard, and after World War 2 the Southern premises became the main Allard factory. See also COACHCRAFT and RANALAH.

STANFORD & GREY

Stanford & Grey of London built an open four-seater body on a 3-litre Bentley chassis in 1923.

STARTIN

Thomas Startin of Birmingham was primarily a commercial bodybuilder and produced the Austin Seven van under sub-contract from Austin in the period 1923-26. However, the firm is known to have bodied a Rolls-Royce 20/25 limousine in 1930. A commercial bodybuilding company with a similar name still existed in Birmingham in the sixties.

STEWART & ARDERN

See CUNARD.

STEVENSON

J B Stevenson of Glasgow was at the 1921 Scottish Motor Show, exhibiting an Austin 20 tourer, and is known to have been still in existence in 1928.

STOREY

A H Storey & Sons, of Holloway in North London, is known to have bodied an Alvis and several Bentleys in the twenties.

STRACHAN & BROWN

The origins of the firm go back to 1894, when Walter Brown started a small coachbuilding business in the Shepherds Bush area of West London. A year later a Mr Hughes joined as a partner, and the firm became Brown & Hughes; it claimed to be one of the first to build motor bodies. James Strachan joined as a partner in 1907, and the name changed to Brown, Hughes & Strachan, with a new factory at nearby Park Royal. Just before World War 1 Strachan and Brown both resigned and formed a new firm, known by their two names, with premises at Kensington, also in West London. During the war this firm built ambulances and other vehicles, later deciding to concentrate on bus and coach building. In 1921 it built a new factory at Acton and by 1923 had closed the Kensington site and moved totally to Acton.

Strachan & Brown bodied the occasional car chassis, including the four 1922 Aston Martin grand prix cars and

SURBICO: 1927 Invicta 3-litre tourer.

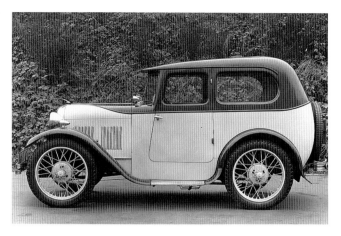

SWALLOW: 1927 Austin Seven sports saloon (above), small but still pleasing to the eye. 1930 Standard Nine sports saloon (below). When William Lyons embraced the long, low look in 1931 for his SS1 he executed it in his usual dramatic style (bottom) – helped by a specially lowered chassis.

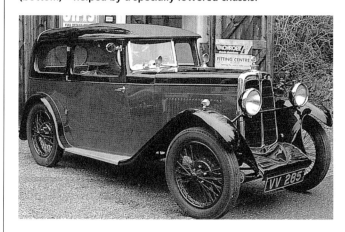

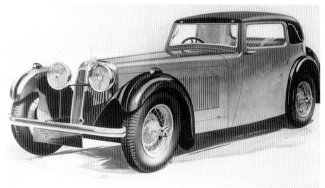

also a 1924 Meteorite, as well as its own 'Aberdonian' marque. In 1928 Walter Brown broke away from the firm, joining Duple as a director, and the next year James Strachan died from a brain tumour aged 64. The firm renamed itself Strachans (Acton) Ltd, but seems to have hit financial trouble as it later became Strachans Successors Ltd. By 1939 this firm was building vans, taxis and RAF vehicles as well as coaches. After World War 2 it became part of the Giltspur group and in 1963 moved from Acton to Hamble, by then being known as Strachans (Coachbuilders) Ltd, which ceased business in 1974.

SURBICO Surbiton Coach & Motor Works, of Surbiton in Surrey, bodied a number of both Bentley and Invicta chassis in the late-twenties, and also Wolseley Hornets a little later. The firm used the brand-name 'Surbico'.

SURREY MOTORS Surrey Motors, of Sutton in Surrey, exhibited at Olympia once only, in 1920, showing work on Standard, Talbot and Phoenix chassis. The Talbot 25 saloon was a distinctive design, being curvaceous in places – such as roof and window-line – where most of its contemporaries used straight lines.

SWALLOW The Swallow Sidecar & Coachbuilding Co Ltd was of course the precursor of the Jaguar car company. Started in Blackpool by William Walmsley, the firm originally made good-looking sidecars for motorcycles under the 'Swallow' brand-name. In 1921 Walmsley took into partnership William Lyons, then only 20 years old. The firm prospered and in 1926 produced its first car body on a Talbot chassis. The next move, however, was the one which made its name, and that was to produce a special body for the Austin Seven. This first offering, a 'saloon/coupé', was an immediate success, and led to a saloon version which became even better known, with its distinctive two-tone colour scheme. The same style was later offered on Standard Nine, Fiat Nine and Swift chassis.

By now, even though production had been put on an organised basis, the firm was hitting problems of space and labour, and in late 1928 it took over an old World War 1 shell factory in Holbrook Lane, Coventry. From 1929 on Swallow was sufficiently confident to start exhibiting at Olympia, and the following year at the Scottish show (where it exhibited a two-seater beetleback Wolseley Hornet). The firm's abilities were by now apparent: not only could it produce striking designs but it could also do so at an unbelievably low price. In 1930 it showed models which were largely unchanged, apart from the addition of a two-seater Austin, but it was at the 1931

Show that the real sensation appeared – the SS1 coupé, initially known as the SS Sixteen.

The SS1, a two-seater fixed-head design, embodied all the visual features which were then fashionable: very long bonnet, very low roofline, sloping windscreen with peakless front, and cycle wings without running boards. *The Autocar* described it as 'the embodiment of speed and efficiency'. Its low appearance was helped greatly by the lowered chassis, supplied by Standard exclusively to Swallow. The SS1 was joined on the Olympia stand by a smaller but similar-looking model on the Standard Little Nine chassis, which later became known as the SS2, and a Wolseley Hornet sports two-seater.

In 1932 the SS1 was considerably improved, mainly thanks to a lengthened chassis which permitted the addition of two occasional rear seats as well as more luggage space. It appeared at that year's Olympia Show, and this was the last occasion that Swallow was seen in the coach-builders' section. The remainder of the firm's history, glorious though it is, belongs elsewhere than in this book.

T & D
T & D Motors, of London NW6, produced a fixed-head 'sports coupé' on the Austin Seven chassis in 1931. Its design was clearly intended to follow the then-current fashion for lowered bodies, but the result was less than graceful.

TANNER
Tanner Brothers, of Fulham, South-West London, was responsible for three sports two-seater bodies on the Frazer-Nash 319/40 model of the mid-thirties.

TAYLOR (LONDON)
H Taylor & Co. appears to have had premises in both Kensington, South-West London, and Kingston, Surrey. The firm produced special bodies on the Austin Seven chassis in the period 1927-30: a 'semi-sports', later known as the Ace, and a 'super-sports' which was known as the Taylor Launch. It also bodied a Singer Junior in 1930.

TAYLOR (WOLVERHAMPTON)
L & L T Taylor Ltd of Wolverhampton, often referred to simply as Taylors, was originally a partnership of three Taylor brothers and two others. However this arrangement broke up in 1922, and two of the brothers formed the new company. The only car bodies it is known to have built were some 3-litre Bentleys in the early twenties and an Austin Seven in 1927. The company changed its name to HOLBROOK & TAYLORS in 1930 when Sam Holbrook bought into it.

THAMES
The only claims to fame which the Thames Motor Body and Engineering Company of Wandsworth, South-West London, could make were firstly that it was the sole bodybuilder for the Storey car, and secondly that the company was run by St John

THAMES: 1920 Storey 20hp limousine.

Cooper, half-brother to actress Gladys Cooper. Neither claim proved to be long-lasting, as Storey production only ran for a few months in the 1919-1920 period, and Thames in turn could not survive the collapse of its major customer.

THORN
W & F Thorn of Norwich was bodying cars as early as 1905. It exhibited at Olympia for the first three post-war Shows, 1919-21, using an eclectic mixture of chassis including Vauxhall, Ruston-Hornsby, Dodge and Dort. At the 1921 Show it not only used a BAC chassis, but was described as 'now trading under the name of the British Automobile Co. Ltd', so it would appear that W & F Thorn had become a subsidiary of that company.

THORNTON
Thornton Engineering of Bradford is known to have constructed all-weather bodies on Vauxhall chassis during 1921.

THRUPP & MABERLY
The London-based firm of Thrupp & Maberly had a well-documented history going back to 1760. In that year Joseph Thrupp set up as a carriage-builder in George Street, in the West End. The firm prospered; in 1844 it opened showrooms in Oxford Street and in 1858 joined up with George Maberly, who had previously operated from premises in neighbouring Welbeck Street and Marylebone Lane. The firm enjoyed considerable prestige, and its reputation was underlined when in 1877 George Thrupp wrote his definitive 'History of the Art of Coachbuilding', still used as a reference book today.

T & M built its first car coachwork at least as early as 1896, when it bodied an electric victoria for the Queen of Spain, and the car side of the business developed rapidly during the early years of the new century. During World War 1 the firm turned to such things as staff cars but after the war was quick to resume the bespoke coach-building business. It was present at the first post-war Olympia Show, with exhibits of which *The Autocar* thought highly: 'in addition to excellent workmanship,

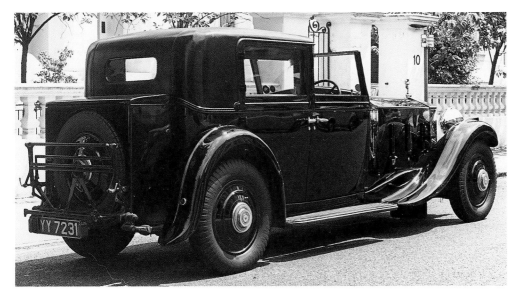

THRUPP & MABERLY: 1932 Rolls-Royce Phantom 2 'sports sedanca'(left); squared-off trunk is unusual. 1933 Bentley 3½-litre four-door saloon (below). The luggage-boot is now an integral part of the design. 1935 Hillman Aero Minx coupé (below middle); note the subtle styling changes compared with the earlier Carbodies version. 1938 Rolls-Royce Phantom 3 'owner-driver saloon with division' (bottom); razor-edge style now predominating.

the outlines follow the latest dictates of fashion'. For the next few years there followed the normal output of a bespoke house – landaulets, limousines, coupés-de-ville, cabriolets and so on, many on imported chassis such as Delage, Hotchkiss, Minerva and Peugeot.

Then two major events happened. In 1924 T&M moved its works to Cricklewood, in North-West London (although it retained its West End showrooms which by this time were in North Audley Street) and in 1925 it was acquired by the Rootes organisation. Whether this second event had been triggered by the cost of the first, or whether both were the result of some master-plan, we shall probably never know. The separate West End showroom promptly disappeared, as Rootes already had its own offices and showrooms at Devonshire House in Berkeley Street.

From this time on T & M seem to have undergone a distinct shift of image – but not in the direction one might have expected. Far from going down-market, or bodying special editions for the Rootes dealerships, it was now seen to body only the very best British chassis. Thus from 1925 on T&M Motor Show stands always had at least one Rolls-Royce chassis, and there was usually a Daimler or a Bentley as well. The coachwork on these chassis was unquestionably luxurious, being usually in the form of beautifully-trimmed limousines or coupés-de-ville. Yet it is to the credit of the Rootes brothers that there was no question of any previous creativity being stifled – quite the contrary. From 1926 onwards there was a succession of ingenious inventions, the first being the glass division which tilted as it dropped, thus releasing more space in the rear for legroom or occasional seats. In 1929 T & M was the first coachbuilder in Britain, if not anywhere, to fit hinged rear quarter-lights for improved ventilation. Then in 1933 came the sliding de ville extension, which was concealed when open and flush with the rest of the roof when closed.

One well-known project which was clearly aimed at publicity was in 1929 when the company provided the

body for Sir Henry Segrave's land speed record contender 'Golden Arrow'.

T & M's creativity was also evident in the overall standard of its designs. The streamlined Bentley four-door saloon at the 1934 Show was an outstanding example of the way such treatments should be executed, as were the Rolls-Royce continental coupés the following year. The firm was also an early exponent of the 'razor-edge' style, although it could not claim to have invented it. By this time – indeed from 1932 onward – it was applying its talents to Humbers (and some Hillmans); no doubt it had become part of the Rootes brother's long-term strategy to let the T & M prestige rub off on their top marque, but again the brothers can be applauded for having resisted the temptation for some time, since they had been in effective control of Humber since 1928.

Purists might say that this was the beginning of the decline for T & M, but at least initially there was no question of Humber quality being any lower, with limousines and sedancas-de-ville being the staple production. Then in 1936 the firm started to body some Talbots and Sunbeam-Talbots, this coinciding with a partial move to the old Darracq works at Acton (the Cricklewood works being retained). These premises happened to be next door to a company called British Light Steel Pressings, and the two companies were merged just before World War 2.

During World War 2 T & M was engaged amongst other things on the manufacture of the famous Humber staff car in both open and closed versions. After the war it went back to its Cricklewood base, but times had changed and there was no question of resuming bespoke coachbuilding. Instead the company's role within the Rootes group became the construction of 'special' bodies, including all open models. Initially this embraced a form of composite body for the Humber Pullman and Imperial, which was not too different from pre-war practice, although the mounting of body to chassis took place elsewhere. Later, however, it became no more than paint-and-trim work on shells supplied by others, namely British Light Steel Pressings and Pressed Steel. T & M made convertible versions of the Minx, Gazelle, Rapier, and special coupés on the same models, as well as finishing the big Humbers. Even this work started to die away in the middle sixties, and the Cricklewood factory closed in 1967.

TICKFORD See SALMONS.

TILBURY

Although the Tilbury Motor Co was located in the Hammersmith area of West London it preferred to exhibit at the Scottish Motor Show, which it did in the years 1923-25. It saved even more money by not taking a stand itself but instead showing its wares – on Delage and Arrol-Johnston chassis – on the stands of local dealers.

TIMMS

W E Timms was a Coventry firm active in the early twenties. The only body of which we have knowledge was on a Lea-Francis C-type in 1923.

UNION

Union Motor Car Co Ltd of London SW1 was a Weymann licensee in the late twenties; nothing more is known about the company.

UNIVERSITY

When COACHCRAFT was bought by University Motors in 1946 its name was changed to University Coachwork. The company is

UNIVERSITY: 1949 Railton drophead coupé – post-war body on a pre-war chassis.

known to have done some work for Lea-Francis, as well as bodying some 'post-war' Railtons (in reality made from 1930s chassis and body parts stored during the war). It also took a stand at the 1948 Motor Show and exhibited a special Bristol saloon and a prototype new Railton.

Thereafter University Coachwork moved to Egham and confined itself to car repair work. The Hanwell address, meanwhile, specialised in commercial body-building and distribution, and this branch of the business was still in business, under the name of University Commercials, right up to the mid-sixties. In the early eighties the Hanwell premises were finally demolished to make way for a DIY store, the end of the road for a building which had started life as a tram depot and had housed no less than six differently-named bodybuilding companies.

VANDEN PLAS

The origins of this firm go back to Belgium, in the last century. Carrosserie Vanden Plas was well regarded long before it made its first car body, and its automobile work only enhanced that reputation. The firm became known in England from about 1906, when Metallurgique cars began to be imported, the majority of them bearing Vanden Plas bodies, and their quality was much admired. Eventually Warwick Wright, a name which was to become well known in the motor trade, obtained the exclusive rights to the Vanden Plas name in England and changed the name of his associate coachbuilding firm, Théo Masui, to Vanden Plas (England) Ltd.

At this point World War 1 intervened and the British company was sold off to the Aircraft Manufacturing Company (the forerunner of de Havilland, based at Hendon Aerodrome) so that it could use its resources on the production of aircraft components. In 1917, with the end of the war in sight, that portion of Airco's interests was spun off into a new company named Vanden Plas (1917) Ltd, and in 1919 bodybuilding restarted, still using part of the Hendon buildings.

Interestingly, it was the Belgian firm – SA Carrosserie Vanden Plas – which started exhibiting again at the London Motor Shows. It was at the White City (the overflow hall from the main exhibition at Olympia) in 1920 and

1921, but the British company was absent. Yet in 1922 there was the unusual sight of both firms existing apparently in harmony on near-adjacent stands. The next year the Belgians were there once again but the British company was absent, battling with bigger problems: trade had dwindled so much that it had been forced into receivership, and there was some doubt whether it would ever reappear.

The company's troubles were all the more unfortunate in that it had already bodied its first Bentleys, starting in 1922, for if it could only have managed to stay afloat a little longer that relationship alone would have been enough to save it. As it was, Edwin Fox and his brothers, who bought the goodwill of the business from the receiver, moved the company over the hill from Hendon to Kingsbury, and immediately resumed the Bentley connection. In 1924 the new company bodied 84 Bentleys alone, and in 1925 leased part of their premises to Bentley for the latter's service department. By 1931, when the 'old' Bentley company went out of business, Vanden Plas had bodied over 700 of its chassis. This dominance by the one make was almost overwhelming during the twenties, although there were occasional appearances from Rolls-Royce, Daimler, Minerva, Alfa Romeo, Delage and so on; the 'sporting four-seater', built on the Weymann fabric system, became a standard design on both 3-litre and 4½-litre Bentley chassis.

All the more credit to the company, then, that when Bentley did crash, Vanden Plas did not go down too. Although it was a severe blow, Vanden Plas managed to switch quickly to other manufacturers, at least until such time as the new Bentley might become available. This ability to win new business must in part be ascribed to a far-sighted decision on the part of the directors: in 1931, at the lowest point of the Depression, they concluded that they needed to strengthen their design capability and recruited John Bradbury from Invicta. Bradbury had made his reputation at Cadogan where he had worked for nearly 10 years. His first move was to create a modern drawing-office, coupled with the introduction of desirable practices such as detailed, full-scale drawings for every body produced. Another major contributor to the

survival was the larger-than-life character of Charles Follett. Follett started selling Alvises just before the launch of the first Speed Twenty, and his influence on both that model and the Vanden Plas bodies with which it was often clothed is clear.

Thus the combination of good trade contacts – not just Charles Follett, but also others such as Warwick Wright, Jack Barclay, and Oxborrow and Fuller – together with a strong design department, ensured the prosperity of Vanden Plas for the duration of the thirties. Alvis, Bentley, Talbot and Lagonda were the predominant chassis used, but there were plenty of other prestigious makes as well – Rolls-Royce, Daimler, Armstrong-Siddeley, and many more. The company's reputation for quality, of both design and workmanship, never slipped – all the more remarkable since it became progressively 'productionised' with standard bodies often being manufactured in batches of six or more.

With war seeming inevitable, Vanden Plas began in 1938 to contract for aircraft work once more, and by the end of 1939 car bodybuilding had ceased. At the end of hostilities, the company lost no time in making proposals to Rolls-Royce, Alvis and even Ford for some or all of these companies' bodybuilding work, but it was an approach in the opposite direction, from Austin, which dictated its post-war history. Austin was looking for someone to build a luxury saloon on its six-cylinder chassis – the project which became the A125/A135 Princess – and the result, in 1946, was that it took over the Vanden

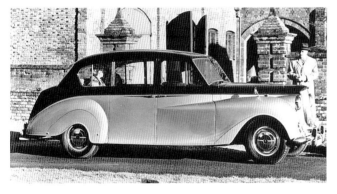

Plas company. This coachbuilt, luxuriously appointed saloon was soon being turned out in surprisingly high numbers for a time of comparative austerity – figures of between five and 10 per week have been quoted – and was subjected to gradual improvements as successive versions were launched.

In 1958, in a significant move, it was decided that the Kingsbury works should also assemble the chassis of the Princess. From there, it was only a short step to envisage Vanden Plas as the manufacturer of the whole vehicle; this was given official recognition by the management of what had now become BMC, who in 1960 dropped the name Austin and described it as the 'Vanden Plas Princess'. The company exhibited at that year's Motor Show as a manufacturer instead of a coachbuilder. In 1967 it ceased to be Vanden Plas (England) 1923 Ltd and became a division of BMC.

VEHICLE DEVELOPMENTS See ALLINGHAM.

VICKERS

The industrial giant Vickers, at its Crayford factory, made an attack on the car coach-building market in 1923. In that year it generated much publicity about its saloon body on a Fiat 10-15 chassis, and implied that many more were going to emerge from a specially laid out shop which had a capacity of 400 bodies a week. Nothing more was heard of the project, however, and the company turned instead to the bus and tram field (it was producing 'many hundreds' of such bodies by 1927).

VICTORIA

Victoria Coachworks took its name from the area of South-West London where it was located. The sole car body of which we have details was a tourer on the Bugatti stand at the 1921 Olympia Show. The firm ceased business in 1924, and shortly afterwards its premises were being used for additional capacity by GORDON ENGLAND.

VINCENT

William Vincent Ltd of Reading was founded in 1805, built its first car body in 1899, and bodied its first Rolls-Royce as early as 1906. Vincent became known in the twenties as an important provincial coachbuilder, claiming at one time to have the 'largest and most up-to-date works in the British Isles', which was moderated later – and probably more accu-

VINCENT: Fiat tourer (above) of the very early twenties. 1934 Rolls-Royce 20/25 shooting-brake (below), an appropriate style for the firm's 'county' clientele.

rately – to '...in the southern counties'. It exhibited at Olympia from an early date; attendance after World War 1 ran from 1919 to 1935. Vincent's particular allegiances, probably reflecting its agencies, were with Sunbeam and Austin (the latter involving only the higher-horsepower chassis). The company's main fame amongst its county clients, however, was for something quite different: it was a specialist in the production of horse-boxes, in which it had been a pioneer ever since 1912.

It would be idle to pretend that Vincent was an innovator, either technically or artistically. If its products were noted for anything, it was for the lavishness of their interior fittings, with inlaid woodwork being a particular speciality. The clientele was the provincial upper classes and minor aristocracy who wanted a landaulet, limousine or saloon that reflected their station in life, and that is what Vincent gave them. When times became harder and the demand for such vehicles dropped, the company decided not to follow its competitors into contract bodies for less expensive chassis and merely wound down its car coachbuilding activities. In fact Vincent can be complimented for having managed to continue such a business for as long as it did.

After the mid-thirties the company turned increasingly to commercial bodybuilding, specialising in horse-boxes. It maintained this aspect of its business after World War 2, and even resumed car coachbuilding, exhibiting a Rolls-Royce at every Earls Court Show from 1948 to 1952. However, it gave up all coachbuilding activities in the mid-fifties, at which time the company was still in the control of the Vincent family.

WAINWRIGHT
This Wolverhampton firm built a tourer on an Itala which appeared on the Itala stand at the 1924 Olympia Show.

WALTER, MARTIN
The Folkestone firm of Martin Walter Ltd started life around the turn of the century as a saddlery business, later moving into sports goods and cycles. The real driving force, though, was not W Martin Walter himself but his brother-in-law, Spencer Apps, who set up the firm's first motorcycle business in 1910, expanding into cars two years later. The move into coachbuilding took place in 1916, when Martin Walter took over another Folkestone firm by the name of Norrington's.

Car-dealing and coachbuilding then expanded side-by-side. MW exhibited at Olympia in 1921, showing what seems to have been a standard all-weather body adapted to two different chassis – a Bianchi and a Panhard. For some reason it then withdrew from the Motor Show for three years, returning in 1925 to show work on a pair of Delage chassis. Thereafter a pattern began to establish itself, with Talbot, Daimler and – later – Lanchester and Vauxhall being the favoured marques, for which standard bodies were available. This is not to overlook the company's work on other makes, however, for MW bodywork appeared on some of the finest chassis, including Bentley, Hispano-Suiza, Lagonda, Mercedes-Benz (a racing-type body) and Rolls-Royce.

It was fortunate for MW that it had a strong car-dealing side to support it during the Depression years. This meant that, far from having to reduce or even close its coachbuilding activities like so many firms, it could take the bold decision to expand them. The company was apparently convinced that, firstly, there was a place for coachbuilders to provide manufacturers with their more specialised bodies, and, secondly, that such bodies would be predominantly drophead designs. It proved to be right on both counts. In 1929 MW began producing a long series of standard designs named after local villages; the first was the Romney 2/3-seater drophead coupé, applied initially to the Daimler 25hp, and the next year to the Austin 12 and 16 models. In ensuing years it was also built on numerous Lanchesters and Vauxhalls. The next design came in 1931 – the Denton four-seater drophead, built first on the Austin 12-6 and then on Lanchester, Vauxhall and Daimler models. In virtually every case the application was approved by the chassis manufacturer and included in his catalogue; many other coachbuilders were to do the same in the next few years, but Martin Walter was amongst the very first.

The company was so successful that it had to find additional capacity for the work which started to come its way, in spite of having already moved to new premises in 1928. Around 1932 it took over a former World War 1 airship hangar at nearby Capel, and dedicated it to the production of drophead bodies. At the same time a licence was obtained from the German coachbuilder

Salmons (Tickford) MG SA drophead coupé c.1938. Could one criticise the front wing line slightly for being insufficiently concave?

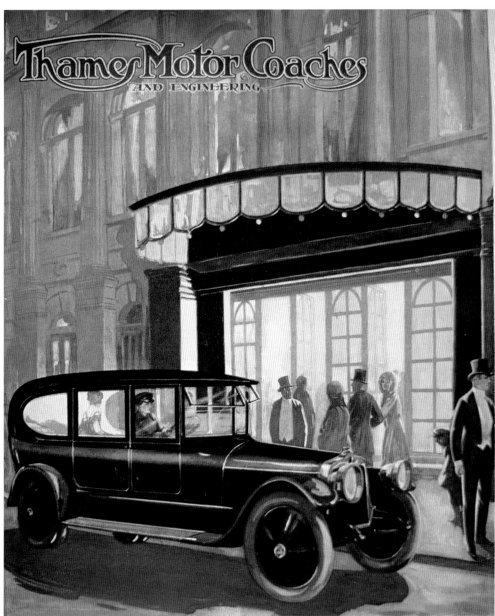

1919 Storey limousine by Thames as the artist saw it.

Swallow Austin Seven saloon, 1930, different from the standard
product and more attractive.

Vanden Plas 1933 Talbot 90 tourer (top). Note this firm's typical rubber inserts instead of a full running-board. MG NA two/four-seater (above), an Allingham design built by Whittingham & Mitchel; rear panel hinges up to form seat-back.

1934 Mercedes-Benz 500K drophead coupé by Windover (above); the body could only be British yet the front wings show a trace of continental influence.

James Young 1930 Alfa Romeo 6C 1750 Super Sport drophead coupé (below). Front wings, valanced and swept into the running-boards, are advanced for their time.

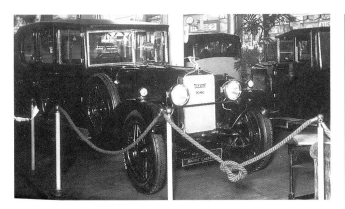

MARTIN WALTER: Talbot 20-60 seven-seater limousine (above left), finished in brown and black, at the 1926 Olympia Show. Vauxhall Big Six 'Wingham' four-door cabriolets (above right) being built at the Cheriton Road works (after the Capel works had closed) in 1936. Vauxhall Big Six 20hp 'Romney' drophead coupé (above) of c.1934, a catalogued Vauxhall model.

Glaser for its 'self-acting cabriolet head'; in this context a cabriolet meant little more than a drophead coupé, but with a better standard of hood lining and padding. The 'self-acting' description was more important: MW's objective was to achieve the true 'open-closed' body, where converting from one form to the other was so easy that it would overcome all previous prejudices. In addition, MW wanted to apply the new head to four-door bodies as well as the two-door designs which Glaser produced, so some development work was needed first.

Martin Walter announced its new Glaser-head designs at the 1933 Olympia Show, and insisted on calling them 'cabriolets', presumably to avoid confusion with their previous range of drophead coupés. The four-door design was designated the 'Wingham', and was shown on a 20hp Daimler; the two-door 'Rye' appeared on a Vauxhall Big Six. They aroused great interest, and over the next two years were constructed on numerous other Daimler, Vauxhall, Lanchester and Hillman chassis. Of the two designs the four-door Wingham was the more popular, so much so that by the 1935 Olympia it was the only one

which MW bothered to exhibit – on five different chassis.

Now it was that the prescience of Martin Walter – or more particularly of Spencer Apps – showed itself for a second time. In 1937, at the height of the cabriolet's success on the British market, he sold the business. ABBEY COACHWORKS was the buyer, and liked what it had bought so much that it even changed it own company name to WINGHAM MARTIN WALTER. Apps himself maintained that he took the decision because he could foresee the end of the coachbuilt body, but whatever the reason, his timing could not be faulted.

Martin Walter went on to make munitions in World War 2, and then started converting Bedford vans into the 'Utilecon', which had windows and seats. This led to the famous 'Dormobile' motor caravan which was launched in 1954 and sold for 40 years. This also caused a brief return to car coachwork in 1956 and 1957, when the company applied the Dormobile name to Vauxhall, Standard and Austin estate car conversions. MW became a public company in 1955, and during the seventies found itself a stock-market 'property play'; the rump company, Dormobile Ltd, went into receivership in 1994.

WARD W E Ward and Co was yet another small Coventry bodybuilder from the twenties of which little is known, apart from it having bodied a C-type Lea-Francis in 1923.

WARWICK: Morris Oxford all-weather c.1923; note this very early example of a luggage-trunk.

WARWICK Warwick Motor Body Works started in 1919 in South London; the name came from its first address, Warwick Mews. A year later it moved to better premises in nearby Croydon. It specialised in commercial bodybuilding but also bodied car chassis including Morris Oxford, Vauxhall 14/40 and 3-litre Bentley.

WATERMAN Waterman Coaches, of Paxton, Somerset, is known to have received six Austin Seven chassis in 1929 and bodied them as tourers.

WATSON P W Watson & Sons Ltd of Lowestoft, founded in 1830, was in existence and bodying cars by 1902. It had interests other than coachbuilding, being involved in motor repairing and dealing, and was even a fishing-boat owner and fish dealer. It started exhibiting at Olympia in 1924, and for four years used only Armstrong-Siddeley chassis to show its work; presumably this reflected one of its dealerships. Later it also used Daimler and Minerva chassis. Unsurprisingly for upmarket chassis such as these, the bodies exhibited were entirely limousines and landaulets. Watson was apparently noted in the trade for the quality of its interior woodwork.

The company ceased attending the Olympia Shows after 1930 but was still listed as car a bodybuilder in 1937 and was still in existence as a commercial bodybuilder in the sixties.

WESTALL S C Westall, of London SW1, is known to have bodied a Fiat brougham in 1922-23.

WESTMINSTER The Westminster Carriage Co Ltd was formed in March 1928, and appears to have had the same address as LONDON IMPROVED, which went out of business about the same time. There is also a hint that MORGAN of Leighton Buz-

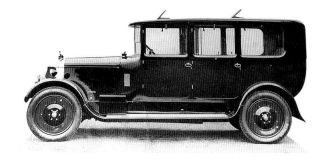

WATSON: Armstrong-Siddeley 30hp limousine c.1924.

zard might have moved to the same address at the same time. The new company clearly prospered for a time, as two years later it opened an additional coachbuilding and painting works in Brentford, west of London. However, nothing more was heard it.

WEYMANN Charles Terres Weymann was a Frenchman with a background in aviation. This experience led him to believe that a body should be as light as possible, and at the same time flexible so that it could absorb chassis movements rather than trying to resist them. Thus was born the Weymann system, which used an ultra-light wooden framework covered with tightly-stretched fabric instead of the usual steel or aluminium panels. Importantly, the components of the framework were assembled not with the usual mortise-and-tenon joints, but with steel plates which could flex slightly. Seats were mounted directly on the chassis, thus relieving the bodywork of yet another job.

Even more ingeniously, Weymann realised that the wooden frame members did not have to be in contact at all: he therefore arranged for the steel plates to hold them apart (by about 4mm). In a stroke he had solved the problem of noise – creaks, squeaks, rattles – which up to that point had affected all classes of coachbuilt body from the

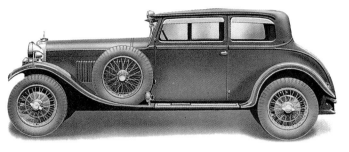

WEYMANN: 1929 Stutz 8-cylinder limousine (top) with American-style horizontal bonnet-louvres. 1929 Sunbeam 25hp two-door saloon (above) came with fitted luggage.

cheapest to the most expensive. Other refinements were added after the system was first announced in 1922: special locks to accommodate relative movement between doors and framework, straining-wires to allow adjustment of the door shape, and so on. Eventually the search for silence even led to greaseproof paper being inserted between the steel plates and the wooden frame.

In spite of the many alternatives being explored, such as sub-frames to insulate the body from the chassis, the superiority of the Weymann approach soon became accepted, both in France and in Britain (where it was launched a year later). In Britain the company's initial approach was to appoint licensees rather than – as in France – set up its own factory; presumably this was simply because of a lack of finance. Weymann set up a subsidiary named Weymann Motor Body Co, which was in effect a joint venture with the Rotax company, and which in 1923 awarded the first sub-licences to Rover, CHALMER & HOYER and ELKINGTON. The latter two showed their new skills at Olympia that year in the form of four-door saloons on Bentley and Peugeot chassis respectively. More licences followed the next year, including CADOGAN, GURNEY NUTTING and WINDOVER.

By 1925 the venture was clearly a success, and raising outside finance was no longer a problem. The British operation therefore decided to emulate its French parent and set up a factory, which it did via the formation of a new company, Weymann's Motor Bodies (1925) Ltd. Bodybuilding facilities appeared overnight through the purchase of the CUNARD company, which brought with it a coachworks in Putney, South-West London; the Cunard name itself was allowed to die. The strategy behind the move to manufacturing, both in Britain and in France, is not clear to this day, since Weymann obviously risked

alienating its licensees by competing with them.

Whatever the thinking, the results spoke for themselves. Not only was there a rapid take-up of licences by coachbuilders, but the Weymann factory's own output grew so fast that the company soon had to move to new premises. These were in the old Bleriot/Eric Longden factory at Addlestone in Surrey, where Weymann relocated in 1928. This, as so often happens in a period of rapid expansion, proved to be its peak year of production.

In the end it was appearance which defeated the fabric body; cellulose paint had arrived on the European scene around 1925, and within a few years its advantages were too overwhelming to ignore. From 1929 on in Britain – and probably a year earlier in France – the numbers of Weymann bodies built, both in the two Weymann factories and under licence, declined rapidly. Weymann counter-attacked bravely, by announcing its 'semi-panelled' system, whereby the lower half of the body was clothed with steel or aluminium panels and the fabric covering confined to the upper half only – ie above the waistline. It could be argued, however, that the 'semi-Weymann' development only hastened its own demise, since it led directly to the Silent Travel system which was to become almost an industry standard during the early thirties.

1931 was the last year that Weymann attended the Olympia Show, and by that time it had already turned its attention to bus bodies. In 1932 it became part of the new Metropolitan-Cammell-Weymann combine.

WHITTINGHAM & MITCHEL

Whittingham & Mitchel Ltd, best known as being in London's New Kings Road, started in 1921 at a nearby address, described as a sheet-metal working business. It was not until 1931 that the Kings Road address appears, by which time the firm was known as a coachpainter. The new premises were clearly suited to coachbuilding, having at one time been occupied by the REGENT CARRIAGE CO. W & M progressed quickly, and took a stand at Olympia in 1932. At that Show it was described as specialising in sports coachwork for the Wolseley Hornet, and four examples were on display; all bore the 'E W' designation, with the 'Daytona' brand-name, indicating that they were made for the London dealer Eustace Watkins. By this time the affairs of the two companies had become so closely bound together that Eustace Watkins decided to buy W & M outright.

W & M had also made the March design of Hornet for a short time, but the conflict of interest was such that the latter contract soon moved to JOHN CHARLES. The EW Hornet models ran for several years, but they were far from W & M's only product. In parallel with the Hornet development, the company was working with Rover to produce a sports four-seater for the 1932-33 catalogue; this was the 'Rajah', available on four different chassis. It continued with minor modifications in the next year's catalogue. By now Whittingham & Mitchel was becoming the main name in the industry for open bodies produced

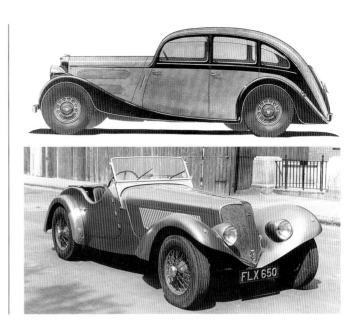

WHITTINGHAM & MITCHEL: 1931 Wolseley Hornet Special 'EW' saloon (above) in a somewhat aspirational setting. 1937 British Salmson S4D 14hp saloon (above right) appears to have been influenced by the Flying Standard. 1939 Allard sports (right), with V-12 Lincoln Zephyr engine, believed to be by this coachbuilder.

WILLIAMS & BAYLISS: 1930 Rolls-Royce 20/25 Weymann saloon obtains maximum room inside only by extending seats beyond rear axle.

under contract and the next client, Vauxhall, was to be its biggest. Starting in 1933 with the 'Stratford' tourer on the Light Six (and later DX) chassis, W & M supplied Vauxhall over the next six years with the 'Airline' coupé (Light Six/DX), 'Cavendish' tourer (Big Six) and the 'Velocity' and 'Sandringham' drophead coupés (DX). Of these, the Airline, Stratford and Sandringham (shared with RANALAH) were ALLINGHAM designs, as was the Rover 14 drophead which Whittingham & Mitchel supplied in 1935-36.

In 1934 there was another new client, Singer, to which W & M supplied a tourer body for the 11hp model. However, 1935 was probably the peak year, with further contracts for British Salmson (sports two-seater), MG (N-type Magnette 2/4-seater – another Allingham design), Lancia (tourer for Kevill-Davies & March), Talbot 10 (tourer) and Ford 8 ('Kerry' tourer for W H Perry, the Ford dealer).

In the last pre-war years Whittingham & Mitchel became involved with some rarer and more upmarket marques – Alvis, British Salmson, Frazer Nash-BMW, Railton and Allard; it even bodied a Rolls-Royce tourer. By the end of the thirties the company seems to have become independent of Eustace Watkins and was in business as a repairer as much as a coachbuilder, under the name W & M Motors. After World War 2 the company moved to Staines and recommenced bodying Sunbeam-Talbot dropheads; the old Kings Road works became one of the Allard company's factories. In 1947 W & M also built a saloon body on a pre-war Railton chassis. Later still, in the mid-sixties, it was said to be in business near Brooklands as a marine engineer.

WINDOVER: 1923 Rolls-Royce 20hp cabriolet (right) with division. 1936 Rolls-Royce limousine (below) with pillarless rear-door treatment.

WILLIAMS & BAYLISS

This Cheltenham firm went through a number of changes of name. It was originally W Mills & Sons Ltd, then Williams & Bayliss, then Williams, Bayliss & Co. Ltd, then F J Williams & Co. Ltd. Under the Williams & Bayliss name it is known to have bodied two Rolls-Royces – a 20hp in 1923 and a 20/25 in 1930. It specialised in Weymann construction at one time, and in 1926 bodied at least one Bentley saloon using this system.

WILSON (KINGSTON)

The Wilson company of Kingston-on-Thames was primarily a commercial bodybuilder, responsible amongst other things for the 'Esanday' range of commercials sold by the London dealers Stewart & Ardern. However it had at least one attempt at the car coachwork market when in 1933 it offered an attractive open two-seater on the Ford 8 chassis.

WILSON MOTORS

Wilson Motors of Victoria, South-West London, was one of the first bodybuilders to offer a coachbuilt body on the Austin Seven chassis. Announced in 1924, it was a sporty-looking boat-tailed two/four-seater which even included walnut deck planking with copper nails. It was known as the 'Burghley', and remained in production until 1928.

WILTON

The Wilton Carriage Co Ltd of Croydon must have been in existence by at least 1920,

since it was reported as opening its 'new' factory in January 1921. At that time it announced that it specialised in Ford saloon bodies, but later that year it began to body the Alvis 10/30 chassis and by November was advertising a full range of Alvis two-seater, four-seater, coupé and all-weather bodies. Also in late 1921 it is known to have built a saloon body on a Rolls-Royce chassis. Nothing more is known of the company.

WINDOVER

The origins of the Windover company of Huntingdon go back to 1856, when Charles Windover, son of a Grantham carriage-builder, came to Huntingdon and bought the business of Frances Armstrong. Windover, 37 years old at that time, initially had only nine employees, but his sales soon climbed, and four years later the firm employed 30. Charles Windover seemed to be able to cultivate the best class of customer even though he was far from London. His clientele included Indian Princes, the Governor General of Australia and eventually the Royal Family. By 1886 the number of employees had soared to 300, and the firm of Windover was being described as 'the backbone of Huntingdon's wealth'; Charles Windover became the town's mayor. One of the secrets of his success was said to be that he was the first to use hickory and steel in his carriages, thus making them much lighter without reducing their strength.

Charles Windover died in 1900, and it is not recorded whether his firm had built a car body by then. That event must in any case have taken place soon afterwards, for at an early stage Windover was well established as a coach-builder on car chassis. It was at the first post-war Olympia Show in 1919 and at every one thereafter (including the two Earls Court Shows) until World War 2. Preferred marques were Daimler, which was on the stand at all of those Shows except one, and Rolls-Royce, which was only absent on two occasions.

In 1924 Windover took the major step of moving

WOODALL NICHOLSON: 1926
Crossley torpedo-style tourer.

from Huntingdon to North-West London, opening a factory at Colindale. Why they did this is not immediately clear; many firms would have made do with a London showroom, which Windover already had and indeed retained even after the move. Certainly it cannot have been a light decision to part with so many long-serving and experienced employees, although it has been suggested that Charles Windover's grandchildren, who were now running the business, far preferred London to Huntingdon. At the least they installed a top manager to run it in the person of R I Musselwhite, previously managing director of CUNARD.

It is a sad fact that, in spite of Windover's association with expensive chassis, and above-averagely attractive designs, quality was generally judged to have declined during the inter-war period. To what extent this can be attributed to the London move is impossible to say; it could be instead that the firm found it necessary to hold down prices during difficult times, and that quality suffered as a result. Nevertheless the two things did happen at the same time, and one cannot avoid at least asking oneself whether they were linked.

During the thirties Windover continued to body Rolls-Royce and Daimler as well as such marques as Alvis, Armstrong-Siddeley, Bentley, Lagonda, Lanchester and Mercedes-Benz. After World War 2, while not giving up car work and indeed exhibiting at the first post-war Motor Show, it concentrated increasingly on building passenger-coaches. In 1956 Windover was bought by the London dealer Henly's, and in the same year gave up coachbuilding work altogether, although continuing in business as a car dealer.

WINGHAM
See MARTIN WALTER and ABBEY COACHWORKS.

WOODALL NICHOLSON
The Halifax firm of Woodall Nicholson was established in 1873 when Thomas Woodall Nicholson took over the old-established coachbuilding firm of Piercy's. After his death in 1914 his sons, Charles and Herbert, ran the business, but Herbert retired early for health reasons, leaving Charles in control.

During the twenties the firm bodied such chassis as Rolls-Royce, Wolseley, Crossley and Austin, but by 1929 it was in financial difficulties, from which it was saved by a capital reconstruction involving investments by several local businessmen. Even this did not restore profitability, and in 1933 Charles Nicholson left the board, dying a year later, aged 57. The new management (which included Charles' son-in-law) started to specialise in the conversion of second-hand Rolls-Royces into hearses, and from then on the company's future was assured. Even so, some car bodying continued, including a Hispano-Suiza V-12 cabriolet in 1937.

From World War 2 onwards the company's coachbuilding activities were confined to hearses and other commercial vehicles, with one exception: this was the 'Cirrus GT', the winning entry in the IBCAM/Daily Telegraph styling competition of 1971, which was constructed from scratch by Woodall Nicholson craftsmen. The company was taken over in 1982 by Coleman-Milne, its main competitor in hearses, and was closed down in 1987.

WOODS, REEVES
Woods, Reeves & Co bodied a Rolls-Royce 20/25 in 1934. At that time it was described as succeeding R Harrison Ltd; since the address was given as London NW1, it would appear to have also inherited the same premises.

WOOLLEY
John S Woolley Ltd of Nottingham bodied at least two Rolls-Royces in the period 1936-38, but nothing more is known.

WRAIGHT
F J Wraight of London SW11 was contracted to body the Whitehead-Thanet car, for which ambitious plans were announced in 1920, but it is not certain that any cars were ever made.

WRIGHT
A E Wright Ltd of Alexandra Park, North London, built sports bodies during the thirties on Wolseley Hornet and, especially, Austin Seven chassis. The latter were sold from 1933-36 under the 'AEW' brand-name; both two- and four-seater versions were available.

WOOLLEY: 1938 Rolls-Royce 25/30 four-door four-light saloon.

WYLDER

G Wylder & Co of Kew, Surrey, was founded in 1923, and maintained an independent existence for 14 years. It exhibited at Olympia only once, in 1931, showing a saloon and a drophead coupé, both on Talbot chassis.

Wylder bodied a number of Bentleys in the twenties, and is also known to have bodied Rolls-Royces and at least one each of M45 Lagonda and Riley 15/6. The workload seems to have declined by the mid-thirties, as the firm was able to rent space to Rapier Cars in 1935 when that company was formed following the Lagonda collapse. In 1937 Wylder was bought by ALPE & SAUNDERS and ceased car coachbuilding. The new owners – who incidentally had put their name to an Austin Seven body in the late twenties, although it is almost certain that they did not build it themselves – were only interested in building hearses. Wylder survived in the hearse business until at least the mid-sixties, and at that time was still connected with the Wylder family.

WYLDER: Talbot 90 saloon as shown at Olympia 1931. Note lack of running-boards.

YOUNG, JAMES

James Young & Co Ltd of Bromley, Kent, went back to at least 1863, when Mr James Young bought an existing firm of carriage-makers. The new firm developed quite a reputation, particularly for a lightweight carriage known as a 'Bromley brougham'. It moved relatively late into car bodybuilding, in 1908, its very first body being for the local Member of Parliament, but soon made the switch completely. During World War 1 the company was occupied in manufacturing bodies for lorries, ambulances and even armoured cars.

James Young was comparatively little known for the first few post-war years; an exception should perhaps be made for the Bentley company, whose chassis started to bear James Young bodies as early as 1921. The firm also seems to have had a reputation as an all-weather specialist, having been an early user of the patent Gwynne head (later known as the Beatonson head). James Young is known to have bodied such exotica as an early Bugatti, a Hispano-Suiza, an Isotta-Fraschini and a Beverley-Barnes and also made an appearance at the 1922 Olympia Show on the Lorraine stand, where one chassis carried an all-weather James Young body. However it was not until

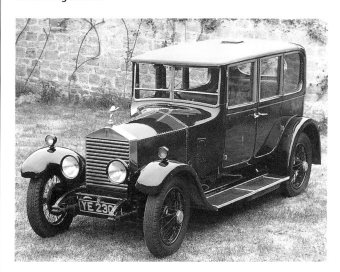

JAMES YOUNG: 1926 Rolls-Royce 20hp saloon; little hint of the elegance to come.

1925 that the firm took a stand in its own name, showing a Chrysler all-weather and a Lanchester saloon. Thereafter it exhibited every year up to 1939, as well as in the post-war years.

For the next 10 years or so James Young survived as a bespoke coachbuilder by steering a middle course. On the one hand, it maintained and enhanced its reputation for quality and exclusivity by carrying out individual commissions on upmarket chassis. On the other it developed alliances with various manufacturers and importers

JAMES YOUNG: 1937 Lagonda LG45 drophead coupé (left); erected hood for once enhances the car's appearance. 1954 Rolls-Royce Silver Dawn saloon (below).

so that it could sell what were effectively standard designs of bodies on those chassis. An early example was with Sunbeam, where for seven years from 1928 the company specialised in both formal coachwork on the 25hp chassis and foursome drophead coupés on the 20hp. Another prestigious speciality was the Alfa Romeo marque, where during the same period – the end of the twenties – James Young became noted for its coachwork on the 1500 and 1750 models; again, its best-known design was a drophead coupé, although tourers and saloons were made as well. In contrast to its normal bodies on these chassis, which were luxuriously appointed, the company also went to the other extreme and built a small number of lightweight fabric-covered four-seater tourers for the racing fraternity.

James Young's next affiliation was with the Talbot marque. From 1932 to 1936 it produced a range of saloons and coupés on whatever was the top model at the time – first the 75, then the 105, and finally the 110 (3½-litre). In the 1933 season it produced a catalogued model for the Rover company, a top-of-the-range sports saloon on the Speed Meteor chassis. Meanwhile two other prestigious makes of chassis were beginning to be associated with James Young – Daimler and Bentley (the latter after a gap while it came under the control of Rolls-Royce). It was presumably this latter connection which brought the company to the attention of London dealer Jack Barclay,

who bought the James Young company in 1937. Already two years previously a James Young Bentley drophead had caused a sensation when it appeared with a 'parallel action' door which moved backwards rather than outwards, and in 1938, under the new owners, the firm's Rolls-Royce 'saloon coupé' with this type of door won the premier coachwork award at the year's Motor Show. The door had been designed by the legendary G H Wenham, who had been with James Young since 1910 and who by then was works director.

World War 2 saw the company's production turned over to munitions, aircraft components and suchlike. The works suffered badly, being completely burned out during the 'blitz' with the loss of all records and then hit a second time by a V1 bomb. After the war coachbuilding resumed, with A F MacNeil now installed as chief designer. Soon, though, MacNeil found himself back in charge of Gurney Nutting as well when that was brought into the Jack Barclay fold. The company resumed exhibiting at the London Motor Shows in 1948, and eventually became one of the last two remaining traditional coachbuilders. By then, however, the work available had become severely constrained by the few chassis available – namely Rolls-Royce Phantom and Silver Cloud and Bentley Continental. In 1967 the inevitable happened and coachbuilding ceased, although James Young continued as a company doing body refurbishing work.

Appendix 1
How to Buy a Coachbuilt Car

After reading in the preceding chapters of the poor reputation which traditional coachwork had in its time, a potential buyer of such a car may be excused for wondering whether any worthwhile examples could possibly still exist. Nevertheless, it is remarkable how many of these fine old cars are still on the roads and apparently in good condition. It is worth reminding oneself that in fact only a tiny minority have survived, and that huge numbers went to the scrapyard quite early on; this was often because of failure of the bodywork, but not necessarily so. If a pre-war car survived in good condition until 1939, it then most likely had a six year rest on blocks in its owner's garage and in the post-war era it would then have been even more carefully looked after as new cars were impossibly scarce for a few years. Gradually, though, such a car would have been passed down the ownership ladder until it was run on a tight budget, with consequences for its mechanical rather than bodywork condition. Very many such cars were scrapped at the beginning of the sixties, for example, when the British 'MoT' testing system on older cars was introduced, and some of the larger, thirstier cars had gone some years earlier at the time of the Suez fuel crisis. We can be confident, therefore, that those cars that have survived until now are those that for whatever reason have been well looked all their lives both bodily and mechanically.

Even so, our potential buyer would no doubt prefer some reassurance that the beautiful object which he or she is contemplating buying is relatively sound and not likely to produce large unforeseen bills for bodywork repairs in the short to medium term. Although there can be no guarantees in this uncertain world, there are certain things to look for, and certain tests which one can carry out, during an inspection of a coachbuilt car, which can at least reduce the risk and increase the buyer's confidence and his or her ability to sleep at night after the deed is done. These tests and observations apply equally to saloons, drophead coupés and sports models. It has to be said that any remedial work found necessary will be easier (and therefore cheaper) to carry out on an open car than on a closed one, and easier on a sports or tourer than on a drophead coupé; however this is a subject to which we shall return later.

When inspecting a car, our starting-point is an assumption that the body structure was potentially long-lasting when it left the coachworks. This may sound strange after the reader has been told of the tendency of coachbuilt bodies to destroy themselves under the influence of chassis flexing, but this was much more a twenties phenomenon, and by the following decade there had been enormous strides both in chassis rigidity – cross-bracing, deeper side-members and so on – and in body design. In any case, if a body has lasted for 50 years or more and is not yet showing any signs of structural problems, then there is no reason to suspect that it may develop them over the next five or even ten.

The most important matter by far is therefore to reassure ourselves that the structure is still sound; panel fit and finish come a long way down our priorities. This is not only to try and avoid problems in the future, but also because any repairs in this area are likely to be expensive; it is not usually possible to repair a body frame, in whole or in part, without removing the relevant exterior panel or panels. In the case of a saloon this usually means cutting apart panels that were welded together when the body was made. Worst of all is to find problems in the 'bottom-sides' – the heavy-section longitudinal members which run from front to rear – since replacing these is tantamount to rebuilding the whole frame from scratch.

Firstly, ensure that the car is absolutely four-square on a level, horizontal surface. Then stand back from the car, sideways on, and look at the shut lines round the doors. Be objective; you are not there to be seduced by those voluptuous lines. If the gaps are even, then the car has made a good start. If not – if, as is the most likely, the gap is wider at the top (of a saloon) or the side (of an open car) than at the bottom – then the door has dropped.

A dropped door may be serious or not, depending on the cause. Items like worn hinge-pins are easily remedied. Even loose hinge securing screws are a minor item, except that they indicate a certain lack of interest on the part of the previous owner; on the other hand they could mean that the previous owner had tried to tighten them but was unable to because the hinge-post had rotted. A dropped door can also mean swelling of the door-frame or closing pillar because of wood-rot, or possibly accident damage in the past.

Now view the door-lines from the front. Does the door conform exactly to the body curvature, especially at the bottom where in all probability there is some 'turn-under'? The ability of a door-frame to retain this complex double-curvature is one of the best indications that the frame is in good condition. Conversely, any tendency of the door to revert to a flatter shape suggests some hard use at some time.

This 1935 Thrupp & Maberly 3½-litre Bentley may look slightly scruffy, but structurally it seems to have possibilities. The bottom front edge of the door has warped outwards ever so slightly, but otherwise the shut lines look quite good – particularly the bottom of the rear edge, which has retained its outward curvature.

On the other hand this 1953 Healey Tickford saloon gives off bad vibrations. Not only are numerous panels dented and wavy, but both the door and the bonnet shut-lines are noticeably irregular. This one would probably be a 'panels-off' restoration – still very worthwhile, provided it was reflected in the purchase price.

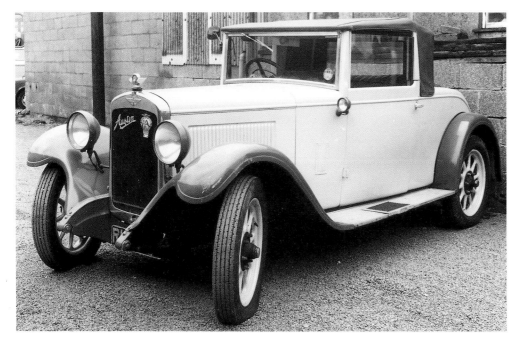

It is hard to judge from photographs, but is there something wrong with the door of this Martin Walter Austin 12/4 drophead coupé? If not, why was it not completely shut before the photo was taken? The likelihood is that the door has dropped so badly that it needs some skill to shut it at all.

One of the vulnerable areas is the boot-lid opening. In order to repair the frame on this Alvis Speed 25 Charlesworth drophead it was necessary to remove the whole of the rear panelling – but on an open car this can be done relatively easily. The rear is now clear (below), and the frame can be built on to the rest of the body without too many problems.

Another Alvis, but this time a Speed 20 Mayfair saloon. The warning signs are there: door-fit is poor, especially at the bottom, and alloy reinforcing pieces have been added to the roof. A thorough job is in progress (below), including repairs to the wood frame and replacement doors, and of course preparation for a bare metal respray.

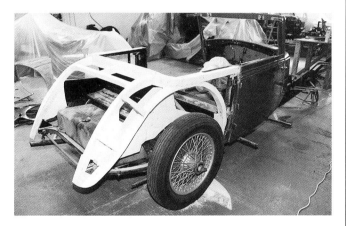

As a further check on the integrity of the door and its mounting, take hold of it at the top and bottom edges, furthest from the hinges, and twist it back and forth gently. Any sloppiness is an indication of something amiss, but be careful to track down exactly where the movement is taking place – for example, that it is not just due to loose or worn hinges. Be aware also that many sports and tourer bodies were so lightly constructed that their hinge pillars and adjacent panels were designed to flex a certain amount even when new. What you are looking for is excessive movement which would indicate weakening of the pillars through rot.

Now move to the rear of the car and apply to the boot-lid and boot opening the same tests as you did for the doors. All the time keep an eye open for damp or corrosion, as this in turn may indicate a long-term problem which could eventually have caused wood-rot. If you are satisfied here, turn your attention to the interior of the car. It should be possible to find places where you can pull back the trim and expose the timber frame; the ideal places, if you can reach them, are at the bottom of the 'standing' (ie upright) pillars where they join the 'bottom-sides', as this is where water will lie if it has been allowed

to enter at all. On drophead bodies, around the bottom of the rear (ie door-hinge) pillar is the absolutely critical area for rot.

Now take a pointed object such as a pen-knife and see how far you can push it in to the exposed wood. Timber which has been around for this length of time should be pretty hard – hard enough not to allow the point to enter more than, say, 1-2mm. If it goes in significantly further than this, and/or the wood feels generally soft, you should consider ending your love-affair with this particular car. If the car passes the test, try and repeat it at other critical places such as door and boot frames.

When dealing with a saloon you should now look at another important part of the interior – the roof-lining. Any stains here are sure signs of water problems in the past; most likely places are around the sun-roof, if there is or was one, and around the rear window. A leaking or sealed sun-roof can indicate that the drains leading from it have become blocked at some time; worse, on some cars these drains were in the form of rubber tubes running down inside the windscreen-pillars, and when these perished the result was often wood-rot in the pillar as well.

Another check for saloons is to look for signs of

The fact that the driver's door of this Lagonda 3-litre saloon of 1932 has dropped is plain for all to see. However this is a Weymann body, and different rules apply; it might even be possible to restore the door to shape with a spanner, if by good fortune the adjusting mechanism at the bottom of its frame is in good condition.

paint-cracking, or worse, in the upper parts of the pillars. Normally a roof adds to the strength of a body, but if (say) the inner member of a windscreen pillar fractures then the inertia of the remaining roof-structure can cause it to flex and crack the panelling around the pillar.

If the car has passed all these tests, there is a good chance that it has a sound body-frame. You can now start thinking about the more cosmetic aspects of the body's condition. To a great extent this is similar to examining a more modern car, except that with the coachbuilt version any work done in the past is more likely to have involved repairs than replacement. With this in mind, walk round the car and assess the gaps between wings and tyres, comparing especially side-to-side. If there is any noticeable lack of symmetry then there could well have been some accident damage which was not repaired very skilfully. Bear in mind also, though, that unlike modern bodywork it is possible to remove individual components such as wings in order to work on them.

We have confined these comments so far to the traditional coachbuilt body – wood-framed, panelled in steel and/or aluminium. There are other varieties which you

might possibly encounter, where some of the comments above do not apply. The by now rare Weymann body, for example, was designed to be extremely flexible, so the tests suggested for door rigidity would tell you nothing. Furthermore the later Weymann doors had a diagonal straining-wire, with an adjusting nut set in the underside of the frame, so that any sag could be immediately eliminated. Another advantage, if one can call it that, of a Weymann body is that the fabric covering – and its padding underneath – will certainly need replacing, so the extra cost of any work on the body frame is rather less prohibitive.

The successors to Weymann – the semi-panelled Weymann and the Silent Travel systems – bring their own problems in restoration, as they both relied on Silentbloc bushes to hold the framework together, and to mount the frame to the chassis. Excellent though these devices were when new, the rubber will by now have certainly perished, and replacing the bushes could be difficult; expert help should be sought.

By now, if you are satisfied with the results of your inspection, you are probably thinking seriously of making a purchase, but if you are still unsure, remember that there are plenty of people available to help you. To begin with, there is the Club for the marque you are contemplating buying; indeed, you really should have joined and asked for advice well before you reached this stage. If you have not already joined, do so immediately. You can find

This Rolls-Royce 20/25 saloon by Park Ward looks at first sight to be in a sorry state. Closer examination, however, shows that the door shut lines and panel curvatures are perfect, the only point of concern being in the boot-lid area. As it turned out, all the car needed was some repairs to the frame around the boot-opening and a total respray.

A post-war all-steel coachbuilt body often corrodes at the points where it is mounted to the chassis. Here a mounting on an S-type Bentley coupé is undergoing repair.

the address from any of the classic car magazines, or if all else fails from Beaulieu Motor Museum. In addition there are experts available who, for a fee, will give you a full report, which could be money very well spent.

We said that we would return to the subject of closed versus open cars. There has been a 'classic car' movement of some kind or other in Britain for at least 70 years, starting perhaps with the first Brighton commemorative runs and then given a boost by the formation of the Vintage Sports Car Club. From quite early on there was an understandable tendency to preserve open rather than closed cars; indeed the early VSCC members would have regarded the concept of a closed sports car as a contradiction in terms. Even in more recent times, however, open cars have been more sought-after than closed ones for restoration and preservation, for a variety of reasons: no doubt a 'hobby' car is always associated with summer,

and the idea of open-air motoring and being able to wave to one's friends is doubly appealing. Another reason, though, is the one which brought us on to this topic: the fear that purchasing a coachbuilt saloon might eventually land its owner with a large repair bill for rebuilding its bodywork.

The result has been that for a long time open coachbuilt cars of the twenties, thirties and forties have been much more sought after than their closed equivalents, with a corresponding effect on prices. In consequence many good-looking saloons in restorable condition were scrapped or – even worse – stripped of their saloon bodies and turned into 'replica' sports models. This has led to today's situation where, in many cases, the saloon version of a model is now rarer than the open one. One has to ask oneself how long it will take before this is recognised in a realignment of their relative prices.

The lesson from our inspection rules, though, is that one should not reject the idea of a coachbuilt saloon just because it might give trouble in the future. Firstly, any coachbuilt body, closed or open, might give trouble but by applying our tests we can minimise that risk. Secondly, not all work on a saloon body will be more expensive than on an open one. Of course if the saloon you are contemplating buying does need major work, then you should think carefully, since as we have discussed this could well involve a complete 'skin-off' reframing. That apart, a saloon does not have to be any more expensive to look after than an open model.

Lastly, though, remember the advantages of a saloon over an open model, which may not occur to you until you are well immersed in classic-car activities: you have far more room both for passengers and for luggage, you can contemplate the journey to any event without wondering about the weather, and you will be the envy of the open-car fraternity when you eat your sandwiches in the dry while all the others are huddled under umbrellas.

APPENDIX 2
GLOSSARY OF COACHBUILDING TERMS

The variety of descriptions of body styles which existed during the heyday of coachbuilding can be both bewildering and daunting. The picture becomes even more confused when one realises that, firstly, particular descriptions changed their meanings over the years, and secondly, coachbuilders had a habit of inventing a new description when a perfectly good one existed already.

To simplify matters as much as possible, this summary confines itself to those terms which were current during the twenties and thirties. In addition, any terms which were peculiar to US or Continental usage have been omitted. Those who seek more detail are directed to *The Complete Book of Automobile Design* by Ian Beattie (now out of print, but available from libraries).

ALL-WEATHER

In the immediate post-World War 1 period this name was applied to cars which could be opened to the elements, but which had comprehensive arrangements against wind and rain when they were closed. This would normally have included glass windows in metal frames, which either folded down into the doors or were stowed away in a special compartment. This was in contrast to a TOURER, which had only a rudimentary hood and, possibly, canvas side-curtains which rolled down. The complexity and expense of these systems meant that all-weather bodies were confined to expensive chassis.

The picture became confused when cheaper versions of all-weather bodies became available with removable side-curtains made from celluloid in a steel frame - a system which was soon appropriated for tourers as well. At the same time, the widespread adoption of 'mechanical' (ie winding) window-lifts allowed them to be used on the more expensive all-weather bodies, and this became the point of difference between all-weathers and tourers.

The term ALL-WEATHER declined in usage during the mid-twenties, in favour of first TRANSFORMABLE and then CONVERTIBLE.

BELT-RAIL

The horizontal bar of a body frame, at the level of the bottom of the windows. The equivalent rail inside a door is the GARNISH RAIL.

BROUGHAM

Based on its horse-drawn forerunner, the brougham was a highly formal design, distinguished by the separate nature of the passenger compartment, which often retained its own carriage lamps. Originally it was of course not ENCLOSED-DRIVE, but even when the chauffeur's area became enclosed the passenger saloon was

Brougham: a less than elegant Beardmore from the early twenties by Lawton-Goodman.

made wider, usually by use of a 'D-front' – so called because of its shape as seen from above. Another distinguishing feature was the brougham's sharp-edged appearance in profile; this applied both to the roof-line and to the shape of the door, and the 'brougham door' – curved forward at the toe – continued to appear as a feature of many otherwise conventional designs well into the thirties.

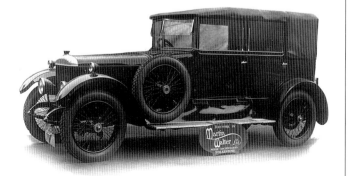

All-weather: Daimler Light 30 by Martin Walter, c.1921.

BROUGHAM LIMOUSINE

This description was virtually synonymous with BROUGHAM, but made it even more clear that there was a DIVISION between the two compartments as in all LIMOUSINES.

CABRIOLET

Of all coachbuilding terms, this is the one whose meaning has evolved the most over the years. Originally a cabriolet was a four-door, four- or six-LIGHT DROPHEAD body with a DIVISION, and without even having ENCLOSED DRIVE. Soon, however, the requirement for the division was dropped, and it came to mean the same as an ALL-WEATHER; it began to replace that name during the

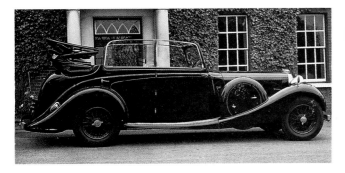

Cabriolet, thirties style: 1937 Lagonda LG45 four-door by Salmons (Tickford).

mid-twenties. (A variation, the COUPÉ CABRIOLET, had only two doors.) The increasing popularity of the style in the thirties, and some borrowing of features from Germany where it was even more popular, led to a further widening of its definition. It could now, for example, describe a body (sometimes known as a SALOON CABRIOLET) where only the fabric roof itself opened, leaving windows and frames standing, and indeed some commentators tried to restrict its use to such bodies (leaving DROPHEAD COUPÉ for the alternative type). Later, the requirement for four doors evaporated, and a cabriolet came to be synonymous with a DROPHEAD COUPÉ.

CABRIOLET DE VILLE

This version of the CABRIOLET implies merely that the front portion of the folding head can be opened separately into the DE VILLE position, usually by being rolled

Cabriolet de Ville: 1920 Rolls-Royce Silver Ghost by Cockshoot.

up. The later term for a similar, although less formal, design was a THREE-POSITION DROPHEAD COUPÉ. See also SALAMANCA.

CANOPY

That part of the roof which is over the driver's seat.

Canopy: this 1938 lwb Humber tourer by Hooper is unusual in having a detachable canopy.

CANT-RAIL

The longitudinal frame member of the roof, running above the door.

CLOSE-COUPLED

Originally implied that all seats were within the wheelbase (often to make more luggage space), and that rear seating room was therefore limited. Later, when engines had been moved forward and seating within the wheelbase had become the norm, the term came to mean merely that the body was shorter than normal.

CLOVER-LEAF

An arrangement of three seats, usually in an open car or COUPÉ, where the third seat is placed behind and between the two front ones so that its occupant's legs are between the front seats. In vogue during the twenties.

CONTINENTAL COUPÉ

A popular style in the late twenties and early thirties. The intended image was of a fast, CLOSE-COUPLED car which would be ideal for Continental touring; it was reinforced by making the luggage container in the form of a separate trunk rather than an integral part of the body, since this was perceived to be a French style of the time.

Continental Coupé: 1938 Rolls-Royce 25/30 by Gurney Nutting.

CONVERTIBLE
An all-embracing term which has come to mean any car with a folding head. See also ALL-WEATHER.

COUPÉ
The French word *coupé* means 'cut'. As applied to coach-building, it originally referred to the centre part of a horse-drawn carriage, between the 'box' in front and the 'boot' at the rear. Thus for a car it also means foreshort-ened – ie close-coupled – but it is applied specifically to a two-door, two- or four-light, close-coupled body with either a fixed or an opening head. In the latter case it must have normal glass windows – fixed, lifting or sliding – otherwise it becomes a SPORTS body. A coupé can have two or four seats enclosed under the head.

COUPÉ CABRIOLET
See CABRIOLET.

COUPÉ DE VILLE
Similar to a CABRIOLET DE VILLE, but the rear part of the head is fixed instead of folding. Where it was intended to make clear that the design had only two doors and no division, it was sometimes called a SEDANCA COUPÉ.

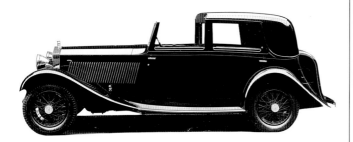

Coupé de Ville: Barker-bodied Rolls-Royce 20/25 of 1934.

COUPÉ LANDAULET
See LANDAULET.

COUPÉLETTE
See LANDAULET.

CYCLE WING
A wing on the front wheel which closely follows the wheel's curvature, like the mudguard on a bicycle. Some-times actually turned with the wheel. See also HELMET WING.

DE VILLE
Implies a body style where the front (ie driver's) com-partment is either open to the skies or can be made to be. Originally all 'de ville' designs had four doors.

DICKEY-SEAT
Usually found on two-seater COUPÉS of the twenties; a lid behind the hood lifted up to form an additional seat.

Dickey-Seat: a glamorous model shows how to get into the dickey-seat of the Grose Talbot 90 sports coupé at the 1930 Olympia Show.

DIVISION
Also known as a partition, this is a glass panel which divides the driver from his passengers. In earlier days it was fixed, and often D-shaped as in a BROUGHAM, but it soon became the norm for it to be removable in some way. In cheaper versions it was made in two halves which could slide sideways; the more desirable method, although this took up more room, was for it to disappear into the back of the front seats, usually by means of a winding mechanism. A later alternative was for the divi-sion to hinge upwards and lie flat against the roof.

Division: Crossley 20/70 limousine of c.1925 by Grose.

DROPHEAD
A design where the head can be folded flat to make the car open.

DROPHEAD COUPÉ
A COUPÉ with an opening head.

ENCLOSED DRIVE
Also known as interior drive, this meant that the driver's compartment was completely enclosed by a roof and side-windows. The term was obviously applied only to formal bodies, and dates from the time (up to the early twenties) when the opposite was the norm – ie the driver was

Drophead Coupé: Martin Walter's 'Denton' design on the 18hp Lanchester of c.1934.

exposed to the elements by having no side-windows and sometimes even no roof. Hence, for example, 'ENCLOSED LANDAULET'.

FAUX-CABRIOLET
The French word '*faux*' means false; these bodies looked like dropheads because they had fabric-covered roofs, and often dummy HOOD-IRONS, but in fact their roofs were fixed.

FINE-LINING
A narrow painted line, often used at the edge of a PICK-ING-OUT line.

FIXED-HEAD COUPÉ
A COUPÉ, with a solid, immovable HEAD (although it might possibly be fitted with a SUNSHINE ROOF).

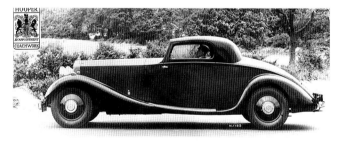

Fixed-head Coupé: 1935 Hooper body on a Rolls-Royce Phantom 2 chassis.

FLAP
A panel which folds out of the way to allow a passenger to enter or leave.

Flap: shown in the open position, on a 1925 Isotta-Fraschini 45hp tourer by Hooper.

FOURSOME
Implies that the body has seating for four under the roof, but that such seating is CLOSE-COUPLED.

GARNISH-RAIL
See BELT-RAIL.

HEAD
Originally meant a collapsible, but not detachable, covering. Later the word became interchangeable with 'roof', as in FIXED-HEAD COUPÉ.

HEEL-BOARD
The vertical board under the front of a seat.

HELMET WING
Similar to a CYCLE WING, but the bottom kicks backwards away from the wheel rather in the manner of a Roman helmet.

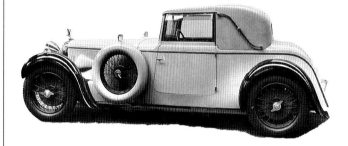

Helmet Wing: 1932 Alvis Speed 20 SA drophead coupé by Charlesworth.

HOOD
Originally meant a collapsible and detachable covering (as opposed to a HEAD), but later came to mean a folding head.

HOOD-IRON
Also known as landau joints or stretchers, or in more recent times as pram-irons, these are the decorative hinged struts on the outside of a hood which stretch it taut when erected.

HOOP-STICKS
The cross bars which support the roof or hood material.

LANDAULET
(Also spelt 'landaulette'.) A very popular style amongst the moneyed classes before and after World War 1. Based on a well-known style of horse-drawn carriage, its distinguishing feature was that only the rear portion of the roof opened – ie that part covering the back-seat passengers. Originally it was assumed not to have an enclosed driving compartment, so in later years the term ENCLOSED LANDAULET (or sometimes LIMOUSINE LANDAULET) made the distinction. It was further assumed to have a DIVISION; when this was omitted, it became a SALOON LANDAULET.

Landaulet: this 30hp Daimler was on Hooper's stand at the 1922 Olympia Show – described, for the avoidance of doubt, as an 'enclosed-drive limousine landaulet'.

Finally, it might be a THREE-QUARTER, SINGLE or COUPÉ LANDAULET (this last sometimes shortened to COUPÉLETTE), according to whether it had six, four or two LIGHTS.

LIGHT

A light in coachbuilding terms is a side-window; hence it is convenient to classify a SALOON, for example, as four-light or six-light.

LIMOUSINE

The essential qualities of a limousine are that it should be roomy (usually through having a long wheelbase), its roof should be fixed, and it should have a DIVISION. The driver's compartment may not have been enclosed in the early days, but the passenger compartment always was. The massive legroom in the rear usually permitted the addition of two further 'occasional', ie folding, seats. What was not normal was a luggage compartment, since a limousine was used for town work rather than touring; there was often, however, a folding luggage grid. Later, a demand grew for a dual-use body which could combine both formal and touring requirements, which became known as a sports limousine or later TOURING LIMOUSINE; this retained the division but sacrificed some rear leg-room, and usually the occasional seats, to permit the addition of a luggage-boot. The sports limousine often dispensed with a QUARTER-LIGHT.

LIMOUSINE DE VILLE

A LIMOUSINE with a folding roof extension above the driver's seat.

Limousine: Rolls-Royce Phantom 2 by Park Ward, c.1930, in 'semi-Weymann' style.

LIMOUSINE LANDAULET

See LANDAULET.

PEAK

The part of the roof which projected beyond the windscreen (a fashion which had finished by the early thirties).

Peak: Bridges bodied this Sunbeam 14hp coupé in 1923, when roof peaks were the rage.

PHAETON

An early description now only used in North America; it is equivalent to a four/five-seat TOURER.

PICKING-OUT

A relief colour used for mouldings, in contrast to the main colour. See also FINE LINING.

PILLAR

A vertical member of a body frame. Sub-divided into scuttle pillars, hinge pillars, shut pillars and so on.

PILLARLESS

A fixed-head body where there is no obstruction above the waist-line between the windscreen pillar and the rear quarter. Can apply to both two- and four-door designs.

QUARTER-LIGHT

Originally a LIGHT, or window, alongside the rear seat which was fixed in the rear quarter of the car rather than being part of a door. Later, when it became common to arrange swivelling ventilation windows in the front section of front doors, these also became known as quarter-lights, and it became necessary to distinguish between front and rear ones.

ROADSTER

The term originated in America, and meant a drophead body with one wide seat capable of taking three abreast, possibly also having a dickey-seat. In recent years it has come to mean the same as a two-seater sports car.

SALAMANCA

Sometimes called a SALAMANCA CABRIOLET, this design was conceived by Count de Salamanca who was the Rolls-Royce agent in Madrid. It was no more than a formal, four-light CABRIOLET DE VILLE, but luxurious in execution. The term was used exclusively in connection with Rolls-Royce chassis.

SALOON
Probably the term which has least changed in meaning over the years. It has always meant a vehicle which has a fixed roof (although possibly with a SUNSHINE ROOF fitted), which is completely enclosed, and which does not have a DIVISION. It can have four LIGHTS or six, and either four doors or two, although during the thirties the last type became increasingly difficult to distinguish from a FIXED-HEAD COUPÉ, and indeed was sometimes named SALOON-COUPÉ.

SALOON COUPÉ
See SALOON.

SALOON LANDAULET
See LANDAULET.

SALOON LIMOUSINE
Similar to a SPORTS LIMOUSINE, in that it had a division but being built on a shorter chassis than a normal limousine had to sacrifice some rear leg-room. Unlike a sports limousine, however, it normally had a QUARTER-LIGHT – ie it was a six-light design – and would not have had a luggage-boot.

Saloon Limousine: 30hp Armstrong-Siddeley by Burlington, from a catalogue of about 1925.

SCUTTLE
That part of the bodywork between the engine compartment and the windscreen.

SEDANCA COUPÉ
See COUPÉ DE VILLE.

SEDANCA DE VILLE
The word sedanca is in theory synonymous with DE VILLE, so to describe a body as a sedanca de ville is illogical in the extreme. In practice it implied a de ville design with a large, saloon-like rear compartment often having four side-windows.

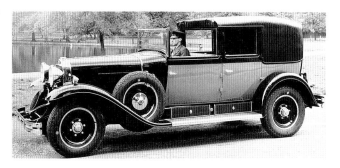

Sedanca: a rare 1928 Cadillac by Hooper.

SINGLE
See THREE-QUARTER.

SPORTS/SPORTING
A term used, often emotively, by both manufacturers and bodybuilders to imply that superior performance is available through either an uprated engine, or a lighter body or chassis, or both.

SPORTS LIMOUSINE
See LIMOUSINE.

SPORTSMAN'S COUPÉ
A two-door, four-light FIXED-HEAD COUPÉ with built-in luggage-locker. The provision of covered luggage accommodation was quite an innovation in 1927, when the intense but short-lived fad for this type of design started. It was achieved by 'close-coupling', ie moving the rear seats forward so that the rear passengers' feet were in floor wells under the front seats.

SPORTSMAN'S SALOON
This was a four-door, four-light CLOSE-COUPLED SALOON; the craze for this type of body took over, around 1929-30, from that for the SPORTSMAN'S COUPÉ. The name was later shortened to sports saloon.

Sports (man's) Saloon: By 1935, when Freestone & Webb bodied this 3½-litre Bentley, the shorter description was in vogue.

SQUAB
The vertical portion of a seat, against which the passenger's back rests.

SUNSHINE ROOF
Otherwise known as a sliding roof; became highly popular on British saloons from the latter twenties onwards. A

steel panel in the roof can be slid backwards – either over or, later, under the rear fixed roof panel – to give the occupants the impression of being in the open air.

SUNSHINE SALOON

During the latter half of the twenties, in the search for the ideal combination of open and closed body, numerous styles were named 'sunshine saloons' by their builders. They ranged from saloons with what we would now call a sliding or SUNSHINE ROOF, to semi-cabriolet designs where the whole roof folded back (while leaving the window-frames and CANT-RAILS standing).

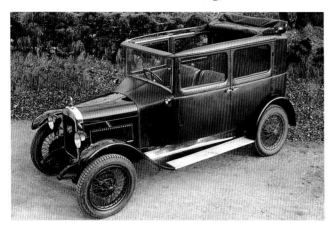

Sunshine Saloon: Austin c.1930 by Penman.

SWAGE-LINE

A decorative line formed by a crease in a metal panel.

THREE-QUARTER

An older coachbuilding term, little used after the twenties. A three-quarter body had a QUARTER-LIGHT; its opposite, a SINGLE body, did not; thus a four-door, six-light landaulet would be referred to as a 'three-quarter landaulet', whereas a four-door, four-light version would be a 'single landaulet'.

Three-quarter Coupé: 1924 Rippon body on a Rolls-Royce 20hp, which also shows a 'brougham door' influence.

TONNEAU COVER

A covering for an open TOURER or SPORTS car for use when no sidescreens have been erected. It comes from a very early motoring term describing the passenger-carrying part of a body (from *tonneau*, the French word for a barrel).

TORPEDO

An early term for what was in effect a large four- or five-seat tourer. Although bearing little resemblance to a torpedo, its name came from its smooth contours, free from intricate mouldings, and from the continuous horizontal line formed by the bonnet and waist-line, often accentuated by a secondary scuttle or apron between the two rows of seats.

TOURER

Always an open body with a collapsible hood, and usually having four or five seats. The feature which distinguishes it from a CABRIOLET or DROPHEAD COUPÉ is that its side windows – if it has any at all – are in the form of lightweight detachable side-screens which can be removed and stowed in a locker.

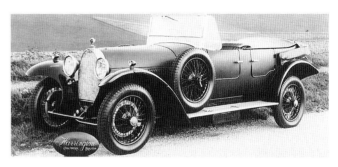

Tourer: Harrington Bugatti of c.1929 also shows its tonneau cover in use.

TOURING LIMOUSINE

The final development of the LIMOUSINE, whereby it retained its division for formal use yet also had sufficient luggage capacity for Continental touring.

Touring Limousine: a late (1957) example by H J Mulliner on a Rolls-Royce Silver Wraith chassis.

TRANSFORMABLE
See ALL-WEATHER.

VICTORIA HOOD

A type of hood which is cantilevered out from its point of attachment to the front of the seat it is intended to cover, with no support from the windscreen. Only feasible for two-seaters (although at least one four-seater design had two such hoods, one for each row of seats).

BIBLIOGRAPHY

Coachbuilding and Coachbuilders

A History of Coachbuilding, Oliver, Cassell, 1962
Automobile Body Design, Beattie, Foulis, 1977
Bodies Beautiful: A History of Car Styling and Craftsmanship, McLellan, David and Charles, 1975
Cars, Carriages and Caravans, Thomson, self-published, 1980
Cars and Coachbuilding: One Hundred Years of Road Vehicle Development, Oliver, Philip Wilson, 1981
Coachbuilding Past and Present, Hooper & Co, published privately, 1928
Coachbuilding in London, Vickers, London Industrial Archaeological Society, 1994
Coachmaking 1844-1944, J Cockshoot Ltd, published privately, 1944
Coachwork on Rolls-Royce, 1906-1939, Dalton, Dalton Watson, 1975
Vanden Plas, Coachbuilders, Smith, Dalton Watson, 1979
Vintage Style: The Story of Cross & Ellis, Bardsley, Brewin, 1993

Cars by Marque

Among the many marque reference books I have consulted, the following have been particularly valuable:
The Complete Encyclopedia of Motorcars, 1885 to the Present, Georgano, Ebury, 1954
A-Z of Cars of the 1920s, Baldwin, Bay View Books, 1994
The Thoroughbred Motor Car 1930-40, Scott-Moncrieff, Batsford, 1963
The Marques of Coventry, Long, Warwickshire Books, 1990
The Vintage Alvis (2nd edition), Hull and Johnson, Alvis Register, 1995
Armstrong-Siddeley: The Parkside Story 1896-1939, Cook, Rolls-Royce Heritage Trust, 1988
Aston-Martin 1913-1947, Hunter, Osprey, 1992
Austin Seven Source Book, Purves, Foulis, 1989
Bentley: The Vintage Years, 1919-1931, Hay, Dalton Watson, 1986
All the Pre-War Bentleys – As New, Sedgwick, Bentley Drivers Club, 1982
HRG: The Sportsmans Ideal, Dussek, MRP, 1985
Jensen, Anderson, Haynes, 1989
Lagonda: A History of the Marque, Davey and May, David and Charles, 1978
Lagonda: An Illustrated History, 1900-1950, Seaton, Crowood Press, 1988
The Lanchester Legacy, 1895-1931, Clark, Coventry University, 1995

Rolls-Royce: 75 Years of Motoring Excellence, Eves, Orbis, 1979
Cars of the Rootes Group, Robson, MRP, 1990

The British Car Industry

Air-Road-Sea Addlestone: The Bleriot-Weymann-Plessey Works 1916-1988, Rowe, DM and JL Barker, Addlestone, 1992
Automotive History Sources in Coventry Archives, Storey, University of Warwick
British Car Factories from 1896, Collins and Stratton, Veloce, 1993
British Motor Car Industry Records, Leng-Ward, unpublished MA thesis for Loughborough University, 1994
Early Country Motoring: Cars and Motorcycles in Suffolk 1896-1940, Bridges, self-published, 1995
Herbert Austin: The British Car Industry to 1940, Church, Europa, 1979
One Hundred Years of Motoring, Flower and Wynne-Jones, RAC, 1981
Out on a Wing: An Autobiography, Thomas, Michael Joseph, 1964
The Coventry Car Component Industry 1895-1939, Beavan, unpublished MA thesis for De Montfort University, 1994
The Motor Makers, Adeney, Collins, 1988
The Car Makers, Turner, Eyre and Spottiswoode, 1963
The Motor Industry, Maxcy and Silberston, Allen and Unwin, 1959
The Motor Car Industry in Coventry since the 1890s, Thoms and Donnelley, Croom Helm, 1985
The Making of the Motor Car, 1895-1930, Ware, Moorland, 1976
Trades and Industries of Norwich, Gurney-Read, Gliddon, 1988
William Morris, Viscount Nuffield, Overy, Europa, 1979

Design and Streamlining

Design 1920s, Benton, Open University, 1975
Harley Earl, Bayley, Trefoil, 1990
In Good Shape: Style in Industrial Products 1900 to 1960, Bayley, Design Council, 1979
Industrial Design, Heskett, Thames & Hudson, 1980
Into the Thirties: Style and Design 1927-1934, Sembach, Thames & Hudson, 1980
Objects of Desire, Forty, Thames and Hudson, 1995
Streamlined Transport, Loewy, Industrial Arts [Magazine], Autumn 1936
The History of the Airflow Car, Scientific American, Aug 1977
The Streamlined Decade, Bush, New York, 1975

INDEX